SOUTHERN LITERARY STUDIES

SOUTHERN LITERARY STUDIES

Edited by
LOUIS D. RUBIN, JR.

A Season of Dreams: The Fiction of Eudora Welty
By ALFRED APPEL, JR.

The Hero with the Private Parts
Essays by ANDREW LYTLE

Hunting in the Old South: Original Narratives of the Hunters
Selected and edited by CLARENCE GOHDES

John Crowe
RANSOM

JOHN CROWE RANSOM

John Crowe
RANSOM

CRITICAL ESSAYS
AND
A BIBLIOGRAPHY

edited by

THOMAS DANIEL YOUNG

LOUISIANA STATE UNIVERSITY PRESS   Baton Rouge

For
Tommy, Terry, and Kyle

ACKNOWLEDGMENTS

I want to express my appreciation to Joe Davis for reading the Introduction and making many valuable suggestions. I am also indebted to Don T. Harrell and Robert Neill, who have assisted me at every stage in the preparation of this book.

T.D.Y.

CONTENTS

John Crowe
RANSOM

INTRODUCTION

Thomas Daniel Young

As poet, teacher, critic, and editor, John Crowe Ransom has been one of the most influential men of his generation. In attempts to place him among his contemporaries, scholars and critics have agreed that Ransom commands an eminent position, but have disagreed on the precise nature of his contribution. Many have felt that his future reputation will depend upon a proper understanding of his poetry, for it is as poet that Ransom is most effective as a spokesman for values and attitudes important among members of his generation. And yet his most enthusiastic defenders admit that he imposed limitations upon both the scope and volume of his poems. Some commentators therefore consider his efforts as critic, editor, and teacher to be his most significant contributions to modern American letters. Not only has he advanced interesting and influential theories on the nature and value of poetry, he has also provided invaluable demonstrations of how poetry should be read. Ransom and his followers have convinced thousands of readers that the reading of poetry, though not an easy occupation, is a uniquely rewarding one. The extent of Ransom's influence cannot be precisely defined; he has been a teacher of great dedication and skill, and for more than two decades he was editor of one of the most distinguished literary journals in the country. As teacher, editor, and friend he has had inestimable influence on such notable figures as

Donald Davidson, Allen Tate, Robert Penn Warren, Andrew Lytle, Randall Jarrell, Peter Taylor, and Robert Lowell. It is necessary, therefore, to include the several facets of Ransom's career in any thorough assessment of his impact upon American literature since World War I.

A collection which proposes, as this one does, to indicate the development of Ransom's literary reputation and to present within limited compass some of the many attempts to find his place among the important writers of his generation must face immediately several problems for which there seems no completely satisfactory solution. Because of space limitations, first of all, many excellent essays must be excluded. Then, too, some aspects of Ransom's career have attracted more and better critical commentary than others. Many illuminating studies of Ransom's poetry, for example, must be omitted in order to include essays concerned with his social and literary criticism. Since no adequate treatment of his career as editor was available in print, George Lanning's informative memoir has been prepared for this edition. The sixteen essays of this collection, along with the introduction and the bibliography, are intended to assist the reader in evaluating the achievements of one of the most articulate men of letters in the twentieth century. The essays are arranged in chronological order according to date of publication.

II

On the occasion of Ransom's seventy-fifth birthday, Allen Tate attempted to place his old friend among the poets of their generation. "I consider him now," Tate wrote, "since the death of Stevens and Frost, the dean of American poetry." Ransom has earned this place of eminence, most critics agree, in spite of his self-imposed limitations. As Tate has pointed out, Ransom has always considered himself "deliberately minor; he very early set limits to the scope of his performance." But within this "deliberately minor mode" he has written a small number of "great poems." And Tate reminds us, "In a deliberately minor mode, Donne, Marvell, Landor, and Yeats wrote their great poems." [1]

Randall Jarrell has proclaimed Ransom "one of the best, most

[1]Allen Tate, "For John Crowe Ransom at Seventy-Five," *Shenandoah*, XIV (Spring, 1963), 8.

original and sympathetic poets alive," whose poems will "always be read and cared for" because he has written ten or twelve poems that are "perfectly realized and occasionally almost perfect." These poems will be read by the "hypothetical generations of the future . . . page by page with Wyatt, Campion, Marvell, and Mother Goose." [2] John L. Stewart calls Ransom "one of the great stylists of modern American poetry." [3] Vivienne Koch has pointed out that Ransom's "structures"—to use one of his own critical terms— are "quite narrow segments of reality," but his "experiences of them are not. His poetry represents the triumph of an original sensibility over an essentially small stock of 'ideas' or 'structures.' " [4] In one of the earliest attempts to assess Ransom's poetic achievement, Richmond Croom Beatty set the pattern for much of the later critical comment. The most striking attributes of that poetry, Beatty wrote, are "its language and its successfully rendered dramatic situations." His poetry, though restrained, is rich in variety and it "will likely remain both significant and exciting among readers who retain a serious esteem for the art." [5]

Ransom's reputation as one of the most significant poets of his generation is somewhat surprising in the light of the fact that his poems, few in number, were written during an unusually brief period. According to Donald Davidson, Ransom's first poem—at least, the first one he was willing to let anyone else read—was apparently written in 1916. "One day of days I remember well. My teacher, John Ransom, beckoned me aside and led me to a shady spot on the campus near the streetcar stop called 'Vanderbilt stile'— though the stile had long yielded to an open entrance. Ransom drew a sheet of paper from his pocket. Almost blushingly, he announced that he had written a poem. It was his very first, he said. He wanted to read it to me." [6] This poem, "Sunset," was included in Ransom's first volume, *Poems About God,* which appeared in

[2]Randall Jarrell, "John Ransom's Poetry," *Sewanee Review,* LVI (Summer, 1948) , 388.

[3]John L. Stewart, *John Crowe Ransom,* No. 18 of *University of Minnesota Pamphlets on American Writers* (Minneapolis, 1962) , 28.

[4]Vivienne Koch, "The Achievement of John Crowe Ransom," *Sewanee Review,* LVII (Spring, 1950) , 261.

[5]Richmond Croom Beatty, "John Crowe Ransom As Poet," *Sewanee Review,* LII (Summer, 1944) , 366.

[6]Donald Davidson, *Southern Writers in the Modern World* (Athens, Ga., 1958) , 14.

1919 while he was serving in the Army in France. Although the poems in this collection were too modern for Davidson, who read them while he too was in service overseas, they were written in what the critics have labelled Ransom's "early manner." The poet's dissatisfaction with their conception and execution is indicated by the fact that all thirty-three of them were excluded when he selected the verse he wished to keep in print.

Although Ransom's discontentment with these early poems was surprising and somewhat disturbing to Davidson, when the two met again at Vanderbilt after the war, Davidson was delighted to see that his friend's creative energy had not decreased. It had merely taken a new turn. Perhaps the early verse appeared to Ransom himself at that time, as it was later to impress Randall Jarrell—"old-fashioned, amateurishly direct jobs that remind you of the Longfellow-Whittier-Lowell section in your sixth-grade reader." [7] At any rate Ransom's poetic development was both rapid and dramatic. From the sonnets which he wrote and exchanged with Walter Clyde Curry when he first returned to Nashville, he quickly turned to productions which foreshadowed his mature poems. During the winter of 1921–22 he read "Necrological" to his fellow Fugitives, and, as Allen Tate has recalled, with that poem almost "overnight he had left behind him the style of his first book and, without confusion, had mastered a new style." [8]

The period from April, 1922, to December, 1925—the forty-five months during which *The Fugitive* was published—was most productive. To most of the weekly or fortnightly meetings of the Fugitive group Ransom brought one or two poems which he read in what Allen Tate has called "a dry tone of understatement" and in an "ironic manner both brisk and bland." The manner of Ransom's oral presentation was well-suited to the "texture" of these poems. Many of his contributions to *The Fugitive* bear the unmistakable stamp of his mature style. From these and a few others he selected the seventy-nine poems and the sequence of twenty-one sonnets he included in his next two volumes, *Chills and Fever* (1924) and *Two Gentlemen in Bonds* (1927). But the stream of Ransom's poetry dried up almost as abruptly as it had begun its initial flow. Almost as if the urge to create poetry were bound to the publication

7 Jarrell, "John Ransom's Poetry," 389.
8 Allen Tate, "The Fugitive, 1922–1925," *Princeton University Library Chronicle* (April, 1942), 83.

of the magazine and the regular meetings of the Fugitive group, Ransom turned his attention to other matters shortly after *The Fugitive* ceased publication and some of the important members of the group became engrossed in affairs less directly literary.

In a period of eleven years, including those spent in World War I, Ransom's poetic career was almost completed. When he collected the poems he wished to preserve in *Selected Poems* (1945), he excluded all of *Poems About God* and the sonnet sequence from *Two Gentlemen in Bonds*. From the seventy-nine remaining poems in the latter volume and all of those from *Chills and Fever,* he selected only thirty-seven, adding five new poems written after 1927. In *Selected Poems* (1963) he added some new stanzas but no new poems; there were five new stanzas in "Prelude to an Evening" and an extensive revision of "Conrad in Twilight" which appears as "Master's in the Garden Again." Ransom has apparently concluded that only a third of his comparatively meager output—and fewer than half of the mature poems—deserves reprinting. The bibliography which follows these essays indicates that Ransom published only 152 poems, of which only 53 appear in the *Selected Poems* (1963).

Naturally, many critics have attempted to explain why "the luxuriant stream of Ransom's poetry . . . dried up . . . into a thin and turgid trickle." [9] Ransom has commented directly on this matter. In response to a question on why he has not produced more poetry, he replied: "My talent was a modest one, and I did the best I could." [10] This characteristically modest statement is as satisfactory an explanation as we are likely to get. Perhaps within the strict limitations he set for himself Ransom said all he had to say; consequently he moved quickly and wisely to a less confining medium, the prose essay. As early as 1927, in a review of *Two Gentlemen in Bonds,* Allen Tate pointed out: "It may be, of course, that further additions to the testament complete now with this volume would cry out redundancy—that Mr. Ransom has overwritten himself." In 1932 Robert Penn Warren pointed out that the sonnet sequence "Two Gentlemen in Bonds" is much less satisfactory than the other poetry in that volume because these sonnets are not in Ransom's characteristic ironic vein; their statement

[9] Beatty, "John Crowe Ransom As Poet," 366.
[10] Rob Roy Purdy (ed.), *Fugitives' Reunion: Conversations at Vanderbilt, May 3–5, 1956* (Nashville, 1959), 81.

of theme is too direct; they present in a "fashion perhaps too obvious and mechanical for full poetic success, the practical and appreciative faculties." [11]

III

Warren's early essay set the pattern for a great deal of the later criticism of Ransom's poetry. In much of Ransom's verse, he wrote, the prevailing theme is the "discrepancies between human desires and their fulfillment." Far more important than the theme, which in itself is certainly not new, is the poet's manner of presenting it. The two properties usually associated with Ransom's poetry are wit and irony, Warren writes, and the critic errs when he asserts that the "wit exists for wit's sake." Such an attitude is entirely wrong, for in Ransom's poetry "wit appears as an instrument"; it is an "attempt at the fusion of the emotional and the intellectual or critical qualities in poetry." In some poetry irony is employed because its author is "enamoured of the effect divorced from any persistent point of view." But such is not the case with the irony in Ransom's verse because it always refers to an ethical center which is constant. To understand and appreciate Ransom's poetry, one must be constantly aware of its center.

It is to be defined in terms of that sensibility whose decay Ransom, along with various other critics, has bewailed. It has been remarked that his poetry deals with "intimate little psychological cruxes." To an astonishing degree, in far more than a majority of the cases, the hero or heroine of the poem is a sufferer from that complaint of "dissociation of sensibility." The poem itself is a commentary on the situation, its irony deriving from the fact that these perhaps otherwise admirable people "cannot fathom nor perform their nature." [12]

Cleanth Brooks agrees with Warren's argument and elaborates its thesis. "To an astonishing degree," Brooks writes, "the problems which engage Ransom's attention turn out to be aspects of one situation: that of man's divided sensibility." [13] This division, Brooks explains, reveals itself in the broken and confused life of the mature man and the innocent and total world of childhood which he has grown out

[11]Robert Penn Warren, "John Crowe Ransom: A Study in Irony," *Virginia Quarterly Review*, XI (January, 1935), 109.
[12]*Ibid.*, 103.
[13]Cleanth Brooks, *Modern Poetry and The Tradition* (Chapel Hill, 1939), 88.

of." The ineffectuality of Ransom's characters as human beings, their standing eternally poised on the brink of self-annihilation, is the result of their inability to attain the "unity of being" which they once possessed. The poems treating childhood give a "suggestion of what such unity can be, but development into maturity, and specialization, break up the harmony of faculties and leave intellect at war with emotion." [14]

F. O. Matthiessen states this essential conflict more explicitly: Ransom's "main theme has been that of the divided sensibility torn between reason and imagination, between science and faith." [15] But Vivienne Koch does not entirely agree; in fact she insists that later critics attempting to follow Warren too closely have been misleading. Although many of Ransom's characters suffer from a dissociation of sensibility, they are not in this condition, as these critics imply, because they have uncritically accepted the myths of nineteenth-century science. "On the contrary," she insists, "the split in sensibility, when present, usually reflects human situations which have always given rise to conflict, and probably always will."

Other critics have concurred with Koch's assertion that Ransom's themes are universal and are not confined to the peculiarities of a specific time and place. Graham Hough points out that the best poems are those that present situations "common to all—old age, love imperfectly fulfilled." [16] John L. Stewart believes the predominant theme is that "man has always been the same and endured the same fate." [17] The central concern of the poems is

. . . established upon a coherent body of convictions which Ransom chose to represent in a few simple themes, all testifying to the ultimate unknowableness of the universe, the tendency of all monistic systems to give man illusions of power over his surroundings and to mislead him into disaster, the ambiguous value of all human experience, and the difference between the simple, carefree, sunny world of the heart's desire and the world we are actually given.[18]

Almost everyone who has written on Ransom's poetry has com-

[14]*Ibid.*, 90.
[15]F. O. Matthiessen, "American Poetry 1920–40," *Sewanee Review*, LV (Winter, 1947), 40.
[16]Graham Hough, "John Crowe Ransom: The Poet and the Critic," *Southern Review*, I (January, 1965), 21.
[17]Stewart, *John Crowe Ransom*, 21.
[18]John L. Stewart, *The Burden of Time* (Princeton, 1965), 222.

mented on his arresting and unusual use of language. Hough says that the poet immediately demands the reader's attention by a "prevailing trickiness of expression, by which expectation is mildly defeated, the mind is made to boggle a little before getting at the meaning." This specific effect is the result of the poet's deliberate use of language that is "a highly mannered fusion of many and disparate elements"; it is neither "of the tribe" nor "of any particular literary tradition." This "stylish idiosyncrasy" of vocabulary is merely Ransom's way of calling attention to his poetic expression in a day when poetry is not widely read and the poet can no longer take his audience for granted.[19]

The juxtaposition of the rare and the commonplace word, Richmond Croom Beatty believes, is a conscious attempt "to strengthen the wit." The poet relies upon his combinations of words not ordinarily used together, and upon the "unusual situations which they assist in portraying," rather than upon "startling similes or metaphors or upon impassioned speech. In Ransom's poetry a 'transmogrifying bee' replaces such images as 'When the evening is spread out against the sky / Like a patient etherised upon a table.' " [20] But this mixing of the rare and commonplace in diction, as John L. Stewart has pointed out, is only part of a technique which "combines the contemporary with the archaic, the lay with the learned, the informal with the formal, the written with the colloquial, and the terse rooted in Anglo-Saxon with the polysyllabic rooted in Latin and Greek." [21]

The critics have commented on the variety of subtle effects Ransom has derived from his sophisticated use of language. Isabel Gamble MacCaffrey says he uses "the precision and formality of Latin" to furnish "a background of austere eternity," and the common English words "that have a hold on our emotions" he uses to express "love and sadness." [22] Cleanth Brooks argues that in many of the best poems the specific effect of the expression comes from the poet's playing "the Latin meaning of a word off against its developed English meaning." The archaic language, Vivienne Koch believes, employed as it often is in poems where the "cast is colloquial and contemporary," serves to remind the reader of the "distance between the situation

---

19Hough, "John Crowe Ransom: The Poet and the Critic," 4.
20Beatty, "John Crowe Ransom As Poet," 356.
21Stewart, *John Crowe Ransom*, 20.
22Isabel Gamble MacCaffrey, "Ceremonies of Bravery; John Crowe Ransom," *Hopkins Review,* VI (Spring-Summer, 1953) , 113.

and the values against which it is judged." The language functions
to point up the essential conflict that is always present in the poetry—
"the conflict between the mythic past and the de-valued present." [23]

Randall Jarrell insists that Ransom's rhetoric has been affected by
his profession (teacher, critic, and editor) and by his classical education and interests. But F. O. Matthiessen suggests that it is the
result of the "lingering rhetoric of the South" and, more importantly
perhaps, that it is a method he developed in order to cope with some
of the difficulties inherent in the writing of poetry in the twentieth
century. He developed his "rhetorical machinery" as a means of
"handling sentiment or emotion without ever seeming sentimental or
over-emotional," as a way of "keeping the poem at the proper aesthetic distance from its subject." This method, Jarrell believes, has
both strengths and weaknesses.

Most writers become over-rhetorical when they are insisting on more emotion
than they actually feel or need to feel; Ransom is just the opposite. He is
perpetually insisting, by his detached, mock-pedantic, wittily complicated
tone, that he is not feeling much at all, not half as much as he should be
feeling—and this rhetoric becomes over-mannered, too protective, when there
is not much emotion for him to pretend not to be feeling, and he keeps
on out of habit.[24]

Almost without exception, the critics agree that Ransom is one of
the most significant poets of his generation. John L. Stewart says
his poetry "is exquisitely balanced and articulated; its texture is as
rich and brilliant as Ransom himself could desire; and from it we
learn things about the world's body that we did not know before."
Isabel Gamble MacCaffrey calls it "a small but accurate mirror of
the modern sensibility. In it are reflected the miraculous virtues of
contemporary verse at its best: its combination of delicacy with
strength, of fervor with restraint, of elegance with earthiness." Louis
D. Rubin, Jr., points out that the verse combines "the urbanity and
hard-wrought decorum" characteristic of his generation. Others have
commented on its "firmness and gentility," its "mockery and playfulness," its "teasing whimsey," "light poise," and "good humored self-
deprecation." But Rubin insists we should not turn Ransom into "a
Good Grey Poet," for throughout the poems there is a "theme of

23Koch, "The Achievement of John Crowe Ransom," 229.
24Jarrell, "John Ransom's Poetry," 379.

death—savage, cruel, terrible . . . an imagery of violence, mocking the gentleness and playfulness." The point upon which these critics agree—and many of the others who have commented on Ransom's verse—is that in a few "perfectly realized" poems he reflects with accuracy and precision some of the almost inexpressible attitudes of his time. His poetry, like the age in which he lives, is one of "perilous equilibrium," of dichotomies and ironies, of tension and paradox. His poems, in the words of Randall Jarrell, portray "the composed and inexhaustible ambiguity of things."

IV

When *The Fugitive* ceased publication in December, 1925, Ransom's career as practicing poet was almost over. His creative talent was already being diverted toward the consideration of aesthetic and social principles which would demand a large portion of his time and energy during the next forty years. In the period when he was deeply absorbed in the publication of *The Fugitive*—and publishing some of his best poetry in its pages—Ransom, like Allen Tate and Donald Davidson, had argued that he was an artist with little or no concern for the social and economic problems of the region to which he belonged. But by 1927 all three of these men had assumed the posture of attacking the New South program of industrial progress and defending the principles of the Old South; the immediate cause of this rather dramatic reversal, Davidson has written, was the famous "anti-evolution trial" and the glaring misrepresentations of the South which "broke in upon our literary concerns like a midnight alarm." [25]

Ransom's shift from a position of unconcern to one of almost complete involvement, as Louise Cowan has pointed out, was less in the "nature of a revelation" than was that of Davidson or Tate.

He was less fundamentally attached to the South than was Davidson and less antagonistic to it than Tate had been, being essentially a detached thinker who concerned himself with the timeless and universal elements in man. Sentimentally he had always valued his native land, with its code of gentility and its fine manners; but the arrogant and ill-natured journalistic attacks on the South attendant upon the Dayton trial roused him to an examination of the philosophic bases of the dispute and placed him finally in the somewhat surprising position of defending Fundamentalism.[26]

[25]Davidson, *Southern Writers in the Modern World*, 30.
[26]Louise Cowan, *The Fugitive Group* (Baton Rouge, 1959), 245.

This examination of "the philosophic bases of the dispute" absorbed so much of his attention during the next ten years that Kelsie B. Harder says he became an "economic polemicist." It was during this period, Harder believes, that Ransom "developed his critical sensibility and sharpened a pointed prose style that served him in good stead when he turned to literary criticism." [27] Ransom's interest in economic and social issues is evident in *God Without Thunder* (1930), as well as in the introduction and the lead article which he contributed to the symposium *I'll Take My Stand* (1930) and in the many articles he published during the thirties in such journals as the *American Review*, the *Southern Review*, and the *Virginia Quarterly Review*. The names of some of these essays give an excellent indication of their subject matter: "The South Defends Its Heritage," "The South Is a Bulwark," "The Aesthetic of Regionalism," and "Modern with a Southern Accent."

Ransom's interest in aesthetic speculation developed concurrently with his political and social concern. Although he had written an occasional short prose piece for *The Fugitive*, he apparently did not turn his attention to probing the nature of art and religion until after he had prepared his third book of poetry. In 1926 he wrote Tate that he was looking forward to the "delicious prospect" of relatively free time for studying and writing. He contemplated writing a book on aesthetics, which he was referring to at the time as "The Third Moment," and he had taken a leave of absence from Vanderbilt to devote full time to the project. In this book, which was never published, he intended to bring together some of the scattered reflections which had appeared in a few brief Fugitive pieces and the critical ideas which a prolonged correspondence with Tate had helped him to develop. Two related problems seemed to him to be the primary concerns of the literary critic in the twentieth century. First he must accept the fact that "it is not a pre-scientific poetry but a post-scientific one to which we must now give our consent." [28] Then he must determine the existing relationship between science and art, and, particularly, he must establish and maintain "a firm ontological position in the face of a dominant scientific knowledge." [29]

To get at these problems, Ransom sought to set forth the three

27Kelsie B. Harder, "John Crowe Ransom as Economist," *Modern Age*, II (Fall, 1958), 390.
28John Crowe Ransom, *The World's Body* (New York, 1958), vii.
29Cowan, *The Fugitive Group*, 231.

"moments" that distinguish the historical order of experience, and he explained the scheme of the proposed book in the lengthy correspondence with Tate. The first moment is the actual experience itself, "pure of all intellectual content, unreflective, concrete and singular; there are no distinctions, and the subject is identical with the whole." In the second moment the experience is recorded and concepts are formed; abstract ideas of the experience are derived through the process of subtracting "from the whole." In the third moment "we become aware of the deficiency of the record. Most of the experience is quite missing from it." The abstract ideas do not reproduce the initial experience, and no amount of philosophical synthesis will recover it.[30] The only way to recall the "fugitive first moment" is through images. If man follows "this recourse to images," what he really gets is a "mixed world composed of both images and concepts; or a sort of practicable reconciliation of the two worlds." [31] He tries to recapture this first moment through dreams, religion, morals, or art. Here Ransom is pondering a problem that has concerned him in much of his later criticism. Because it can reconstitute experience through concrete images, poetry has epistemological and ontological significances that one cannot find in science.

After abandoning "The Third Moment," Ransom began work on *God Without Thunder*. Walter Sutton believes that this book, the first extended prose work Ransom published, "reflects many of Eliot's views, which are, however, more boldly stated by Ransom in his role of an unabashed Southern fundamentalist." [32] But, though the focus has shifted from poetry to religious myth, Ransom is still concerned with the dual nature of the universe, with the inadequacies of scientific abstractions as revelation of the relationship existing between the physical and metaphysical realms, and with the necessity of man's resorting to religious myth (which employs the supernatural "to represent the fulness of the natural") if he would not unnecessarily limit his vision. John L. Stewart contends that *God Without Thunder* "holds the central position in Ransom's prose writing" because in it "the ideas of the letters and the miscellaneous essays preceding it are summarized, systematized, illustrated, and defended in detail." Too, it anticipates many of the ideas more fully developed in later essays, and it "clarifies and enriches one's understanding and

---

[30]Letter to Tate, September 5, 1926, quoted in Cowan, *The Fugitive Group*, 236.
[31]*Ibid.*
[32]Walter Sutton, *Modern American Criticism* (Englewood Cliffs, N.J., 1963), 107.

appreciation of his poetry, for many of its conceptions expand upon convictions and attitudes implicit in the poems." [33]

Ransom argues for the need of an inscrutable God, one that cannot be explained by scientific fact or comprehended by man's reason. His "unorthodox defense of orthodoxy" favors the wrathful God of the Old Testament, and he seeks institutional support for his ideas. Since he can find no established church with which he is compatible, he can suggest only one position for the modern man who feels the need of a sustaining orthodoxy:

> *With whatever religious institution a modern man may be connected, let him try to turn it back towards orthodoxy.*
> *Let him insist on a virile and concrete God, and accept no Principle as a substitute.*
> *Let him restore to God the Thunder.*
> *Let him resist the usurpation of the Godhead by the soft modern version of the Christ, and try to keep the Christ for what he professed to be: the Demigod who came to do honor to the God.*[34]

That Ransom perceived a kinship between religion and poetry is demonstrated in a passage that appears later in the same work:

[Religion is] the system of myths which gives a working definition to the relation of man to nature. It always has to join together in some fashion two quite different views of this relation. The first is that of nature as usable and intelligible for man: nature as humane order, devoted to man's welfare, created by a benevolent God for the purpose of man's service. The second is that of nature as unintelligible and contingent, and therefore alien and unusable for man: nature as an order that is not the humane or ethical order.[35]

Ransom wrote *God Without Thunder* while he was involved in what some have called his agrarian phase, and it is clear that he believed the mythic way in which man should regard nature and God is possible in an agrarian society.

Religion is our submission to the general intention of a nature that is fairly inscrutable; it is the sense of our role as creatures within it. But nature in-

33Stewart, *The Burden of Time*, 268.
34John Crowe Ransom, *God Without Thunder: An Unorthodox Defense of Orthodoxy* (New York, 1930), 327–28.
35*Ibid.*, 156.

dustrialized, transformed into cities and artificial habitations, manufactured into commodities, is no longer nature but a highly simplified picture of nature. We receive the picture of having power over nature, and lose the sense of something mysterious and contingent. The God of nature under these conditions is merely an amicable expression, a superfluity, and the philosophical understanding ordinarily carried in the religious experience is not there for us to have.[36]

At the time when Ransom was most intensely involved with the agrarian controversy, he continued to speculate on the nature of poetry, and in 1938 he brought together fifteen of his literary essays under the title *The World's Body*. This collection includes some of Ransom's best known literary ideas, and it represents adequately the form in which he was to express these ideas, with "a prevailing trickiness of expression." Hough cites as an example of this manner the use of "ontology," a word which to Ransom does not mean a branch of metaphysics but "the reality of an object's being." But to John L. Stewart the "informing principle" in the criticism, as in the poetry, is contrast.

It is everywhere: in the style, in the organization of the discourse, in the topics. Contrast between the tone and the topic; between the sophisticated hypothesis and the homely example; between the colloquial diction and syntax and the learned terms and Great Names; between what Ransom regards as monistic, even totalitarian philosophies and pluralistic, rebellious particulars that will not submit to confinement; between logic and feeling; between science and art; between mind and body; between East and West.[37]

In *The World's Body* Ransom continues his attack against science, but now his interest is in ritual rather than in dogma. "It is my idea," he wrote, "that religion is an institution existing for the sake of its ritual, rather than . . . for the sake of its doctrines." A work of art is a more valid source of knowledge than a scientific account because the work of art connotes the "whole substance" of the object. Not only is poetry a source of knowledge; it seeks through presentation of concrete particularities to restore the world's body, which science, with its eternal tendency to draw abstractions, tends to destroy. "What we cannot know constitutionally

[36]John Crowe Ransom, "A Statement of Principles," in Twelve Southerners, *I'll Take My Stand: The South and the Agrarian Tradition* (New York and London, 1930), xxiv.
[37]Stewart, *The Burden of Time*, 258.

as scientists is the world which is made of whole and indefeasible objects, and this is the world which poetry recovers for us." The artistic rendering of an object is usually better than the object itself, for when confronted with the object one may wish to use it, to discover the "physical satisfaction which it contains"; but in the face of the artistic representation one "may wish to know it for its own sake and conceive it as having its own existence." Thus in contemplating a work of art one may see in it qualities which he cannot perceive in the object itself.

The critical method underlying this collection of seemingly unrelated essays—they deal with a broad variety of subjects, from Shakespeare and Milton to Edna St. Vincent Millay and George Santayana—provides its author, Morgan Blum writes, with "a machinery of approach" to a wide range of problems both literary and nonliterary. "With a few purely practical alterations, it can damn the Platonism in a Shelley's poetry or a Santayana's philosophy; it can judge the inadequacy of a religion or a metric with equal facility." [38] Ransom's essay on "Lycidas," Graham Hough believes, with its central theme of the "virtual disappearance of the author, with his historic personality, his private and social passions, behind the formal and conventional structure of the elegy," is "one of the most valuable studies" of that poem. Blum contends that Ransom's discussion not only "illuminates . . . the text at hand, but also the complex psychic process we call creation." But Winifred Lynskey demurs; instead, she sees the piece as a classic example of Ransom's myopia. The criticism is "motivated by Milton's failure to live up to Mr. Ransom's critical theories. To Mr. Ransom logical structure or form is a messianic device by which the poet attains ontological truth and indicates this truth to the reader." Since Milton "deliberately wrote an irregular pastoral solely to gain publicity," his motive was suspect; and its irregular structure "means an obscure conception of truth and an inferior poet." Many readers would doubt that Lynskey's objections do serious damage to the central thesis of Ransom's argument.

In "Criticism, Inc.," the concluding essay of *The World's Body,* Ransom deplores the lack of the proper kind of criticism in the universities, where good criticism should be practiced; wherever he looks, he finds the academic critic absorbed in textual, philologi-

38Morgan Blum, "The Fugitive Particular: John Crowe Ransom, Critic," *Western Review,* XIV (Winter, 1950) , 96.

cal, and historical scholarship. He calls for a criticism that is more concerned with formal analysis and aesthetic values, one that is centered on the work of art itself. The poem is the basic document and the critic's attention should be focused on it, not on facts about it or its author's life. Ransom's call was soon answered. In the same year in which *The World's Body* was published, *Understanding Poetry* appeared. Edited by Cleanth Brooks and Robert Penn Warren, two of his former students, this textbook effected many of the changes that Ransom desired. To say that it initiated a virtual revolution in the way literature is taught to undergraduates would scarcely be an overstatement.

V

In the fall of 1937 Ransom left Vanderbilt, after almost thirty years, to become editor of the *Kenyon Review*. Under his direction this journal quickly became one of the most important and influential literary quarterlies in America. In its pages he published excellent poems and stories by many of the established writers of Europe and America. He also introduced to the serious students of literature in the Western world some of the most significant of the promising new writers who were just beginning to publish during and after World War II. But the extent of Ransom's contribution to the world of letters through this journal can best be ascertained by reviewing the impressive volume of first-rate criticism published by the *Kenyon Review* while he was chief editor. Hardly an issue appeared that did not include contributions by Ransom and by one or more of the men whom he called the "New Critics": Allen Tate, Cleanth Brooks, Robert Penn Warren, R. P. Blackmur, Kenneth Burke, and William Empson.

After many years of deliberation on the subject, Ransom was convinced that the critic should devote his attention to the text of the poem. The critic's function was to indicate precisely what a given passage of literature actually *means*, how a poem says that which cannot be said in any other literary medium. Among the many critics whose work he had been reading for almost two decades, he found a relatively small group who seemed to him to be practicing their craft in the proper manner. His next book, *The New Criticism* (1941), is devoted primarily to a systematic study of the theories and practices of some of the best known of these: I. A. Richards, William Empson, T. S. Eliot, and Yvor

Winters. Ransom's first intention, apparently, was to conclude his study of significant contemporary criticism with his discussion of the critical theories and practices of these men, but Delmore Schwartz, who was asked to read the manuscript, insisted that there was one glaring omission. Characteristically, Ransom had not included himself among the important New Critics, and Schwartz urged him to present his own critical views in more detail. Following Schwartz's suggestion, Ransom added the chapter "Wanted: An Ontological Critic," in which he attempts to give his current views on the responsibilities and functions of the literary critic.[39]

Most of the assumptions in *The New Criticism* can be found in *God Without Thunder* and *The World's Body*. With new details and additional evidence, Ransom reasserts his belief in the basic distinction between the language of science and the art of poetry, arguing for the sensuous particularity of poetry. Specifically, he indicates the two components of all poetry. First there is *structure,* which Ransom defines as "the prose of the poem, being a logical discourse of almost any kind and dealing with almost any content suited to a logical discourse." The structure of the poem, then, includes not only conventional rhyme and meter but also the poem's logical content, with its beginning, middle, and end, and its appropriately interspersed transitions. But there is also a second necessary component:

What is the value of a structure which (a) is not so tight and precise on its logical side as a scientific or technical prose structure generally is; and (b) imports and carries along a great deal of irrelevant or foreign matter which is clearly not structural but even obstructive? This a– and b– formulation is what we inevitably come to if we take the analysis our best critics offer. We sum it up by saying that the poem is a loose logical structure with an irrelevant local texture.

This "local texture" is composed of diction, imagery, sound—the "irrational" elements of art, the details which furnish inexhaustible new insights. These details are ordered and interrelated, although their organization is not logical and their relationship is not always obvious. Both *structure* and *texture* are essential components of poetry, for, in Ransom's words, a "beautiful poem is one which proceeds to the completion of a logical structure, but not without at-

39Stewart, *The Burden of Time,* 280.

tention to the local particularity of its components." The true function of the critic, furthermore, is to perceive the relationship that
exists between the two. "To define the structure-texture procedure of
poets," he writes, "is to define poetic strategy." The "indeterminate
final meaning" of a poem results from the interaction of structure and
texture, and the understanding of this meaning is the "vocation *par
excellence* of criticism." In other words, the critic's responsibility is to
inform his reader of what the poem *says* or *means,* and the only way
he can fullfill this function is to read the poem and not something
else.

VI

Although Ransom has not published a book of criticism since
1941,[40] in the past twenty-five years he has produced more than
forty critical essays, many of which are on literary subjects.

These essays demonstrate that Ransom has altered his critical opinions in several important ways. If the earlier writing seems to emphasize texture and particulars, these later essays are more concerned
with structure and universals. In 1947, reacting to Cleanth Brooks's
The Well Wrought Urn, Ransom expressed a fear that some of his
earlier remarks might have been taken too literally:

. . . about fifteen years ago I was thinking of the poem as having a logical
structure or framework, and a texture whose character was partly irrelevant
to the logical form and purpose. My "texture" in particular has given offense,
and the fact is that I had no sooner uttered it than it struck me as a flat
and inadequate figure for that vivid and easily felt part of a poem which we
associate particularly with poetic language.[41]

Now he would recast his definition, using a figure that had had a
particular appeal to eighteenth-century critics: "Suppose we say that
the poem is an organism. Then it has a physiology. We will figure
its organs, and to me it seems satisfactory if we say there are three:
the head, the heart, the feet." [42] Although there is considerable co-
operation among these various organs, "the peculiarity of the joint
production is that it still consists of the several products of the organs

[40]*Poems and Essays,* a Vintage paperback issued in 1955, contains eight critical
pieces.
[41]John Crowe Ransom, "The Concrete Universal: Observations on the Understanding of Poetry," *Kenyon Review,* XVI (1954) , 559.
[42]*Ibid.,* 560.

working individually." Each organ speaks a different language: "the head in an intellectual language, the heart in an affective language, the feet in a rhythmical language."

Criticism must be aware of all three languages, not the least of which is that of the head. The New Critics, with their strong focus on language, have achieved a "linguistic revolution" in the reading of poetry. But their emphasis upon the "total connotation of words," their minute scrutiny of the "detailed phrase," and their deliberate movement from phrase to phrase have created a "sense of disorder" and suggested to some readers that a poem cannot be perceived as a whole.[43] These critics are neglecting the intellectual language of the poem. Since a poem has an intellectual action, it contains a beginning, a middle, and an end. To be aware of the poem as a "logical whole," the reader must perceive each of these parts and the relationships among them. Since these relationships are rather difficult to determine, particularly in some modern poetry, the reader must perform an *explication de texte*. But the process of reading is not yet complete. Since the poet uses the "mode of feeling rather than logic," the "composite language" must be translated into the "exclusive language of the intellect." Thus Ransom comes to accept the value of "logical paraphrase," a term which had been anathema to him a few years earlier. There was a time when he had insisted that intellectuals were "abusing and spoiling our poems" but now he feels that such an attitude is "arrogant and wrong":

There is nowhere in the world for the logical paraphrase to have come from except the poem, where it is implicit; and it is the intellectuals (in their capacity of formal logicians) who are the masters of the science of explicating what is implicit. Nor do they harm the poem by taking their use of it. When we look again, the poem is still there, timeless and inviolable, for other uses.[44]

The New Critics, he fears, may be spending too much time with what he had earlier called the poem's texture; consequently they tend to neglect the "theoretical constitution of poetry" and to "create a sense of its disorder." "I would put the emphasis," he wrote in 1943, "on the positive or prose elements of the poem first, and

[43]John Crowe Ransom, "Poetry: The Formal Analysis," *Kenyon Review*, IX (1947), 436.
[44]"The Concrete Universal," 561.

regardless of another element [45] which proposes to make a poetry out of it." [46] Only in this way can one be fully aware of the eternal human values contained in a work of art.

During the forties, too, Ransom commented on what some scholars have regarded as the too restrictive range of much modern literary criticism. Literary judgment, he contended, has two margins. The lower of these employs the tools of academic scholarship: the language, the milieu out of which the literary work came, and even biographical facts about the author. But the other level, and the higher of the two, should employ the principles of psychology and philosophy. Because their concern has been almost entirely with language, some critics have made themselves vulnerable to their enemies, those who know and use the methods of the Freudian psychologists. Following his own advice, Ransom went to philosophy in an attempt to state more precisely his notion of the dual nature of poetry and his belief in the distinctions between science and art. A term useful for this purpose, he found, was the Concrete Universal, which he borrowed from Hegel. "A Universal in Hegel's favorite sense," Ransom believes, "is any idea in the mind which proposes a little universe, or organized working combination of parts, where there is a whole and single effect to be produced, and the heterogeneous parts must perform their several duties faithfully in order to bring it about." And by Concrete Hegel means the "objective element in which the universal in all its parts is to be materialized." [47]

There are two kinds of Universals: the practical and the moral. The first of these is exemplified in the "operations of applied science." The scientist insists that there be "no unused remainder of the Concreteness"; consequently, if he does not find the "right parts already existing in the state of nature," he alters the material he finds there until he makes it perfect: "Not one necessary part missing; not one unnecessary part showing; nor a part showing which is either excessive or deficient in its action." [48] Because the literary critic is concerned with the second kind of Universal, he should not expect to find this same rigorous kind of organization within a poem. The "logical plan" of a poem is not "borne out perfectly in the sensuous detail which

[45] That is, the texture: "interpolated material which does not relate to the argument."

[46] John Crowe Ransom, "The Inorganic Muses," *Kenyon Review*, V (1943), 286.

[47] John Crowe Ransom, "The Concrete Universal: Observations on the Understanding of Poetry," *Poems and Essays* (New York, 1955), 162.

[48] *Ibid.*, 164.

puts it into action"; neither is the "Concrete . . . used up so completely in the service of the Universal that there is no remainder."
These things are true because of the nature of the moral Universal:

> The moral Universal of the poem does not use nature as a means but as an
> end; it goes out into nature not as a predatory conqueror and despoiler
> but as an inquirer, to look at nature as nature naturally is, and see what
> its own reception may be. The moral Universal takes a journey into nature,
> so to speak, and the concrete element is an area of nature existing in its
> natural conformations as these are given, and discovered, not a concrete
> element which it means to ransack for materials which have already been
> prescribed.[49]

Again Ransom points out that the poetic statement does not achieve
a synthesis between the general and the particular. The knowledge
which art carries is different from the facts of science; poetic language expresses metaphorically a truth like that of religion or myth.
Ransom still insists that the critic's role is to discover the "indeterminate final meaning" of a poem by perceiving the relationships that
exist between its "logical plan" and the sensuous detail that puts
this plan "into action."

This indication of the critic's responsibility to his reader defines,
perhaps, the area of Ransom's greatest influence. If his theorizing about
the nature and uses of poetry is not startlingly original, he is a sensitive reader of poetry, and his demonstrations of how a poem should
be read furnish convincing evidence that a work of art can be a more
valid source of information than a scientific treatise. Properly read,
the poem informs us of the full range of our limitations and potential-
ities as no other instrument can. But if the poem is to provide this
kind of illumination, it must be read as poetry and not as biography,
history, or philosophy. To read in this manner any good poem—including "Painted Head," "Antique Harvesters," "Captain Carpenter,"
or any of the other of Ransom's nearly perfect lyrics—is to "restore the
world's body" and to gain insights into the nature of human existence
that are otherwise unavailable.

49*Ibid.*, 166.

JOHN CROWE RANSOM: A STUDY IN IRONY

Robert Penn Warren

The poetry of John Crowe Ransom is peculiarly systematic.* It refers regularly to a center which is precise and has been objectively formulated by the poet himself, although not in relation to his poetry. Items of his poetic performance which appear the most innocent and peripheral are usually, on inspection, to be interpreted in relation to that basic idea of his work. The poetry must stand or fall in, and of, itself; but meanwhile, if it is to be fully understood, if its theme is to be stated, if certain effects of the poetry itself are to be appreciated, it must be read in terms of that center to which it refers.

The problem at the center of Ransom's work is specially modern—at least we are accustomed to think it so—but it implies some history. For more than a century men have speculated about the possible effect of science on the poetic impulse. Wordsworth, living at the time when science was beginning to afflict the poet's consciousness, regarded the whole matter with a certain complacency. Let the objects of science become familiar enough, and they would become the objects of poetry. Wordsworth could be complacent at the moment because he assumed that the poet would regard those objects in precisely the same way he had regarded, for century on century,

*This essay originally appeared in *Virginia Quarterly Review*, XI (January, 1935), 93–112.

the horse or the tree. He did not consider what would be the case if the poet, or the reader of poetry, or anyone for that matter, habitually regarded the erstwhile tree in the same way the scientist looks at it. Other poet-critics of the period, even Shelley at times, were less optimistic, and Wordsworth himself suffered twinges of suspicion, as when he wrote the incredible twaddle about one who would peep and botanize upon his mother's grave.

In 1904 Paul Elmer More, in an essay on Tolstoy which was, in fact, devoted to a study of the "age-old quarrel between philosophy and poetry," with a polite hankering after the kalokagathia of Greece, could casually remark on the "new antinomy of literature and science," or say that "the most notable conflict today is undoubtedly between the imagination and the analytic spirit of science." One result of that conflict, the private effect on the poet in the act of exercising his craft, is indicated, almost a quarter of a century later, by I. A. Richards when he writes: "A poet today whose integrity is equal to that of the greater poets of the past is inevitably plagued by the problem of thought and feeling as poets have never been plagued before."

Poets of the past, that is, poets living up to the middle of the seventeenth century, possessed, according to T. S. Eliot's theory in the now well-known essay on the Metaphysical Poets, "a mechanism of sensibility which could devour any kind of experience." But a dissociation of sensibility set in; later poets "thought and felt by fits, unbalanced." By way of cure for the resulting situation he suggests a certain poetic regimen: "The poet must become more and more comprehensive, more allusive, more indirect, in order to force, to dislocate if necessary, language into his meaning"; he must have the faculty of "transmuting ideas into sensations, of transforming an observation into a state of mind." Eliot's diagnosis attributes the disease to literary influence: Milton and Dryden performed special poetic functions so well that collateral deficiencies passed unobserved. But he does not describe the result as a mere narrowing of the sphere of poetic activity. It was a "dissociation of sensibility" causing the poets to think and feel by fits, a dissociation ultimately to be equated with the issue raised in Romantic criticism.

It may be objected at this point that science of itself need foster no such dissociation. Certainly the official view of science in the matter, when science has deigned to consider the matter at all, admits to no such responsibility. J. B. S. Haldane says that poetry, if the poets only knew more science, would interpret to the average man "that beauty in his own life"—which, I suppose, is what Tennyson set out to do in terms of his science, with a degree of success now obvious. But some poets have not been properly grateful for the sop thrown them; for instance, Robert Graves once retorted to Haldane with some heat that it is hard to see exactly what—poetically speaking—all this interpretation would mean. The point at issue for present purposes, however, is not that science need foster the dissociation. The issue is that English poetry experienced a profound change which seems to be coincident with the rise of modern science, and that some generations of poets have feared the danger that the abstract, quantitative world known to science would, as Santayana puts it, "dry up the ancient fountains of poetry by its habitual presence in thought."

Science, perhaps, need not foster this dissociation of sensibility, which, if permitted to proceed unchecked, might end in drying up the ancient fountains. It is on the premise that the situation is, after all, remediable that Eliot, for instance, has put the question. For the poet, by way of cure, he once proposed a private discipline; but since that time he has advocated a public discipline. He has announced himself as a royalist in politics and an Anglo-Catholic in religion; and it is instructive that the disrepute of the dogmas of royalism and conservative religion attended the rise of science. The problem is, finally, social. In paraphrase of Whitman it might be said: to have poetry of the complete sensibility one must have an audience whose sensibility is unimpaired.

On the assumption that the matter is remediable, but not remediable in a purely private discipline on the part of the poet, Ransom has written his criticism. A very small proportion of this criticism is purely literary. The imperfect mythopoeic faculty exhibited in English poetry of the past two and a half centuries is merely an aspect of a progressive attenuation and poverty of the myth-making faculty in general. "For, after all," Ransom says in the prefatory letter of *God Without Thunder*, "look and see how roundly the world has of late been disabused of the most and best of its myths . . . and as a consequence been stricken with an unheard-of poverty of mind and unhappiness of life." Although the principle is capable of extension, it is of religious myth that he speaks. "What a sorry reputation the true priest, the devout keeper of the myths, enjoys now in this Western world,

and particularly in this most Western world of America! It has
occurred to me therefore that I might undertake to explain to it,
as if in simple untechnical monosyllables, the function of myths
in human civilization. This seems to me an important thing to
do; and going with it is the task of explaining why one myth
may be better than another."

Now what is meant precisely by myth? Ransom has not, at any
point, given a vest-pocket definition, but the meaning appears
clear and not specially devised. A myth is a fiction, a construct,
which expresses a truth and affirms a value. It is not an illustration
of doctrine. It differs from allegory in that its components, not
to be equated with anything else, function in their own right. It
is the dynamic truth, the dynamic value. The philosophy of a
given myth may be defined, but the definition is no more the
myth itself than the statement of the theme of a poem is the
poem: in each instance the value becomes static, it may be discussed but not felt, the conviction of experience is forfeited. (The
position of the Platonic myth in relation to the particular topic
of discussion is beautifully in point.) In other words, myth represents a primary exercise of sensibility in which thought and feeling
are one; it is a total communication.

The myth-maker, Ransom says, sets up his God in response to
two motives: an extensive and an intensive. God means, in response
to the former, a universe of "a magnitude exceeding its own natural history"; in response to the latter, of "a richness of being
that exceeds formulation." The myth, then, defines the myth-
maker's world, his position in it, his destiny, and his appropriate
attitude. What is the content of our modern mythology, and wherein is it wanting?

The Semitic God of the Old Testament was mysterious, and
he was the author of evil as well as good. That is, the old God
was not reasonable; He was the God of contingency, of the unpredictable. But Satan, in the Garden myth, was the Demigod, the
"Prometheus, the Spirit of Secular Science, who would like to set
up falsely as the God, the Ruler of the Universe." He would give
of the tree of knowledge, he would have man take comfort in a
purely reasonable order. Christ the Word was likewise a Demigod
who gave man, sick with uncertainty, the hope of reason, but a
Demigod who *refused* to set up as God. Man, however, has forced
the more modest Demigod, Christ, into the role of usurper; the

new religion, thoroughly in harmony with the practical ideal of the Western world, is the worship of the Logos, that is, the God of Reason and Science, the Great Scientist. For instance, I have heard, in Memphis, Tennessee, in the Sunday morning service of a church once concerned with the awful mysteries of atonement and election, a sermon on the four modern "saints," those men who now walk hand in hand with god: i.e., Mr. Pupin, Mr. Millikan, Mr. Ford, and Mr. Rockefeller.

Properly speaking, it seems that there has been no quarrel between science and religion; rather, there has been a quarrel between the older, more conservative faiths, with their elements of irrationality and contingency, and the new religion preached by the apostolic scientist, whether from pulpit or laboratory. The scientists have, finally, offered myths, constructs which are not demonstrable. They have been shy of personalities in their myths, especially in the more professional ones, but such terms as Evolution, Vitalism, Principle, Impersonal Intelligence, look like "poorly disguised versions of personality." Now science has perpetual need in its professional business of these myths; but even in this professional business the myths must be generally recognized as such. The layman who has put his faith in these myths must realize in this respect their limit as knowledge. He should also realize that, although the basic myth of the God of Reason and the professional scientific myths may testify to the presence of the mythopoeic faculty, they testify to it in a peculiarly attenuated, incomplete, and unsatisfying form. The myth of rationality, with all the little myths comprehended under it, does not take care of the contingencies of his being and adventures.

The myth of rationality is deficient, because science "drives too hard after its objective, and pays no attention to the setting." It provides a form of knowledge concerned, not with the concrete, but with the abstract; not with quality, but with quantity. It professes to fit its items into a system, but any one item, in its richness of being, may defy the system until Doomsday. Science provides only one type of chart for the experience of man in the world; in so far as this becomes the basis of education, that is, the basis of interpretation for other charts, a violence is done to human sensibility, which likewise has an appreciative concern with persons, objects, and events of this world—a concern called, in its formal aspect, art. But under the scientific civilization, according to Donald

Davidson, the artist "is *against* or *away from* society, and the disturbed relationship becomes his essential theme, always underlying his work, no matter whether he evades or accepts the treatment of the theme itself." (Under the present order one may observe that when the artist determines to be "social-minded" he generally becomes a propagandist, employing the technical resources of an art for the purpose of thesis. His art becomes a mere instrument; and he a scientist, albeit an imperfect one.)

The way of life congenial to the terms of the myth of rationality is called industrialism. The God of Reason has offered a machinery, a technique, and a gospel of production which provide theoretically at least, a maximum of efficiency in the gratification of desire. Two objections may be raised to the easy acceptance of this way of life prescribed by the myth of rationality. First, such blessings as the myth may afford are the property of a relatively small number of believers. But even if a more equitable distribution of its blessings should be contrived, the second objection would remain in force: the very superiority in efficiency may brutalize desire, for reason, pure and simple, dictates an immediate gratification without let or irrelevancy. This superior efficiency separates man from brute creation, but a sensibility which the exercise of reason in this fashion would destroy or impair might differentiate him even further. In the experience of love, as a case in point, man dwells on the extraordinarily complex qualities which are possessed by the beloved, so that the experience becomes a rich concern not exhausted by physical satisfaction. This total process involves the basic desire and its satisfaction, which is the "reasonable" objective, but it also involves much more than unassisted reason would prescribe in fulfilling that desire. In a system dedicated to the gratification of appetite by the most competent, the most reasonable, process, effective action becomes the ideal of human conduct: Progress, or the perpetual violation of nature. But to be human at all, "we have to have something which will stop action, and this something cannot possibly be reason in its narrow sense." It is sensibility.

Ransom's recommendation of an agrarian economy depends on the foregoing principles. The practical details of that prescription are here irrelevant; it is sufficient to point out that the objective is not the abolition, but the correction of industrialism, just as the objective on the theoretical side of Ransom's argument is not the abolition, but the correction of science; that is, the interpretation of science in the total context of human experience. The agrarian establishment, presumably, would provide fuller opportunity for the play of man's sensibility, or in other words, for the play of his proper humanity. The essential qualities of that establishment—order, tradition, stability—are merely aspects of that sensibility.

Now for a moment of recapitulation. Man has been unable to dispense with myth, but his new myths, the basic one of modern religion and the more special ones of science, are of peculiar poverty. They neither represent nor provide for the exercise of man's complete sensibility. The terms of actual existence dictated by the basic myth and propagated by the application of science create a *milieu* further opposed to the exercise of that sensibility. Ransom's fundamental motive is the defense of sensibility, by which, I take it, he means the harmonious adjustment, or rather unified function, of thought and feeling. This will sound very tame to some, who, if pressed, would probably explain that it is a truism, is not new, is not original, or to sum up, is not "revolutionary"; and revolutionary is precisely what it is not. Ransom has merely been concerned to defend man against a revolution which, by a dogma of unadulterated reason, has endangered his sensibility; which has, in fact, promoted its dissociation.

II

It is time to ask to what extent and in what fashion this fundamental motive appears in Ransom's poetry, on which, to date, his literary reputation is chiefly founded. To answer this I shall, perforce, be roundabout. Wit and irony are the two properties most generally ascribed to his poetry, but their meaning and reference in this particular regard have gone uninvestigated. And to investigate them seems to me the shortest way, after all, to the answer of my question. "Most of Ransom's poetry," George Williamson writes in his essay "Donne and the Poetry of Today," "combines an amusing texture with a serious emotion." This "witty texture," use of the conceit, and occasionally something of "conceptual form," he relates to the Donne tradition, especially to the Cavalier heirs of Donne. In Ransom's verse, he writes, "wit has become a poetic attitude." This seems to be the conventional description of Ransom's work.

Williamson's last remark, I presume, means that wit exists for wit's sake, that it is the "poetic attitude" and not a functional aspect of the general state of mind from which the poetry is written. In other words, it is implied—I hope I do the critic no wrong—that the wit is irresponsible; the poet merely elects subjects which will provide scope for his talent of agility and shock. This approximates Johnson's criticism of the Metaphysicals, although Williamson does not speak in any pejorative sense.

But the poet in question is not a child with such a precocious toy. As a matter of fact, in only two poems, "Survey of Literature" and "Our Two Worthies," the latter of which, according to Williamson, is the closest approach to Eliot, do I feel that the interest is primarily in the wit as such. Elsewhere in the poet's three volumes the wit appears as an instrument. The precise business of this instrument can, perhaps, be best illustrated by a comparison with metaphor. Metaphor, we are told, implies a comparison which, on factual basis and according to strict science, is not defensible, but which justifies itself in terms of the emotional enrichment of a poetic theme, or more ambitiously sometimes, as the vehicle of its communication. Now wit is a critical and intellectual quality; when it appears in a poem, that poem, if otherwise successful as poetry, is enriched, but in another direction. Again, like metaphor, it may be a device toward resolution of a theme. Contrary to opinion among softer readers of poetry, usually those whose taste has been formed on nineteenth-century models, wit and emotional quality in poetry are not mutually exclusive, or necessarily opposed, but indeed may be so interfused that only a violence of abstraction may define them individually. The examples of this readiest to my mind would come from Donne and Marvell, or perhaps in rarer instances from Dryden. In the present case, the wit represents an attempt toward the integration I have been discussing, an attempt at the fusion of the emotional and the intellectual or critical qualities in poetry. This is a technical aspect of the general theory implied in the following quotation from one of Ransom's essays which appeared in *The Fugitive* in 1925: "It is evident that not Byron nor Keats nor Shelley ever became quite sophisticated, or grown-up, though Byron showed an indefatigable and alarming tendency to devote a complete act of cerebration to each of his poetical themes; and Keats missed writing a second English epic because he was too young when he tried it,—he did not know how to bring his whole mind to bear on his subject. . . . Nobody in the whole century knew how to put his whole mind and experience to work in poetry. . . ." (It is interesting to note that Eliot sees in the second "Hyperion" "traces of a struggle toward unification of sensibility.")

This instrument of wit in Ransom's poetry, whether it is employed in incidental imagery, in a certain pedantry of rhetoric, or in the organization of the entire material, is usually directed to a specific and constant effect. This effect is ironical. Something of this nature may be intended in the remark that his "poetry combines an amusing texture with a serious emotion," but such scarcely appears a complete account. It would make the irony an unessential one of manner only.

Irony, like wit, may be used because the writer happens to be enamoured of the effect divorced from any persistent point of view. On this basis it is entirely unphilosophical, a constant flight from "centrality." It is that romantic irony which, by its lack of ethical reference, has provoked such agitation in the Humanists. But the irony of Ransom's poetry is not one of irresponsible contrasts and negations. Babbitt might not have sanctioned the ethical propriety of the center to which it refers, but that center, at all events, is constant.

I hope that by this time I shall have been anticipated by those readers familiar with Ransom's poetry in the definition of its center. It is to be defined in terms of that sensibility whose decay Ransom, along with various other critics, has bewailed. It has been remarked that his poetry deals with "intimate little psychological cruxes." To an astonishing degree, in far more than a majority of cases, the hero or heroine of the poem is a sufferer from that complaint of "dissociation of sensibility." The poem itself is a commentary on the situation, its irony deriving from the fact that these perhaps otherwise admirable people "cannot fathom nor perform their nature." In general they represent a disorder contrary to the principles of order which the poet, in his more explicit, non-poetic work, has defended. Here the poet, from the security of his position, yet with that concrete realization of detail which is any poet's faculty, dramatizes the commentary.

When I say from the security of his position, I do not mean to imply that the sensibility of the poet himself is, necessarily, integrated. The individual cannot, even with a clear diagnosis of his predicament, will himself into the desired state of being; he is, by far, too much a part of all that he has met. But awareness, let it be said, merits the prerogative of commentary. This awareness constitutes the "ethical" reference of the irony. (In the Socratic irony, to employ Babbitt's analysis, the reference is not to perfect knowledge but to a consciousness of man's limitation in attaining truth.) To restrain the poet from his commentary because he has only awareness would be a sort of *argumentum ad hominem,* forbidden by the manuals. Now, as a matter of fact, the poet's own insufficiency has on occasion been the theme of a poem, "Blackberry Winter," or, better, "Philomela"; and a sympathy with the situation in which the heroes and heroines are troubled does something to account for the particular feeling which invests a good many of the poems.

Naturally enough, this type of irony does not appear in the earliest collection of Ransom's poems, but even in that collection, *Poems About God,* there is an occasional tartness, a certain astringency, which must have come gratefully enough in 1919. In these poems of conventional rhythm and simple idiom, so different in these respects from Ransom's later verse, there is a more obvious provincialism of theme, which once betrayed a foreign critic into the absurdity of saying that the poor whites of Tennessee had at last found an interpreter.This provincialism seems to have derived from an instinctive, perhaps nostalgic, turning to an order of life which the poet since that time has analyzed and defended with more formidable social and economic doctrine. But the relation of Ransom's later poetry to his agrarianism is of another type, a type probably more fundamental. In the later poetry the relation is not that of a bucolic background, but of the primary impulse behind the poetry and the defense of an agrarian order.

The irony present in the first volume is largely of the circumstantial sort. The cherubim rebuke an abused woman's prayer to the Lord because it "shrewed His splendid features out of shape." Or there is

> God's oldest joke, forever fresh:
> The fact that in the finest flesh
> There isn't any soul.

In other words, the poet simply observes and records certain discrepancies in the nature and conduct of human affairs. This is essentially an anecdotal and external irony; the poet merely offers the situation, with its obvious contrasts, for what it is. It is the type of

irony so persistent and systematized in the poetry of Hardy, whose
success, perhaps, has influenced Ransom's general preference for the
little objective fable, with a kernel of drama, rather than lyric ru-
mination concerning an experience or situation. But Ransom has,
even in the later volumes, his own satires of circumstance, such as
"Night Voices," "Miriam Tazewell," "Piazza Piece," or "Husband
Betrayed," though these are less sardonic and indeed less mechani-
cally exact in execution than some of Hardy's more celebrated con-
trivances. The reason is not far to seek. In Hardy's "Satires" the
contrast is usually based on some idea of justice, arbitrary discrepancies in the conduct of the world—a theme running through much
of his prose as well. In Ransom's pieces of this anecdotal type the
theme is not so specific; it is rather the discrepancies between human
desires or expectations and their fulfillment. Variety is easier of attainment than under Hardy's more rigid scheme.

But in the second and third collections, *Chills and Fever* and *Two
Gentlemen in Bonds,* titles which in themselves bear a critical implication, the more mature version of Ransom's poetry appears. The
prefatory piece of *Chills and Fever* gives a clue to the poet's intention:

> I will be brief,
> Assuredly I have a grief,
> And I am shaken; but not as a leaf.

That is, a poem is not to aim at representation of emotion; nor is
the "grief" of the natural man merely subdued by the ritualistic ob-
jectifying function of verse, certainly not by what Tennyson termed
"the sad mechanic exercise of dull narcotics." Rather, the pure emotional cry is only a fragmentary expression of the experience of which
the complete sensibility is capable. To be more specific, let me call
attention to "Bells for John Whiteside's Daughter," which, as a matter of fact, is a poem of grief.

> There was such speed in her little body,
> And such lightness in her footfall,
> It is no wonder that her brown study
> Astonishes us all.

> Her wars were bruited in our high window.
> We looked among orchard trees and beyond,
> Where she took arms against her shadow,
> Or harried unto the pond

The lazy geese, like a snow cloud
Dripping their snow on the green grass,
Tricking and stopping, sleepy and proud,
Who cried in goose, Alas,

For the tireless heart within the little
Lady with rod that made them rise
From their noon apple dreams, and scuttle
Goose-fashion under the skies!

But now go the bells and we are ready;
In one house we are sternly stopped
To say we are vexed at her brown study,
Lying so primly propped.

Now the peculiar effect of this admirable little poem is largely implied in the words *astonishes* and *vexed*. First, simple grief is not the content of the primary statement. We are astonished at this event, which, though common to nature, has upset our human calculation. Second, it is not a poem whose aim is unvarnished pathos of recollection. Third, the resolution of the grief is not on a compensatory basis, as is common in the elegy formula. It is something more modest. The word *vexed* indicates its nature: the astonishment, the pathos, are absorbed into the total body of the mourner's experiences and given perspective so that the manly understatement is all that is to be allowed. We are shaken, but not as a leaf.

The premises of "Agitato ma non troppo," however, are clearer when the ironist speaks out in proper character. This speaker observes a world of "Plato, Scythian, dog and wart," and is scarcely consoled by the monistic fable rehearsed by the Doctor of Genealogy "with wisdom on his red eyeball," who would reduce the infinite and contradictory richness of the items into a system and perfect relationship; is "tricked by white birds or tall women into no wonder, and no sound"; tests with his stick the unsoundness of the vaunting oak which the lady regards as "an eminent witness of life"; is "vexed" at the little girl's "brown study, lying so primly propped"; is shaken, in staring at the Miller's Daughter, by "primary chrome of hair, astronomied Oes of eyes" more than by books or "a tale told"; and is in despair if the "bantering breed, sophistical and swarthy," to which he himself belongs, may be made worthy of Philomela.

The speech of this character, in comparison with the earlier poems, is more complex, at the same time more witty and pedantic, can make a bolder, because more self-conscious, use of rhetorical resource, is less lyrical and more dramatic. The rhythms are more intricate and disciplined; they are no longer founded on the line, but are organized for the effect of stanza or even longer division. (One of the difficulties of giving an idea of the quality of Ransom's poetry by mere extract springs from the fact that the poetry, being dramatic rather than lyrical, has been largely purged of merely local excitement. This difficulty is particularly great in a poem like "Persistent Explorer," from which I am forced to give extracts farther on in this essay.) The effect is one of subtle or passionate, but never vehement, statement, rather than song. An appropriate idiom, in fine, has been devised for that character, the ironist.

But to return to the actual working of that irony. In point of composition "Necrological" is, I believe, the first poem in which the particular effect appears. Likewise, it is the first poem in the general style that has become characteristic, although its rhetoric is more elaborate, more tapestried, and less witty than has since been common. The debate of the young man in "Nocturne" who cannot decide between the ball and his book, which is "flat and metaphysical," is also an early and more unsure example.

> The centuries have blown hard and dried his blood
> Unto this dark quintessence of manhood;
> Much water has passed beneath the bridges, fretfully,
> And borne his boats of passion to the sea; . . .

> But still the plum tree blooms, despite the rocks at its root,
> Despite that everyone knowns by now its wizened and little fruit,
> And the white moon plunges wildly, it is a most ubiquitous ghost,
> Always seeking her own old people that are a long time lost—

The last volume is more fruitful, although in the previous one I should not neglect to point out "Armageddon" with its confusion of doctrines which relates to the same background as the poems already mentioned. I shall take a few instances which, to me, seem clear-cut. There is the "poor bookish hind with too much pudding in his head of learned characters" who stares at the Miller's Daughter—

> A learned eye of our most Christian nation
> And foremost philosophical generation—
> At primary chrome of hair,
>
> Astronomied Oes of eyes

and is puzzled because all of this has no reference to the experience that shakes him. In "Morning," as soon as the "true householder Learning" comes back "to tenant in Ralph's head," it is "simply another morning, and simply Jane" who is beside him. But "Man Without Sense of Direction" is the most disordered of all the heroes and heroines. He is "spaced round with perfect Forms," but "there is no moon of them that draws his flood of being"; he "cannot fathom nor perform his nature." No matter where he walks, he cannot care "for the shapes that would fiddle upon his senses," and "for his innocence walks in hell."

> He flails his arms, he moves his lips:
> "Rage have I none, cause, time, nor country—
> Yet I have travelled land and ships
> And knelt my season in the chantry."

And when he rushes back to his love,

> But let his cold lips be her omen,
> She shall not kiss that harried one
> To peace! as men are served by women,
> Who comfort them in darkness and in sun.

His is the special form of loneliness which, we are sometimes told, is a modern predicament: he can find community with neither man nor nature.

Others with similar complaints are "Amphibious Crocodile," who tries travel, projects, *affairs de coeur,* religion, psychoanalysis, and metaphysics, but in the end can only, with nostalgic tears, resort to his primal mud; the two lovers of "Equilibrists," who present a theme treated with less distinction in "Spectral Lovers" of the second volume; and the "Two Gentlemen in Bonds," brothers who present, in a fashion perhaps too obvious and mechanical for full poetic success, the practical and appreciative faculties. From the tomb their father laments the resulting pow-wow in his house:

> . . . now I see
> My manhood halved and squandered, two heads, two hearts,
> Each partial son despising the other's parts;
> And so it is, and so it always will be.

There is one addition to this catalogue, which, in all probability, has even now violated the reader's patience as well as the poetic quality of the examples. But this is an example very pertinent to the present purpose, for the hero appears as something of a poet. In "Persistent Explorer" he walks where "noise of water teased his literal ear," but thinks "that is more than water I hear." The thunder smites him "somewhat as the loud/Words of the god that rang around a man/Walking by the Mediterranean," but the sound and spectacle can, finally, spell nothing to him. He does not even know what he would have it spell. It is by definition the insipid chemical H_2O.

> So be it. And no unreasonable outcry
> The pilgrim made; only a rueful grin
> Spread over his lips until he drew them in;
> He did not sit upon a rock and die.
>
> There were many ways of dying; witness, if he
> Commit himself to the water, and descend
> Wrapped in the water, turn water at the end
> And flow with a great water out to sea.
>
> But there were many ways of living too,
> And let his enemies gibe, but let them say
> That he would throw this continent away
> And seek another country,—which he would do.

He demands, as a man, the privilege of his myths, the privilege of the complete experience. He would seek another country—which is the sum of the whole matter.

But this catalogue, if it has served its intention, has made clear the basic theme of Ransom's poetry. Under ideal conditions, perhaps, this very theme might not exist, just as one of the central themes of Eliot's early work and "The Waste Land," that of tradition, would not exist, certainly in its present form, under such conditions. Even in "Ash Wednesday" something of the theme persists, most obviously in Section VI.

Eliot and Ransom have been concerned with the same problem. The method of irony in Ransom's poetry, for want of a better word, may be called psychological. Factors in the make-up of his heroes which might work for strength actually work toward weakness. Eliot's method may be called historical: the ignoble present is suddenly thrust into contrast with the noble past. This matter has been frequently analyzed. For instance, in "Sweeney among the Nightingales" the nightingales sing while the host of the vulgar dive plots at the door apart,

> And sang within the bloody wood
> When Agamemnon cried aloud,
> And let their liquid siftings fall
> To stain the stiff dishonored shroud.

And in the seduction scene of 'The Waste Land," Tiresias has

> . . . foresuffered all
> Enacted on this same divan or bed;
> I who have sat by Thebes below the wall
> And walked among the lowest of the dead.

Further, Eliot's use of quotation, either directly or in parody, derives its ironical effect from the same basis. This difference in method, however, merely conforms to the difference in critical approach. The literary nature of Eliot's ironical devices is consistent with the fact that his principles have, in most cases, emerged through essays which took the apparent form of literary analysis; Ransom, on the other hand, has written a very small amount of specific literary criticism, having chosen to be more general and to use literature, if at all, as illustration.

But the theme in the poetry of both men is similar: "Where there is no vision the people perish." Both have experienced a necessity for order, and, in consequence, have concerned themselves with disorder as the overt subject matter of their poetry. Both have diagnosed the disorder in terms of dissociation of sensibility, although Ransom, on this point, has been more general.

Neither man as poet, however, has been able to avoid the consequences of that disorder about which he has written. Each, as Donald Davidson said of the artist in the scientific civilization, "is *against* or *away from* society, and the disturbed relationship becomes his essential theme, always underlying his work, no matter whether he evades or accepts the treatment of the theme itself." Eliot has more obviously accepted it; Ransom, not evading it, has merely given himself to greater indirection. Neither is in the position which Eliot attributes to the Elizabethan dramatists: "We feel that they believed in their own age, in a way in which no nineteenth- or twentieth-century writer of the greatest seriousness has been able to believe in his age. And accepting their age, they were in a position to concentrate their attention, to their respective abilities, upon the common characteristics of humanity in all ages, rather than upon the differences." Further than this, both of the present poets have suffered, along with most others of the day, from their situation in another respect. Their dependence for theme on the private critical point of view has produced a certain lack of variety in the poetry itself, a certain predictability about the performance; in the weaker pieces of both a formula may obtrude.

It is fruitless to speculate about what might have been their achievement in another age. As it stands, these writers have developed what, on a priori grounds, might be regarded as a poetic liability into a poetic resource, limited but real. It is not inappropriate, however, that I quote here from the lad in Ransom's poem who climbs Bagley Hill at Oxford to hear the nightingale, only to find, after all, that her classics register a little flat.

> Philomela, Philomela, lover of song,
> I am in despair if we may make us worthy,
> A bantering breed, sophistical and swarthy;
> Unto more beautiful, persistently more young,
> Thy fabulous provinces belong.

AN EXAMINATION OF MODERN CRITICS:
JOHN CROWE RANSOM

Edwin Berry Burgum

There has been much talk of humanism in our day and earlier. The war has been defined as a defense of humanist values against the fascist revival of barbarism.* Even before the First World War there was in this country a strong movement to rescue what was taken for the humanist tradition from neglect and decay. This movement had several objectives. It was opposed to the romantic heritage, to the levelling tendency of democracy, to the corruption of literary standards by an invasion of scientific influence. But there was an ominous contrast between the abstract ideals of these revivalists and the tone of their expression. If humanism were to be defined, as they said it should be, in Renaissance terms, no one of them could be said to have a humanist personality. If Erasmus was a humanist, the creed did not obligate a contempt for the masses. But such a contempt, whether it was Babbitt's crude belligerency or More's spinsterish cold shoulder, was the only emotion our American humanists had in common. A certain virility suffused Renaissance humanism and made its pendantry come alive because of the linguistic needs of the moment. But Paul Elmer More's pedantry was a lusterless complacency as he reduced the best that had been thought and said to insipidity. The leader of the movement was virile

*This essay originally appeared in *Rocky Mountain Review*, VIII (Spring, 1944), 87–93.

in all conscience, but always in the spirit of sadistic negation. Indeed, what Babbitt advocated, the "inner check," was itself a negation. The few who came nearest the ideal of tolerant and zestful experiment seemed to justify Babbitt by their loss of standards. Once Stuart Sherman had outgrown his belated defense of Puritanism he paid for his recovery from the distemper of dogmatism by a growing vacuity of content.

After these sallies from the campus into the areas where literature was produced and published, humanism, baffled and routed by the indifference of the public, retired to the shelter of academic walls once more. Norman Foerster rallied the cohorts and assembled a few disciples from the thin young men exercising the right of asylum within. But the group had lost both gusto and originality, and proved capable only of repeating the old precepts in a monotone of petulance. President Hutchins salvaged a curriculum for academic use. But the Hutchins plan, requiring a blood transfusion from somewhere, went into uneasy alliance with a quite new phenomenon in our intellectual life, a neo-Thomism transplanted from France. If humanism, as a movement, has a future, it will probably be as an ingredient of a trend in education which keeps the old associations but becomes predominantly neo-Thomist, concealing under a grave and tactful urbanity its shift to a philosophical base of spiritual authority. Should such a trend become dominant, the era of Renaissance influence might well be said to have ended.

Meanwhile, one of our critics who seems to me to approach nearest to the old humanist ideal is a man who was never closely allied with the movement. It is a curious fact that the attachment of John Crowe Ransom has been to a different group whose orientation he has never shared. His friendships have been with the Southern Agrarians, who, under the leadership of Allen Tate, have waged a shrewd and aggressive campaign to promote their program. Tate has not found the bitterness and the contempt of the Harvard professor entirely uncongenial. But what in part forbids his being called a Southern Babbitt has been his sociological interests. The Southern Agrarians have been more concerned with the restoration of an aristocratic conception of society than the revival of an aristocratic literary ideal. As the name suggests, they have been the promoters of a social movement towards decentralization, the return to the soil, the encouragement of the small farm. They have recognized that an aristocratic literature is likely to find a more congenial nutriment in the country than the town. But Ransom has not been attracted to politics of any specific cast. In terms of his personal development, he seems to have reacted away from his friends' loss of the traditional humanist temper and emphasis in their agrarian program, while at the same time his lack of personal experience in the humanist movement has kept him from sharing its corruption of professed beliefs. It is ironic commentary upon the state of criticism among us that these delicate relationships of divergent influences should be needed to keep a critic of our day on an even keel of humanism.

However this may be, I find what seems to me central in humanism preserved in Ransom's work. He sees art as concerned with what the tradition has called "the whole man," and he opposes valiantly every approach that would make it concerned with anything else. The forces which have corrupted the values of poetry by shattering its proper concern with the whole man he defines at different times as Puritanism, Platonism, and science. Puritanism he regards as more than a religious faith. It is a divisive frame of mind. What Arnold called "the dissidence of dissent," described with less prejudice, becomes the habit of schism. It always justifies itself by assuming the value of new methods and aims, but what it actually accomplishes is a division of human interests into an increasing number of unrelated specializations. Science itself, from this point of view, is a category of the Puritan temper with a conception of the world that is especially deleterious to poetry and tends to become more and more dominant as a common method to a diversity of discrete ends. Ransom does not object to science in its own place. But those very techniques which have proved so valuable in their own sphere precisely because they have abandoned the old anthropomorphic view of the objective world, when transferred into the area of poetry, by dehumanizing it, have destroyed its essence. There is left of creative power scarcely more than the chill dissections under the miscroscope of the Imagists, who have accepted the scientific attitude completely, and the tortured obscurities of the poets of the unintelligible, caught in the contradiction of using the alien means of science to an end which they recognize to be social and human rather than scientific. In another way, the older tradition of Platonism, Ransom believes, has promoted a similar dehumanization of literature. It has reduced our rich and valid emotions, that are the sinews by means of which man's "wholeness" operates and is revealed, to a static series of innate ideas, as lifelessly abstract as the dissections of the man of science.

These charges, I believe, are correct, but the terminology through which they are put seems to me misleading. Though Puritanism has been a divisive force, as the number of Protestant sects testifies, it can be made the chief divisive element only by accepting the very "Platonism" which Ransom rejects and regarding abstract ideas as the basic motivating forces in human conduct. The divisiveness which Puritanism introduced into the realm of religious and ethical ideas was succeeded in time by the more inclusive analytical methods of science, which have reduced the wholeness of man to manifold fragments of aspects, however sharply defined. But both Puritanism and the scientific method are themselves projections into the area of abstract thought of the all-pervasive temper of bourgeois society. Such a view is consonant with Ransom's preference for the Aristotelian theory of poetic imitation and his rejection of the transcendentalism of both Plato and Coleridge.

For this reason it is unfortunate that his use of the term Platonism is more limited than customary. Ransom uses it to denote a poetry that is didactic or preponderantly ideational, which, by neglecting the representation of emotions, reduces the whole man to a collection of abstract propositions. This is to be sure a disturbing state of affairs. But it seems awkward to call such poetry Platonic, when the supernatural quality of Plato's abstract ideas, by the paradox of themselves being beyond reason, has smuggled into Platonism a vast amount of emotionalism which may be unpleasant because of its vagueness but is nevertheless not abstract idea and hence is "poetry" in the definition which Ransom himself accepts. For his definition is stated clearly and affirmatively though metaphorically in the title of one of his books. Poetry is "the world's body." It is the mechanism which gives "body," life and function and tangibility to our feelings, specific embodiment to the abstract character of the world as science views it. Here again Ransom has, I think, restated a valid proposition. Art is by its nature anti-mystical. The extraordinary difficulties which authentic mystics have found in any sort of artistic representation is proof that the very nature of art rejects mysticism as its philosophical foundation. The artist cannot belittle or negate the evidence of his senses. If he must be a mystic, it is only through the use of his senses that he can achieve the metaphors through which by analogy alone he seeks to realize the unrealizable. The case for mysticism can be less awkwardly presented through the concepts of philosophers which are the more readily detached from the life and blood of experience. But art begins with what the mystic disdains and glorifies the possibilities the mystic rejects.

In his own rejection of the mysticism of Plato, Ransom seems to me not only to remain true to the essence of Renaissance humanism, with its immense and legitimate respect for the body and the body's environment, but he seems actually to have cleared away an inconsistency which the vagueness of Renaissance thinking endured. For there can be no doubt that humanism, when it was under Italian instead of Reformation influences, absorbed as "poetry," as undifferentiated emotional satisfaction, a considerable amount of Platonic drapery of its fundamental acceptance of the body's reality and its inherent possibilities for the good and the beautiful. All this is stripped away in Ransom. But when one looks for some more positive interpretation to take its place one gets the impression that Ransom is not entirely certain what sort of implementation is needed. Like other American humanists, he seems more sure of the implementations to be rejected. In his latest book, *The New Criticism,* he discusses the limitations of a number of contemporary critics. He objects to Richards for approaching criticism as though it were a problem in psychology, to Eliot for viewing it as a branch of history, and to Yvor Winters for being a "logical critic." What we want instead, he says, is an ontological criticism. But this is taking refuge in a term rather than elaborating its implications.

A few examples may clarify the strength and the limitations of Ransom's determination to avoid modern heresies and stay within the traditional area of Renaissance concepts. His distinction between the world of science and that of art admirably preserves and clarifies the Renaissance attitude.

The world of predictability—is the restricted world of scientific discourse. Its restrictive rule is: one value at a time. The world of art is the actual world which does not bear restriction; or at least is sufficiently defiant of the restrictiveness of science, and offers enough fullness of content, to give us a sense of the actual objects. A qualitative density, or value-density, such as is unknown to scientific understanding, marks the world of the actual objects. The discourse which tries systematically to record this world is art.

This is a helpful distinction. Furthermore we may agree with Ransom that the means through which the two different approaches of art and science are communicated can be defined as the "symbol" and the "icon," the one being a general, the other a specific, statement of several values combined into a specific whole, on the basis of which one generalizes with varying degrees of risk. These clarifications of traditional attitudes are excellent. But there comes a point, I believe, when traditional attitudes have to be abandoned and the aesthetician must strike out along new lines. But in place of pursuing into a greater and more helpful detail this distinction between the symbol and the icon, Ransom prefers to leave the statement general. He turns to another, and a less plausible, traditional distinction, which he takes over, makes somewhat more specific, but leaves similarly without an adequate development. I am referring to his acceptance of the traditional separation of the enjoyment of the meaning and the meter in poetry. This well established conception seems to me to demand so many qualifications that it had better be entirely discarded. But Ransom, as usual, prefers to accept it and attempt to qualify it, as contemporary investigations into semantics would appear to necessitate. If the finished poem, therefore he says, is to be regarded as dependent upon the opposition of these two elements of meter and meaning, their fusion enriches the poem by compromising their purity. The pure logic of the meaning is affected by the pure non-logic, or pattern of pure sensations, in the meter; so that the actual poem lacks the specificity of either, its actual pattern having a large amount of the "indeterminate" in both sound and meaning. The weakness of this interpretation is that it makes any form of prose an imperfect approach to poetry since no prose work presupposes a particular metrical pattern to be modified and made indeterminate by its conflict "meanings."

Now one must grant that there is a large amount of vague allusive meaning in poetry. But it would seem desirable to make our understanding of this penumbra of overtone in poetry as lucid as possible. Critics are under no obligation to remain vague about the vague. The matter to be investigated and the tools of investigation do not have to be of the same quality. One can agree with Ransom's rejection of Yvor Winters whether as a "logical" critic or simply as a man unable to read poetry in the first place. But one would have thought that he would have sensed a critic of a kindred aim to his aim in Eliot, for whom the label of "historical" critic is certainly inadequate. Ransom fails to see that Eliot has been desperately searching to escape history, but cannot do so for the very reason that he accepts even more definitely than Ransom that conception of art as "the world's body" which Ransom himself believes in.

In a similar way one might have expected that Ransom would have recognized more explicitly Richards' great service to readers of poetry in his investigations into those indeterminate meanings with which he is so much concerned. I should agree with him in rejecting Richards' philosophy of poetry with its increasing dependence upon Coleridge. But I see no essential relationship between his theory of the nature of poetry and his psychological analysis of a reader's enjoyment of a poem. Doubtless it is a criticism of the hypothetical character of Richards' psychology, its failure to be a really scientific account, that it can be fitted into any number of philosophies of aesthetic. But for the time being it may serve the useful purpose of keeping us aware of the complexity of the experience of reading poetry and particularly of a relationship between idea and emotion in poetry that is more involved and, I think, more valid than Ransom's own analysis. His work in this area has not only been pioneer and revolutionary, but has had the corroboration of a most sensitive application to the poetry itself in the interpretations of such critics as Bowra and Empson and Matthiessen. He has taught us all to read. His weakness lies in his failure to recognize the extent to which the production of the meanings he isolates and the reader's acceptance of them is conditioned by the specific nature of the historical period. At this point Ransom would have done better if he had drawn Eliot and Richards together by recommending that Richards face as squarely as Eliot the inescapable effect of the historical period upon our awareness of the particular "indeterminateness" of a poem. Eliot's consciousness of the influence of the social environment has produced all sorts of conflicts in him, may have left his thinking as a critic unsystematic and his poetry confused. But both he and Richards have been thinking towards a science of criticism, and have been calling our attention to the inadequacy of the rule of thumb methods with which Ransom's humanism leave him too content.

In his hostility to this aspect of their work, Ransom fails to make a distinction between the nature of criticism and that of creative work in the arts, which Eliot himself has ironically suggested. When

Eliot stated that critics are often thwarted poets who transfer into an alien area a creative talent not adequate for direct expression, he was implying also that the critical and the creative methods should not be confused. Ransom's objections to the unfortunate influence of science upon the writing of poetry do not carry over into the quite distinct field of its criticism. Since criticism is not a form of poetry, it demands a different methodology. Those critics like Eliot and Richards who sense the need at long last for a critical method that is free from this confusion of aims may not yet have achieved any notable results; but they are on the right track. It is a pity that Ransom, whose general orientation is sound and promising, should ignore the aid which history and psychology, properly interpreted and properly associated, might bring to their tangible application in the specific poetic situation, and should remain content with the old humanist view that common sense and the spontaneous response of the well-read man are enough. We ought not deny the potential service of science and history to literary criticism merely because they are recognized to have caused great damage to the spirit of poetry. Its spirit can be crushed also by the vagueness of the good intention. Perhaps poetry would be aided the faster to revive if our critics had the boldness to investigate why we live in an era of great prose. But they can do so only if they go beyond the limits Ransom sets and relate the psychology of the contemporary personality to the idiosyncracy of the contemporary social environment. Merely to discover the reasons in this way might give body to Ransom's admirable awareness of the general significance both for the individual and for society of that sense of "value density" which poetry reveals in the "world of actual objects."

INSTRUCTED OF MUCH MORTALITY:
A NOTE ON THE POETRY OF JOHN CROWE RANSOM

Delmore Schwartz

The appearance of Ransom's *Selected Poems* (Knopf, 1945) suggests reflections, full of a modest joy, about the modest triumphs of virtue, both in poetry itself and in the weird, vague, treacherous amphitheater of poetic reputation.* When most of the poems in this book appeared, American poetry was dominated by such trumpeters and maestri as Carl Sandburg, Vachel Lindsey, Edgar Lee Masters, and Edwin Arlington Robinson. It is unfair to join Robinson with the other poets, except in terms of the functioning of poetic reputation. Reputation is the point; the poets who seemed significant and big and what I believe is known as major have suffered the fate of huge balloons. Meanwhile such poets as Marianne Moore, Wallace Stevens, and William Carlos Williams have emerged through the strength of a genuineness which was perhaps the reason for their not being recognized at their true worth immediately. Ransom is another such author, and there is a moral for publishers in the persistence of his reputation. Some authors, good as well as bad, appear to think that they must publish a book every year, if the great beast which is the public is to remember and read them. Ransom has published perhaps six new poems, some of them his best ones, in the past twenty years. Meanwhile, despite the absence of renewal, his poems have remained important in the one truly

*This essay originally appeared in *Sewanee Review*, LIV (Summer, 1946), 439-48.

indubitable way that poetry can remain important: namely, they have been read again and again by other poets and—purest of all laurels—they have been read by those who are beginning to write poetry, those who want to write poetry, and those who are trying to learn how to write poetry. This may seem a somewhat meager existence; but it is the only alternative, given literary curiosity in America, to not being read at all.

A strange instance of this modest triumph of genuineness occurred when, in 1935 in England, Geoffrey Grigson suddenly published a brief essay in praise of Ransom's poetry. The instance is strange in several ways. No new volume by Ransom had appeared, for one thing; and then, it has been clear in general that, were it not for the existence of T. S. Eliot, America to British literati would be virtually indistinguishable from Australia; and strange most of all because Grigson had labored in vain to make head or tail of modern American poetry, finding only that Frost was provincial, James Agee wrote as if he had no roof to his mouth, William Carlos Williams was bogus, and Wallace Stevens was a "stuffed goldfinch," "a Klee without rhythm"! Yet Grigson's comments on Ransom, however inconsistent with his other judgments, were very perceptive. He guessed that Ransom had studied Hardy, he said that "there was not much else in American poetry like Ransom," and that Ransom "defended himself by irony against an inclination to the pathetic," and that, in fine, Ransom's two books, *Chills and Fever* and *Two Gentlemen in Bonds,* were "two of the most delightful collections published since the War." Not too much ought to be made of this praise, though it is always cheering when American literature is not identified abroad with such authors as Steinbeck, Saroyan, Robinson Jeffers, and Carl Sandburg. For Grigson's remark that there was not much else in American poetry like Ransom is both true and false. It is true that the total effect of his poems is unlike that of any other poet. But nonetheless there is a significant resemblance to other poets so far as language and style are concerned, and the sum of this significant resemblance can perhaps best be stated by citing Wallace Stevens. Both poets make a like use of dandyism of surface, of irony, and of a mock-grand style. Here are samples which, so far as the texture of the style goes, might have been written by either poet:

When this yokel comes maundering,
Whetting his hacker,
I shall run before him,

Diffusing civilest odors
Out of geraniums and unsmelled flowers.
It will check him.

* * * * * * *

I placed a jar in Tennessee
And round it was, upon a hill.
It made the slovenly wilderness
Surround that hill.

* * * * * * *

If the lady hath any loveliness, let it die.
For being drunken with the steam of Cuban cigars,
I find no pungence in the odour of stars,
And all my music goes out of me on a sigh.

* * * * * * *

But now, by our perverse supposal,
There is a drift of fog on your mornings;
You in your peignoir, dainty at your orange cup,
Feel poising round the sunny room

Invisible evil, deprived and bold.
All day the clock will metronome
Your gallant fear; the needles clicking,
The heels detonating the stair's cavern.

The first two are excerpts from Stevens, and the second two are passages in Ransom. I have deliberately chosen samples in which there is a likeness of subject-matter to some of Stevens's best known poems. It is not, however, such a likeness which is important, but the way language is used and the attitude *toward* language. Both poets use the grand style with mockery and playfulness, and both poets correct the excess inherent in this mock grandiloquence by that use of the colloquial and the concrete which may seem to the future to be the most marked aspect of modern poetry. Of the two poets, Stevens has followed out the possibilities of this idiom with much greater intensity and consistency. But the irony in Stevens is defensive; he seems at times to be discounting or trimming the serious emotions with which he is concerned, as if he were suspicious of them. In Ransom, however, the irony is most often an expression of the very painfulness of the emotion:

> The little cousin is dead, by foul subtraction,
> A green bough from Virginia's aged tree,
> And none of the country kin like the transaction,
> Nor some of the world of outer dark, like me.

Here the wryness of tone accomplished by rhyming *subtraction* and *transaction* should serve as an instance of how the irony is part of the emotion, and not, as in Stevens, a kind of guard which surrounds it.

It is natural to speculate about this likeness in style, in attitude toward language, of the two poets. There can be no question of the influence of one poet upon the other, although, insofar as a period style may be said to be the source of the resemblance, it is true that there may be some common influence upon both. If one went through the files of *Poetry: A Magazine Of Verse, The Smart Set,* and *The Dial,* one would come upon many poems—by such very different authors as Conrad Aiken, Maxwell Bodenheim, Donald Evans, and even Edna St. Vincent Millay!—in which the convention of the high poetic is used with irony. And there is even, I think, a resemblance to the exotic, foreign, and bravura quality of the prose styles of H. L. Mencken and James Branch Cabell. But these resemblances, far from being a matter of literary influence, suggest a common situation which involves the whole human being, namely, the relationship of the author to the age. The way that the language is used would thus have as its fundamental cause the attitude of society to poetry and the consequent attitude of the poet to his art. When the poet is regarded as a strange, rare, and abnormal being, it is natural that he should mock at the same time as he enjoys the language of the grand manner. Perhaps there is further illumination, in literary history which has not yet been written: the overstuffed upholstery which is the rhetoric of late Victorian poetry was rejected by the poets who began to write between 1910 and 1920. One has only to cite the concern with speech, direct statement, and concreteness which were the declared aims of the founders of the *vers libre* movement. Now if we suppose that poets like Stevens and Ransom were caught, so to speak, in the midst of this shift from rhetoric in the grand manner to the direct concreteness of (what was then) the new poetry, we have perhaps placed the kind of literary energy which is the source of their ironic styles and their resemblance to each other. The irony of their language can thus be attributed to the tension and conflict they felt with regard to the two conceptions of what poetry ought to be.

In "Philomela," a poem which has had the misfortune to be much anthologized so that, like a famous symphony, repetition has imposed a transient triteness upon it, Ransom deals directly with the fate of poetry in our time:

> Procne, Philomela, and Itylus,
> Your names are liquid, your improbable tale
> Is recited in the classic numbers of the nightingale.
> Ah, but our numbers are not felicitous,
> It goes not liquidly for us.
>
> . . . .
>
> Up from the darkest wood where Philomela sat,
> Her fairy numbers issued. What then ailed me?
> My ears are called capacious but they failed me,
> Her classics registered a little flat!
> I rose and venomously spat.
>
> Philomela, Philomela, lover of song.
> I am in despair if we may make us worthy,
> A bantering breed sophistical and swarthy;
> Unto more beautiful, persistently more young,
> Thy fabulous provinces belong.

It is probably needless to suggest that to compare this poem with Keats's "Ode to the Nightingale" is to see the distance between the Romantic and the modern poet. But since I have not quoted the entire poem, perhaps it is necessary to emphasize the fact that the poet's doubt of the nature of modern poetry—he has said in an unquoted stanza that he felt "sick of my dissonance"—is a mixed one. He is not entirely displeased that he belongs to "a bantering breed sophistical and swarthy," and if he feels that "our numbers are not felicitous" nor liquid, he also finds Philomela's classics "a little flat." Indeed there is a pleasure in the use of the language throughout which suggests that far from preferring felicitous and liquid numbers, the poet prefers to be able to write verses in which he can say that he "venomously spat," an instance of the kind of diction which the Romantic poet would be incapable of using, and which the Elizabethan dramatic poet found more and more necessary as he moved from the liquid and empty felicity of Spenser to the choppy and perception-burdened versification of Donne and Webster.

To return to the comparison between Ransom and Stevens, they are alike in their attitude toward language and their themes are often alike. But the ultimate direction is quite different. Stevens moves toward a contemplation of symbols and ideas abstracted from any time and place; and when in his recent poems he returns to the time and the place of the present, the present also becomes some kind of abstraction. Ransom on the other hand returns always to the relationship of human beings to each other and to the immediacy and particularity of existence. The human beings are present chiefly for the sake of declaring an attitude toward existence. Robert Penn Warren has pointed out that Ransom's characteristic form is "the little objective fable, with a kernel of drama." *Kernel* is exact, for it is hardly more than a kernel of drama. Neither the drama nor the characters are important for their own sake, as in many of the lyrics of Robinson and Eliot. It is the meaning of the fable which determines the place or role of all the other properties of the poem. And this meaning comes through so much by way of the tone of the poem—a tone which is by turns playful, charming, gay, off-hand, and sardonic—that the seriousness of the meaning and of the whole poem may easily be missed. Consider, for example, a poem such as "Conrad in Twilight":

> Conrad, Conrad, aren't you old
> To sit so late in your mouldy garden?
> And I think Conrad knows it well,
> Nursing his knees, too rheumy and cold
> To warm the wraith of a Forest of Arden.
>
> Neuralgia in the back of his neck,
> His lungs filling with such miasma,
> His feet dipping in leafage and muck:
> Conrad! you've forgotten asthma.
>
> Conrad's house has thick red walls
> And chips on Conrad's hearth are blazing,
> Slippers and pipe and tea are served,
> Butter and toast, Conrad, are pleasing!

Still Conrad's back is not uncurved
And here's an autumn on him, teasing.

Autumn days in our section
Are the most used-up thing on earth
(Or in the waters under the earth)
Having no more color nor predilection
Than cornstalks too wet for the fire,
A ribbon rotting on the byre,
A man's face as weathered as straw
By the summer's flare and winter's flaw.

Butter and toast, Conrad, are pleasing! How readily the careless
reader may be put off by the seeming triviality of such a line, so
that he misses its essential connection with the extraordinary last
stanza and the theme of the body's decay and death over which
this poem, like so many others by Ransom, agonizes. The prose
quality of the last stanza, the shift in rhythm from the jingling
with which the poem begins to the flat, direct statement of the
last stanza, the significance of the image of "a ribbon rotting on
the byre," the conclusiveness and the beauty of the last line (which
is secured by means of assonance as well as by the visual and emotional connotations of "the summer's flare") —all of these qualities
may be disregarded if the reader does not grasp the easy tone and
jingling rhythm as a *preparation* for the last stanza.

As this poem is concerned with death, so the hard fact of death
is the most frequent subject, and the reader encounters an astonishing
number of funerals and corpses. (In one of his essays, Ransom
remarks in passing that a man may go out of his mind if he thinks
too much about death.) And where the conclusion is not as radical
as that, there is frustration, disappointment, and despair. When the
subject is not a dead boy or a dying lady, it is the impassable distress
that lovers feel at the thought of death, as in "Vaunting Oak,"
where a lady *"instructed of much mortality"* cites a great oak as an
instance of permanence and then, when the oak is struck, hears in
the reverberance "like a funeral, a hollow tone." A mind instructed
in mortality has a natural love of the body, and it is without sympathy for any denial of the body's beauty or actuality, a denial to
which the mind is often tempted. Thus, in "The Equilibrists," two
lovers who are separated by honor forever are told that "great lovers
lie in Hell," "they rend each other when they kiss," and "the pieces

kiss again," while in Heaven there is not only no marriage but the soul is bodiless; and the implication is that in this way Hell is preferable to Heaven. So, in another poem, the head is accused of seeking decapitation, of seeking "to play truant from the body bush," of traducing the flesh, but "Beauty is of body," the body's love is necessary to the head, and without the body's love the living world is colorless and empty. So too, in "Address to the Scholars of New England," we hear that

> There used to be debate of soul and body,
> The soul storming incontinent with shrew's tongue
> Against what natural brilliance body had loved,

In the psychomachy of this poet, the character of the debate has reversed itself, the soul storms against itself for being in the least faithless to the body. Furthermore, to be faithful to the body and to love the body is to be aware of its degradation, its decay, and its death. Here again a detailed comparison with Stevens would be fruitful. I have in mind particularly Stevens' "Sunday Morning," and "The Emperor of Ice Cream": "Let be be finale of seem/The only Emperor is the Emperor of ice cream." And Ransom's best poem must be quoted as a whole, if one is to see how this concern with death can mount to a vision of life in which everything (from children and "the pretty kings of France" to a dressing-gown, buckberries in blue bowls, the "warning sibilance of pines," and "the heels detonating the stair's cavern") is seen in the cold, cloudy light of the fact of mortality:

PRELUDE TO AN EVENING

> Do not enforce the tired wolf
> Dragging his infected wound homeward
> To sit tonight with the warm children
> Naming the pretty kings of France.
>
> The images of the invaded mind
> Being as the monsters in the dreams
> Of your most brief enchanted headful,
> Suppose a miracle of confusion:
>
> That dreamed and undreamt become each other
> And mix the night and day of your mind;
> And it does not matter your twice crying
> From mouth unbeautied against the pillow

To avert the gun of the same old soldier;
For cry, cock-crow, or the iron bell
Can crack the sleep-sense of outrage,
Annihilate phantoms who were nothing.

But now, by our perverse supposal,
There is a drift of fog on your mornings;
You in your peignoir, dainty at your orange cup,
Feel poising round the sunny room

Invisible evil, deprived and bold.
All day the clock will metronome
Your gallant fear; the needles clicking,
The heels detonating the stair's cavern.

Freshening the water in the blue bowls
For the buckberries, with not all your love,
You shall be listening for the low wind,
The warning sibilance of pines.

You like a waning moon, and I accusing
Our too banded Eumenides,
While you pronounce Noes wanderingly
And smooth the heads of the hungry children.

THE DORIC DELICACY

Cleanth Brooks

Modernist poetry is characterized by a complete revulsion against poetic diction.* It has banished the *e'ens*, and *thou's*, the *pleasant leas*, and *soft gales*, and with them archaic diction in general. But the poetry of John Crowe Ransom, though its modernity is patent, makes constant use of archaic diction, some of it as quaintly antique as that of Spenser, whom Ben Jonson chided for having "writ no language." For example, in Ransom's verse the enemy "up clomb . . . in no airy towers"; "the rooster" is seen "footing the mould"; a melancholy young friar becomes a "lugubrious wight"; the poet can even frame such a salutation as "Sweet ladies, long may ye bloom, and toughly I hope ye may thole."

Ransom's use of the archaic, it scarcely need be said, is not Spenserian, either in method or effect: the ancient words are not chosen to poetize the matter; they are not amiably decorative; as Ransom employs them, they are absorbed into a special idiom of distinct character whose very principle is a kind of tough-minded modernity. Yet it is startling that the archaic occurs at all; and among the modern poets, the fact is almost unique. It is worth pondering, for it may indicate a way in which to engage the special quality of Ransom's work. And though this use of the archaic does not point

*This essay originally appeared in *Sewanee Review*, LVI (Summer, 1948) , 402–15.

back to the poetry of Spenser, there is one elder poet to whom it does point unmistakably: John Milton.

For Milton too devised an idiom which was at once highly personal and yet for his time distinctively modern; and in it he too incorporated elements of archaic diction such as one hardly finds in contemporaries like Donne or Denham or Marvell. We can, to be sure, isolate out of Milton's verse Chaucerian forms arrived at pershaps *via* Spenser, but the total impact of the verse is not Spenserian. It is sharply contemporary. Most of all, it is distinctively Miltonic.

But I should hesitate to suggest this parallelism between Milton and Ransom if I did not feel that it was simply one item in a larger parallelism; and, in any case, I hesitate to raise the question of parallels without some rather precise qualifications.

The use of literary parallels is nowadays a somewhat discredited critical device, and justly so; for the matching of "parallels," like source hunting, has too often been pursued as a mechanical exercise. The statistics which it yields are usually quite barren. Yet, a comparison of the work of one poet with another can, on occasion, be illuminating—most of all, perhaps, when we have put away any pre-occupation with borrowings and influences, and are content to use the one case merely to provide a perspective from which to view the other.

The minor poems of Milton seem to me to stand in some such relation to Ransom's poetry. Ransom's poetry enables one better to discern the Miltonic strategy, and the poems which Milton published in the 1645 volume can throw a good deal of light on *Chills and Fever* and *Two Gentlemen in Bonds*.

But having claimed so much for this relationship, I want to make doubly clear what I do *not* maintain: that there is any conscious imitation on Ransom's part. I have collected no specific "borrowings." So far as I know they do not exist. In any case, they are not to my purpose here.

Even the more general parallels between the two men are scarcely to my purpose, though I think that it may be interesting to mention a few of the more striking ones: their common "Protestantism," their learning, their sense of tradition, and their insistence on maintaining the continuity of the tradition. The poetry of both men shows the deep impress of classical letters. (Ransom read "Greats" at Oxford.) Yet there is in both men something which at a first glance seems at variance with the suavity which we associate with a predominant training in humane letters: there is a kind of logical rigor, something of a penchant for positivism. It is not quite fair to say with Saurat that Milton is unhappy with all mysteries including the great Christian mysteries, and demands that everything be plain as a pikestaff. But there is in Milton what amounts to an inveterate rationalism; and there is a comparable quality in Ransom, as his interest in positivism, particularly as displayed in his critical volumes, indicates.

One is tempted to go on and name an even more curious parallel: Milton wrote, and Ransom has written, on theology. Ransom has wryly called his *God Without Thunder* "home-brew theology," but it is a descriptive term which somewhat scandalously applies to *De Doctrina Christiana.* For Milton's book is a brilliant personal reordering of his own position rather than an ecumenical document, and, whatever Milton's intention, was scarcely calculated to win any more converts, had it been published, than the publication of *God Without Thunder* actually did win.

But this parallel is probably too special and accidental to be significant. Better to return to the common trait of a highly personal idiom, a striking trait which has already been mentioned. In this quality Ransom certainly matches Milton. Someone has remarked that, if he found any three consecutive lines of Ransom scribbled on a scrap of paper on a desert island, he would have no difficulty in pronouncing them to be Ransom's. Milton's individual quality is almost as indelible; yet, as we know, it is won from a mélange of borrowings. Any one of Milton's poems is a tissue of allusions, semi-quotations, and echoes from the classic writers and the Elizabethans; but the borrowed matter is always digested and absorbed. The Miltonic poem is not a mosaic; it is an articulated whole; the tone is unified, individual, almost unique.

I have already forsworn source hunting in this examination of Ransom's poetry. But the nature of his characteristic fusion of the archaic and the contemporary, of the Latinized diction and the native idiom—the terms on which the fusion is made, the tensions involved, the tone thereby established—an examination of such matters as these can tell us a good deal about the essential poetry of both Milton and Ransom.

In the case of Ransom, of course, the prevailing tone is ironic, and Ransom's consistent role as an ironist was brilliantly treated some years ago by Robert Penn Warren. With Ransom, one of the obvious functions of the Latinity and the hint of the archaic is to parody the grand manner and to establish the ironic tone which is the consistent tone of Ransom's verse. There is no need here to repeat Warren's discussion. In what follows I have something a little more special in mind: the examination of further qualities which are related to irony, but which transcend irony, being indeed common to Milton's minor poetry as well as to Ransom's.

It scarcely needs to be observed that Milton too is a witty poet, and nowhere more so than in his diction. Milton early gave up the metaphysical conceit, at least in the form in which we associate it with Donne. But, even in his latest poetry, he continued to make use of what I should call a submerged wit, and his more verbal wit (corresponding to the puns in Donne) is characteristically achieved by playing the Latin meaning of a word off against its developed English meaning. The earth, for example, becomes "this punctual spot" (Latin *punctum*, a dot) ; or "Hell saw/Heav'n ruining from Heav'n," i.e., Heaven sloughing off from Heaven as a ruin and Heaven falling (Latin *ruina*, a falling down). The witty quality is easily obscured by the academic habit of regarding these instances as merely the result of Milton's scholarship or pedantry. But when Milton has Heav'n ruin from Heav'n, or writes, of the fallen angels' rebellion, that God "tempted [their] attempt," there can be no question of the wit.

Much of Ransom's more verbal wit takes precisely this form; one can find half a dozen examples in a single poem. Consider, for example, his "Vaunting Oak." The anecdote around which the poem is built is slight. The girl walking with her lover, in her happiness, points to a great oak tree as a proper symbol of the endurance of their love. But her lover, with sorrowful irony, is forced to point out that the aged tree is hollow, already prepared to fall.

It is the Latinized diction (along with archaic diction and a rather formal patterning of sentence structure) which the poet uses to invest the anecdote with its special quality. The great tree, imagined as fallen, is described as "concumbent." Its massive bole (symbol of the eternal) rears up against the sky: "Only his *temporal* twigs are unsure of seat. . . ." The leaves flutter in the wind "in panic round the stem on which they are captive"—literally *held (captivus)* though the poet is glad to retain the English sense of *captive* also. That is, the leaves would flee in their panic if they were not held prisoners.

Thus far in the poem, the Latinisms have been used primarily for a kind of conscious grandiloquence, a kind of parody of the grand manner. But the instances that follow play meaning against meaning for witty ironical effects. The heart of the young girl has been "too young and mortally/Linked with an unbeliever of bitter blood." *Mortally* is darkly, ominously, but the word is presumably used also because the two are linked by marriage, irrevocably, "till death do them part." The girl finds in the great tree an "eminent witness of life"; *eminent,* of course, in the general sense of "signal" or "remarkable," but the specific Latin sense of *eminent* becomes a normal extension of the metaphor of the tree—Latin *eminens,* projecting, lofty. The great tree projects above the humbler "populace/Of daisies and yellow kinds," which are too ephemeral to serve as symbols for the perdurability of love.

Suddenly the poem shifts into the colloquial (though the Latinized diction and formalized phrasing intermittently occur for ironic effect) :

> And what but she fetch me up to the steep place
> Where the oak vaunted?

As they run up the steep hill the girl knows better than to make her boast among the ephemeral flowers of a season. But once arrived beneath the great tree, she murmurs

> "Established, you see him there! forever."

But the "unbeliever of bitter blood" cannot allow her to remain in her "pitiful error." He tests the tree:

> I knocked on his house loudly, a sorrowing lover . . .

At the hollow reverberation,

> "The old gentleman," I grieved, "holds gallantly,
> But before our joy shall have lapsed, even, will be gone."

Up to this point the poem is a half playful, half wistful commentary on the frailty of human love. But the opening measures of the poem, even if we regard them at a first reading as an almost wicked parody on the grand style, have done something to universal-ize the experience. The little anecdote has been told against a background. The lover's original mockery of himself as an "unbeliever of bitter blood" now becomes more than playful. His challenging the oak is not trivial and special: it is typical. The highly personal little anecdote has thus been taken out of a merely personal context. When, therefore, he proceeds to knock more sternly, the tone of the poem modulates into a deeper and more serious note in which the grand manner, earlier parodied, is reasserted this time with full seriousness, so that the answering reverberation from the hollow tree can be justly called a "dolorous cry."

> I knocked more sternly, and his dolorous cry
> Boomed till its loud reverberance outsounded
> The singing of bees; or the coward birds that fly
>
> Otherwhere with their song when summer is sped,
> And if they stayed would perish miserably;
> Or the tears of a girl remembering her dread.

The poem achieves a proper climax and a powerful one as the boom from the hollow oak is made to swell into a great cry of lament which smothers every sound in the spring scene—the singing of bees, the calls of the birds, and the sobbing of the girl. But if we are to express the poet's strategy in terms of diction, we have to say that the ironic use of the formal and pompous diction of the earlier lines of the poem has guaranteed and made possible the powerful and utterly serious use of "dolorous" and "reverberance" in the closing lines of the poem.

But the most important special characteristic which Ransom shares with Milton is what must be called, for want of a better term, aesthetic distance. Indeed, the poem just discussed provides an instance: it employs a considerable measure of aesthetic distance. The scene is given an almost formal quality; the reader is kept well back from the scene; characteristically, the "unbeliever" is not revealed as the "me" of the poem—the speaker—until the poem is half over.

With Milton, the measure of aesthetic distance is nearly always great. This aesthetic distance is not aloofness: the prim young Puritan keeping his distance from the common world that lies about him. It is not to be characterized merely as a sense of form: Donne's "Canonization" is as firmly and as exquisitely "formed" as anything in

Milton. (Both Donne and Milton at their best give us poetry in which form and content cannot be separated.) The quality to which I refer is not even to be defined as a high degree of formality, for whereas Milton is rarely casual, he can be surely "informal" enough. He does not stand on his dignity in "L'Allegro" and "Il Penseroso."

Yet there is in all of Milton's work a large measure of aesthetic distance. The scene is framed, the stance of the observer is carefully implied, a sense of perspective is definitely, if quietly, indicated. Even in "L'Allegro" and "Il Penseroso" a certain detachment is always indicated, and it is this detachment as much as anything else that gives these poems their special flavor of coolness. Indeed, an inspection of Milton's earliest show piece, the "Nativity Hymn," will reveal that Milton's sense of aesthetic distance is already fully developed. The scene is panoramic—the whole world, quieted and stilled, is laid out beneath our gaze. We see the dove of peace descending through the successive spheres; and later, from a comparable vantage point, we are allowed to view the slinking away of pagan gods in Greece, in Syria, in Lybia, as the divine influence flows over the whole known world. Even at the end of the poem, we are not brought up to the manger to kneel with the poet. It is evidently from a distance that we see the whole scene, for it is a tableau conceived amply enough to include "Heaven's youngest teemed star" shining above the stable, "and all about the Courtly Stable, bright harnessed angels . . . in order serviceable."

I would not make too much of what may be thought an accidental quality of Milton's poetry, but I am convinced that it is not accidental. As a device it is closely related to the characteristic tone which is set and sustained in one after another of the minor poems. It is closely related to Milton's particular vision of reality—his characteristic way of "seeing" his world.

The measure of aesthetic distance in Ransom's poetry is thoroughly comparable to Milton's. It is controlled by the poet for his own effects, to be sure. But it is quite as pervasive as in Milton and as fundamental to Ransom's variations of tone.

"Necrological" will furnish a nice and apposite example. The youthful friar who views the battlefield is quite removed from the issues. The battle is over, "the living all were gone," and the young friar himself as observer is withdrawn, at the end of the poem, lost in a "vast surmise," as still as the dead men themselves.

But this last example is rather special. The very theme of the poem is the remove at which the young friar stands from the issues of a torn and violent world. "Spectral Lovers" will provide a less specially weighted and therefore more cogent illustration of Ransom's characteristic use of aesthetic distance.

> By night they haunted a thicket of April mist,
> Out of that black ground suddenly come to birth,
> Else angels lost in each other and fallen on earth.
> Lovers they knew they were, but why unclasped, unkissed?
> Why should two lovers go frozen apart in fear?
> And yet they were, they were.

The lovers are spectral indeed: they are, as it were, made to materialize out of the mist. They "haunt" a thicket of April mist; it is as if they had suddenly come to birth out of that black ground; or else they are angels "fallen on earth," and perhaps fallen in that they are lost in each other. But they are spectral also in the sense that is to provide the torment described in the poem: their lack of grossness, the restrictions which they impose upon the flesh, their ideal quality.

A less tough-minded poet, a less ambitious and brilliant poet, would scarcely have dared to humanize and agonize these creatures of the mist. He would have left them a shade too ethereal, glimmering "white in the season's moon-gold and amethyst." It is typical of Ransom that he should be able to present them realistically.

Ransom presents the man even wittily:

> And gesturing largely to the moon of Easter,
> Mincing his steps and swishing the jubilant grass,
> Beheading some field-flowers that had come to pass,
> He had reduced his tributaries faster
> Had not considerations pinched his heart
> Unfitly for his art.

But if the realistic and witty description jars with the spectral quality of the lovers, it would seem to jar also with the uncolloquial and "literary" language that the lovers are made to speak.

This for the woman:

> Should the walls of her prison undefended yield
> And open her treasure to the first clamorous knight?

"This is the mad moon, and shall I surrender all?
If he but ask it I shall."

This for the man:

"Blessed is he that taketh this richest of cities:
But it is so stainless the sack were a thousand pities.
This is that marble fortress not to be conquered,
Lest its white peace in the black flame turn to tinder
And an unutterable cinder."

The power of the contrasts and of the tensions which are thus set up is obvious. The interesting question will be how, in view of the violence of these tensions, the poem holds together at all. The answer surely lies in the last stanza and the perspective which it establishes.

The first line of this last stanza, "They passed me once in April in the mist," pushes the whole scene back into a past time. It does something more. This is the first time that the "me" of the poem, the observer who speaks the poem, has been mentioned. The speaker, then, is not one of the lovers. The lovers have been described actually from the outside. The calculated language which the lovers have spoken has been imagined for them, since the words are not audible even to each other. The formalized, almost ritual-like quality of their action is thus accounted for. For the spectral lovers prove to be, now that the vantage point of the speaker is established for us, a construction evoked with pity, with understanding, with irony, by the "me" of the last stanza, out of himself and out of the two forms which have silently passed him in the mist.

It is much the same kind of effect that one gets at the end of Milton's "Lycidas" when the "I" of the poem, he who has spoken the passionate though formalized lament, suddenly is reduced to a figure mentioned in the third person, the uncouth swain whose thought is "eager," but who, in spite of his confident declaration that Lycidas, like the day star, has risen and now "flames in the forehead of the morning sky," himself inhabits a workaday world in which suns rise and set and in which now, at the end of his song, the actual sun has dropped again "into the western bay."

I have said that the effect is much the same. Perhaps I should say rather that the effect is comparable, for the device as Milton uses it just reverses Ransom's: we conclude with a figure in the third person rather than, as with Ransom, with a first person, a "me" whom the spectral lovers have passed. But the effect gained by the sudden establishment of a controlling perspective is much the same.

I should like, however, to conclude these notes with a later poem and a finer poem than those I have discussed. For the large measure of aesthetic distance is a constant in Ransom's poetry and can be illustrated from his latest work as easily as from his earliest. The poem I have in mind is the beautiful "Prelude to an Evening." On the surface it is an intensely personal poem with a husband speaking to a troubled wife and addressing her directly as "you." The directness suggested by the "you" is further enforced by his imagining her in the domestic scene "dainty at [her] orange-cup," her "heels detonating the stair's cavern," "freshening the water in the blue bowls," "smoothing the heads of the hungry children," etc.

But the poem must not be allowed to work itself out as an intensely personal poem, for managed so it would violate its theme. If there were real closeness between the speaker and the "you" to whom ostensibly he speaks the poem, the "drift of fog on your mornings" would be dispelled. For her there would be no "warning sibilance of pines."

The speaker of the "Prelude" apologizes wryly for himself as the "tired wolf/Dragging his infected wound homeward." But he has succeeded in infecting his mate, and for her the "images of the invaded mind," because only hinted at, become more monstrous than for him. This he knows, and the poem is a delicate and tender account of her day as he imagines it from his vantage point of guilt and tender concern. He can see the "too banded Eumenides"; she cannot see them, but can only sense them through their troubling effect upon him.

But the tenderness must not be permitted to cloud the picture. Each detail must be registered with clean detachment and with full realism if the experience presented is not to be robbed of its significance. The details in their realism and in their domesticity are faithfully rendered: her "mouth unbeautied against the pillow" as she cries out in her sleep from some nightmare; the "needles clicking" as she knits; her abstracted air as she makes her "Noes but wanderingly" to the questioning children.

All of this means, however, that the imagined scene must be patterned, ordered in a particular perspective, "seen" by the tired husband from his stance outside the room and outside the context of a special day. He has said that it is by "our perverse supposal" that the drift of fog has come upon her mornings; but the re-created scene too is a "supposal," his supposal, his imagined recreation of the scene, and it gains its intimacy and its tenderness because it is "supposed" with clarity and detachment.

> You in your peignoir, dainty at your orange-cup,
> Feel poising round the sunny room
>
> Invisible evil, deprived and bold.
> All day the clock will metronome
> Your gallant fear; the needles clicking,
> The heels detonating the stair's cavern.
>
> Freshening the water in the blue bowls
> For the buckberries with not all your love,
> You shall be listening for the low wind,
> The warning sibilance of pines.
>
> You like a waning moon, and I accusing
> Our too banded Eumenides,
> You shall make Noes but wanderingly,
> Smoothing the heads of the hungry children.

Like so many of Ransom's finest poems, this poem is a triumph of tone; and aesthetic distance is, of course, an aspect of tone, a special ordering of the poet's attitude toward his material, a liberation of the elected poem from the particular and accidental emotions of the poet as man rather than as artist.

Ransom's poems, I have suggested, are always ordered very carefully in this fashion, just as Milton's are so ordered, and it is this control of perspective that constitutes Ransom's special claim to a kind of classical decorum. It is a claim well worth pressing. It is a quality which is rare enough in modern poetry and for the want of which the modern poets have suffered, and, one predicts, are likely to suffer more.

Be that as it may, there is in modern poetry nothing else quite like this quality of Ransom's. Wallace Stevens, our other special master of perspective and of tone, is perhaps a comparable figure, but his general method is quite other than Ransom's and perhaps much more special and limited than Ransom's. In any case, our age has produced nowhere else a poetry so fine grained, so agate hard, so tough-minded as that contained in *Chills and Fever* and *Two Gentlemen in Bonds*. It wears well. After some twenty-odd years, it has worn very well indeed, outlasting verse that once appeared a great deal more exciting or profound. It belongs to that small body of verse which, one predicts, will increasingly come to be regarded as the truly distinguished poetry of the twentieth century.

JOHN RANSOM'S POETRY

Randall Jarrell

The subject matter of Ransom's poems is beautifully varied: they are about everything from Armageddon to a dead hen.* All their subjects are linked, on the surface, by Ransom's persistent attitude, tone, and rhetoric; underneath they are joined, passively, by being parts of one world—joined, actively, by fighting on one side or the other in the war that is going on in that world. On one side are Church and State, Authority, the Business World, the Practical World, men of action, men of affairs, generals and moralists and applied mathematicians and philosophers you set your watch by— efficient followers of abstraction and ideals, men who have learned that when you know how to use something you know it. There is a good deal of rather mocking but quite ungrudging credit— if little fondness—given to this side of things, the motor or effector system which, after all, does run the world along its "metalled ways" of appetency (our version of Tennyson's "ringing grooves of change"). But Ransom's affection goes out to that other army, defeated every day and victorious every night, of so-lightly-armed, so-easily-vanquished skirmishers, in their rags and tags and trailing clouds, who run around and around the iron hoplites pelting them with gravel and rosemary, getting killed miserably, and—half the time, in the pure pleasure or pain of being—forgetting even that

*This essay originally appeared in *Sewanee Review*, LVI (Summer, 1948), 378–90.

they are fighting, and wandering off into the flowers at the edge of the terrible field. Here are the "vessels fit for storm and sport," not yet converted into "miserly merchant hulls"—the grandfather dancing with his fierce grandsons, in warpaint and feathers, round a bonfire in the back yard, having "performed ignominies unreckoned/Between the first brief childhood and the second," but now "more honorable . . . in danger and in joy." In these ranks are children and the old, women—innocent girls or terrible beauties or protecting housewives, all above or below or at the side of The Real World—lovers, dreams, nature, animals, tradition, nursery rhymes, fairy tales, everything that is at first or at last "content to feel/What others understand." Sometimes the poems are a queer mixture of pastoral and child-cult; though the shepherds are aging and the children dead, half of them, and the fox-hunters not making much headway against the overweening Platonism of the International Business Machine Company, it is all magical: disenchantment and enchantment are so prettily and inextricably mingled that we accept everything with sad pleasure, and smile at the poem's foreknowing, foredefeated, mocking, half-acceptant pain. For in the country of the poems wisdom is a poor butterfly dreaming that it is Chuang-tze, and not an optimistic bird of prey; and the greatest single subject of the romantics, pure potentiality, is treated with a classical grace and composure.

The most important thing to notice about this treatment, the rhetorical machinery of the poems, is that it is not a method of forcing intensity, of creating a factitious or at least arbitrary excitement, as most modern rhetoric is. Instead of listening through the hands, with closed eyes, as one is sucked deeper and deeper into the maelstrom, one listens with one's eyes open and one's head working about as well as it usually works. Most writers become over-rhetorical when they are insisting on more emotion than they actually feel or need to feel; Ransom is just the opposite. He is perpetually insisting, by his detached, mock-pedantic, wittily complicated tone, that he is not feeling much at all, not half as much as he really should be feeling—and this rhetoric becomes over-mannered, too-protective, when there is not much emotion for him to pretend not to be feeling, and he keeps on out of habit. Ransom developed this rhetorical machinery—tone, phrasing, properties, and all the rest—primarily as a way of handling sentiment or emotion without ever seeming sentimental or over-emotional; as a way of keeping the poem at the proper aesthetic distance from its subject; and as a way for the poem to extract from its subject, no matter how unpleasant or embarrassing, an unembarrassed pleasure. He was writing in an age in which the most natural feeling of tenderness, happiness, or sorrow was likely to be called sentimental; consequently he needed a self-protective rhetoric as the most brutal or violent of poets did not—such a poet, on being told that some poem of his was a sort of delirium of pointless violence, had only to reply, with a satisfied smile, "Yes, isn't it?" One can say, *very* crudely, that Ransom's poems are produced by the classical, or at worst semi-classical, treatment of romantic subjects. Both the subjects and the treatment of the poems are Impractical, so far as Ransom's war of the worlds (of Feeling and of Power) is concerned; but the Latinity, mixed generality and peculiarity, and mocking precision of the vocabulary, the sharp intelligence of the tone, are always acknowledging or insisting that we can live only by trading with the enemy—that the heart has its reasons, a mighty poor grade of them, too—that the poet himself is an existence away from the Innocent Doves he mourns for.

I suppose that the quality of Ransom's rhetoric—so different from Laforgue's and Corbière's in form, though fairly similar in some of its functions—was suggested by his profession, by Oxford, by the lingering rhetoric of the South, by the tradition of rhetoric in the ministry, and by his own thoroughly Classical education and interests. And I imagine that he had before his eyes, as haunting, more-than-embarrassing examples of the direct treatment of sentimental subjects, some of his own early poems. But by the 1930's— as you can see from "Prelude to an Evening," in which most of his rhetoric has disappeared—he could afford an exact, grave directness.

Ransom seems in his poems, as most modern poets do not, sympathetic and charming, full of tenderness and affection, wanting the light and sorry for the dark—moral and condemning only when he has to be, not because he wants to be; loving neither the sterner vices nor the sterner virtues. He has the personal seriousness that treats the world as it seems to him, not the solemnity that treats the really important things, the world as everybody knows it is. His poems are full of an affection that cannot help itself, for an innocence that cannot help itself—for the stupid travelers lost in the maze of the world, the clever travelers lost in the maze of the

world. The poems are not a public argument but personal knowledge, personal feeling; and their virtues are the "merely" private
virtues—their characters rarely vote, rarely even kill one another,
but often fall in love. The poems have none of that traumatic passion for Authority, any Authority at all, that is one of the ugliest
things in our particular time and our particular culture. To tell
the truth, the poems are out of place in this most Pharisaical of
ages: a time that wanted its artists ruins among its ruins, or else
signposts pointing from them to some Heavenly or Earthly City as
different as possible from everything, everything; a time that damned
Gentile and Jew alike for lacking—of all possible things—the proper
relationship to, or appreciation of, Evil; a time that told each random smile that a smile is nothing but repressed hostility, or sexual
sublimation, or ignorance, or evasion, or an escape, or Original Sin,
or bourgeois complacency, or a hundred other things each worse
than the last; a time that had learned, as no other ever had, that
it was a time different from all other times, a last age different
from all the ages. It tried, with little success, to forgive the poems
for having made a small garden, and not a large crater—for having
saved no one by joining a Party or attacking a Party, by exposing
the shallowness and corruption of our middle-class culture, by maintaining a paradoxical and ecstatic relationship with God, or by doing
anything else that one would expect a poem to do. Instead the
poems told stories. Stories!

The attitude of the poems is quiet and complicated; it neither
satisfied the expectations nor spoke for the causes of any large body
of readers. Any of the poems could have been called "With Mixed
Feelings"; and the feelings of most of their readers may have been
mixed up, but they certainly weren't mixed. The poems were so
transparently dialectical that nobody even called them that: they
set out both struggling sides of things, saw both as catercornered,
corrugated, kaleidoscopic mixtures—all their steady states, even, were
hardened and habitual struggles of opposites. (Look at "Painted
Head," "The Equilibrists," "Spectral Lovers," "Here Lies a Lady,"
and many other poems, where all this is plain.) Once I took a
little girl to a Tarzan movie; and as each new actor, each new
cannibal, each new leopard and monkey and crocodile came on the
scene, she would whisper to me desperately: "Is that a *good* one?
Is that a *bad* one?" This great root-notion, this imperative at the
bottom of our beings, is ill satisfied by Ransom's poems, anomalous

things that keep whispering to us, "Both"—that keep whispering to us, "Neither." Perhaps it is best to call them, as Winters does, an "ambiguous and unhappy connective" between the Experimental Generation and the Reactionary Generation; and certainly, to one so precariously assured of certain certainties as Winters, poems that speak of uncertainties with such ambiguous sureness must seem unhappy.

In Ransom's best poems every part is subordinated to the whole, and the whole is realized with astonishing exactness and thoroughness. Their economy, precision, and restraint give the poems, sometimes, an individual but impersonal perfection; and Ransom's feel for the exact convention of a particular poem, the exact demands of a particular situation, has resulted in poems different from each other and everything else, as unified, individualized, and unchangeable as nursery rhymes. Who could want or imagine anything different in "Here Lies a Lady," in "Captain Carpenter"? They have the composed and inexhaustible ambiguity of things; some of Ransom's queer fabulous allegories are close, in form, to some of Kafka's. If you read "Captain Carpenter" (or *Metamorphosis,* for that matter) to a quite uncultivated audience, it will be delighted with what happens but puzzled about what it means—even "Here Lies a Lady," which seems to an ordinarily cultivated reader almost too immediate to be called allegory, is a puzzling joy to such an audience, since the identification between one's own life or lives in general and the "six little spaces of chill and six of burning," the automatic application of the conceit, occurs with difficulty to such an audience. But Ransom's poetry is not "modernist" poetry at all, normally; and it is remarkable how much narrative, dramatic, non-lyric, non-highbrow interest the best poems have.

Sometimes Ransom uses a version of that ironic-familiar treatment of the past that was so common in the 1920's, but he uses it for freshness, sensation by shock, and not for "debunking." More often he does the exact opposite, and treats the present—or future or what has no time at all—in terms of a specific past:

> Till knowing his need extreme, and his heart pure,
> Christ let them dress him his thick chevelure,
> And soon his beard was glozed and sweetly scented.

Often he is mocking, and pretends to discredit, by the extravagance or incongruity of his terms, precisely what he wishes to make us realize that we do believe and cannot help believing.

It is interesting to compare one of Ransom's mock-medieval, carefully mannered poems inside a chosen convention, with one of those pieces of music, composed at the same time, which also were set inside some arbitrarily chosen convention out of the past. And this reminds one of Stravinsky's remark that Wagner "made an organ" of his orchestra—which could also mean, interpreted past reason, that in Wagner all the contradictions are synthesized in a sort of transcendental unity of intensity. In Ransom the contradictions are clear, exactly contradictory, not fused in arbitrary overall emotion; one admires the clear, sharp, Mozartian lightness of texture of the best poems. And occasionally their phrasing is magical—light as air, soft as dew, the real old-fashioned enchantment:

> Go and ask Robin to bring the girls over
> To Sweetwater, said my Aunt; and that was why
> It was like a dream of ladies sweeping by
> The willows, clouds, deep meadowgrass, and the river.
>
> Robin's sisters and my Aunt's lily daughter
> Laughed and talked, and tinkled light as wrens
> If there were a little colony all hens
> To go walking by the steep turn of Sweetwater.
>
> Let them alone, dear Aunt, just for one minute
> Till I go fishing in the dark of my mind:
> Where have I seen before, against the wind,
> These bright virgins, robed and bare of bonnet,
>
> Flowing with music of their strange quick tongue
> And adventuring with delicate paces by the stream,—
> Myself a child, old suddenly at the scream
> From one of the white throats which it hid among?

Not Nausicaa, not Pharoah's daughter bending among the rushes, gazed with a purer astonishment.

It seems to me that Ransom's best poems are "Captain Carpenter," "Antique Harvesters," "Painted Head," "Judith of Bethulia," "Here Lies a Lady," "Prelude to an Evening," "Janet Waking," "Bells for John Whiteside's Daughter," "Dead Boy," "Tom Tom the Piper's Son," "Vision by Sweetwater," and "Old Mansion." Besides these, "The Equilibrists," "Necrological," and "Armageddon" are elaborately mannered but fairly successful poems of an odd kind; the new version of "Vaunting Oak" has kept all the charm of the old, and has got rid of most of its embarrassing pieces of mannerism and rhetoric; and "Piazza Piece" and "Lady Lost" are good examples of Ransom's microscopic successes. And the last stanzas of "Puncture" and "Conrad in Twilight" are plainly Ransom at his best.

Only one of the poems I have mentioned—"Vision by Sweetwater"—is omitted from the *Selected Poems*. One can imagine Ransom's "Mighty slight, mighty slight" as he left it out, but this was a real mistake, the only important mistake in the book. Few poets have ever picked their own best poems so surely, or disliked their weak or impossibly mannered poems so effectively: the whole *Selected Poems* is a little triumph of omission and revision, a piece of criticism that makes a great deal of the criticism one might otherwise write entirely unnecessary. Perhaps "Her Eyes," "Survey of Literature," and "Dog" might have been replaced. "Survey of Literature" is a fairly popular poem, but it seems to me no more than a recipe, a few half-fleshed-out rhymes, and a moral. "Then there was poor Willie Blake/He foundered on sweet cake" is so queer a judgment, about a poet whose favorite word was *howl*, that one decides it is not a judgment but a rhyme. And "Dog" reminds one of what Goldsmith said about the way Johnson's little fishes would have talked.

A good many people, wondering what Ransom's poems grew out of, must have gone back to the book he published in 1918. At first reading *Poems About God* is shockingly, almost impossibly different from Ransom's later poetry. (Though in the opening poem one comes upon *escheat,* the word that, along with its backward brother *estopped,* was later to become the "little phrase of Vinteuil's" or national anthem of the Fugitives.) Most of the time one is bumping over the furrows of a crude, broad, direct, Southern pastoral, full of reapers and sermons and blackberry pie, quite as country as anything in the early Frost. Many people might recognize, in "Hurrying home on a windy night/And hearing tree-tops rubbed and tossed," the familiar accents of a marginal Arcadia; but who would suppose them Ransom's? Most of the earlier *Poems About God* are old-fashioned, amateurishly direct jobs that remind you of the Longfellow-Whittier-Lowell section in your sixth-grade reader, and there are a few surprisingly close to popular doggerel:

"There's a patch of trees at the edge of the field/And a brown little
house that is kept so warm. . . ." A poem about a practical farmer
who, by cutting away the roses at the edge of his field, always got a
bigger yield than his neighbors has a name like a steam-roller: "One
Who Rejected Christ." But along with the raw innocence of some
of the poems there is the raw knowledge that replaces innocence:
the "hulk of heaving meat" who "in his vomit laid him down" to
die. Some of these earlier poems are nothing but the revulsion and
condemnation that are the direct response of innocence and goodness to the evil of the world: at first one is separated from the other
absolutely, but afterwards, occasionally, they begin to be joined in
the sweet-sour, good-and-evil, steady struggle of opposites that is
usual in Ransom's mature poems. The practical and impractical
are already at their war: the swimmer floating far down in the cool
green depths, with no more need of senses, work, wife, life itself,
hears the scolding watch of the world ticking grimmer and grimmer,
"O *wicked* swimmer!" The preacher being resolutely Christian at
Christmas to the little daughter who impatiently says, "I know, I
know," begs her father to talk about Santa Claus, and at last weeps,
defeated—this is the first of many such poems about children, the
first of many such defeats by the world of morals, business, and
science. And in "Prayer," when God groans despairingly over the
prayers of a poor old woman, several seraphim forget their harping
to scold: "O what a wicked woman,/To shrew his splendid features
out of shape!"

"The Power of God" is the first poem to have some of Ransom's
elaborate Biblical-pedantic rhetoric; but in many of the poems one
can already see his characteristic use of the situation or tone or
gestalt of the ballad or fairy tale. One smiles at the plain broad
beginning of his many-branched myth of Woman: "I have seen wom-
en by these bad roads,/Thank God for that"; but in the poems at
the back of the book one finds very different things; and, remembering "Antique Harvesters," one smiles delightedly at Ransom's
sympathetic and mocking account of that young Hellenist in Tennessee who

> Cursed the paternity that planted me
> One green leaf in a wilderness of autumn;
> And wept, as fitting such a fruitful spirit
> Sealed in a yellow tomb.

One realizes, "Why, it wasn't a mutation—this is Ransom after all"; one has not only seen some of the cruder attitudes, afterwards refined or contradicted, that underlie the later poems, one has wound up among the later poems.

Ransom's poetry shows no individual influences of any real importance. (The Bible, Märchen, and such are important general influences.) Once, in the early "Geometry," Ransom rewrote Hardy in Hardy's own language: "Unprofited by the centuries/He still plants on as crazily/As in his drivelling infancy." And the beginning of "Night Voices," from Ransom's second book, is Hardy being Biblical. Occasionally in *Poems About God* there is a slight flavor of Robinson; and "Tom Tom the Piper's Son" is the working out of a Robinson theme with more grace, concentration, and purity than Robinson could have brought to it himself. Ransom must be almost the only person in the world who has been influenced (though too slightly to talk about, except for fun) by both early and late Yeats; so that as one reads, in *Poems About God,*

> Must I confess before the pack
> Of babblers, idiots, and such?

one remembers a couple of late-Yeats phrases in Ransom's "Address to the Scholars of New England." But when one reads, in "Old Mansion," the phrases "we beautifully trusted" and "with my happier angel's own temerity," one decides that this is a natural similarity, not simply James.

Ransom has noticeably influenced at least three good poets: Robert Graves, Allen Tate, and Robert Penn Warren. But all three were influenced more by his accident than by his essence, and their best poems show no trace of him. To expect Tate's and Warren's poems to be much influenced by Ransom's is like expecting two nightmares to be influenced by a daydream; and Graves, who might have been more affected, ended with a style all his own only after undergoing considerably more mesmeric American influences.

As Blake said, there is no comparison between true poets. Ransom is plainly a member of that strange wonderful family, with about as much individual difference and as much family likeness as is common; and his poems profess their limitations so candidly, almost as a principle of style, that is hardly necessary to say they are not poems of the largest scope or of the greatest intensity. But it is only fair to say that Ransom is one of the best, most original, and most sympathetic poets alive; and it is easy to see that his poetry will always be cared for, since he has written poems that are perfectly realized and occasionally almost perfect—poems that the hypothetical generations of the future will be reading page by page with Wyatt, Campion, Marvell, and Mother Goose.

But one hates to end on such a grave yew-like note, and had rather cover the last page with a picture, a recollected Breughelish landscape of the country of Ransom's poems. In the center of everything—but unseen, like the blind spot in the middle of one's eye—is the practical world of business and science and morality, a vortex that is laboring to suck everything into its transforming revolutions. In the foreground there is a girl weeping for a dead pet; or simply a girl, dead; and her parents are mourning—in their dry, wistful, pedantic way, full of sentiment and knowledge—this pure potentiality which they have tried helplessly to shelter, but which existence itself has brought to nothing. Nearby the girl, grown up now, stands under the great hollow oak that whispers gently to its daughter—stands torn with pure love, pure pain, as she watches the "serpent's track" of the bicyclist pumping his winding way uphill, carrying the last of all letters to her lover: who walks with blank bitter dryness through the bare wet woods, slashing with a cane at weeds, full of abstraction, morality, and baffled oblivious non-attachedness, a man who has seen through everything except the process of seeing through everything. Children are playing in the vacant lots, animals are playing in the forest. Everything that the machine at the center could not attract or transform it has forced out into the suburbs, the country, the wilderness, the past: out there are the fairy tales and nursery rhymes, chances and choices, dreams and sentiments and intrinsic aesthetic goods—everything that doesn't pay and doesn't care. Out there are the old men, like children now—the defeated Way of an old world—and the gods of that way: Christ and Anti-Christ arming themselves for their tourney; Lamb and Paraclete and Exegete; the friar poring doubtfully over the bloody leaves of the battlefield; Grimes, the old scapegoat, old campaigner, hardened and professional in the habit of atonement, careless of those he dies for:

> Blue blazed the eyes of Grimes in the old manner,—
> The flames of eyes which jewel the head of youth
> Were strange in the leathery phiz of the old campaigner,—

Smoke and a dry word crackled from his mouth
And the wind ferried them South.

And there are beauties dangerous as Judith of Bethulia, tender-hearted plant-loving spinsters, lovers embracing like acrobats wrestling on a tight-rope, lovers quarreling and wandering through the dewy night like ghosts. Out there are things queer and unchangeable as anything in Grimm: a Quixote who loses on his quests arms, legs, eyes, everything but his tongue and the "old heart in his bust"—and at last those; Tom Tom the Piper's Son, the changeling pulling his little black coat tight about him, glaring around with little grey eyes; the Maiden accosted among the roses of the trellis of the piazza by Death, who has come for her in a dustcoat; the "fine woman" turned into a timid lady bird; the lady whose life was "six little spaces of chill and six of burning. . . ." Was she not lucky? Here is old Robert Crocodile: who went to Oxford, carried an umbrella, rode to hounds, turned into a society psychoanalyst—an echoingly metaphysical one—and at last sank back into the ooze of the Ohio Everglades, where to this day "floating he lies extended many a rood" among all his kinsfolk.

PRIMARILY LANGUAGE

F. O. Matthiessen

We have not had enough good minor artists in America.* The early
nineteenth century, when the traditions of our literature were being
established, was the time of expansive aspiration, of gigantic projections; and if it brought us a Whitman and a Melville, it also left us
with the inflated ideal of the epic bard and with the dubious dream
of the great American novel. One trouble with that ideal was that it so
easily confused size with value. One trouble with that dream was that
it set up a sterilizing tension of all or nothing. It invoked a spectral
absolute into the realm of the finite and concrete. It did not perceive
that one sign of a rich culture is variety rather than singleness, not
the striving for one impossible masterpiece but a more resilient and
far more fertile practice of writing as a craft.

As we look back now to the second phase of the American renaissance, to the period between 1910 and 1930, we can observe, at least
so far as poetry is concerned, the pervasive growth of the conception
of the poet as craftsman instead of as inspired seer. We can observe
also that during that period far more gifted poets emerged than during any other period in our history. The most influential have been
Frost and Eliot, although the increasing reputation of Wallace Stevens
may now rival theirs. But quite apart from any scale of relative

*This essay originally appeared in *Sewanee Review*, LVI (Summer, 1948),
391–401.

greatness, we can be aware that among our most valuable heritages from that period are the numerous examples of integrity of style, of artistic wholeness within whatever limitations the given poet recognized as his own. In many cases this has meant a spareness of production, as in that of Marianne Moore; or, in that of Cummings, a tendency to keep on producing fresh versions of essentially the same poem. But at the present moment, when so many novelists have lost the sense of social direction in which they were advancing a decade ago, and when both novelists and dramatists have in general failed to dominate the vulgarizations of taste that have flowed back upon them from Hollywood, the usefulness of good minor art should be more and more cogent.

The almost perfect instance of what is implied by the term is the poetry of John Crowe Ransom. The conventional approach to his work is to note that he has not published a book of new poems for twenty years, and so to begin by deploring his lack of capacity for growth or the cultural circumstances of our time that may have crippled him. Such issues are not negligible, but they deflect us from what he has done to what he has not. That kind of critical approach is a phase of the demand for the great American novel. Through its excited attention upon what masterpiece lies next over the horizon, it loses sight of the quality of the work of art at hand.

The limitations of Ransom's production are both natural and self-induced. According to the preface to *Poems About God,* he did not start writing poetry until he was twenty-eight, and in that first book, not one poem of which he has subsequently collected, he showed few traces of his mature style. He did not find his own voice until he was past thirty, and before he was forty he had almost discontinued the writing of verse. But in the interval he had reached such a consistently high level of skill that when he finally came to issue his *Selected Poems* in 1945, it was astonishing that he excluded more than half of both *Chills and Fever* and *Two Gentlemen in Bonds.* From the years after 1927 he added only five poems.

He might well argue that he had provided instances of all his chief themes, and he would be right. His feeling for his region and his particular contrast between the Southern past and present are represented by "Old Mansion" and "Antique Harvesters." His particular contrast between America and older cultures comes out in "Philomela." His absorption with the fragility and impermanence of love and his awareness of death form his most recurrent subjects, and give rise to

the most notable element in both his style and attitude: the irony
that Warren has examined in the best essay devoted to Ransom so
far. The theme which—as Warren saw—brings out the fullest resources of this irony is that of the divided personality "who cannot
fathom or perform his nature." It is phrased most explictly in "Man
Without Sense of Direction."

Ransom was probably wise in omitting "the tale in twenty sonnets,"
the title poem of *Two Gentlemen in Bonds,* since it is a too facile
expression of one of his main absorptions, the contrast between the
body and the mind—a theme to which he gave his most condensed
embodiment in the later "Painted Head." He has never shown any
great aptitude for the longer poem, and his Biblical narratives, "Armageddon" and "Judith of Bethulia," along with his Harvard Phi Beta
Kappa poem, "Address to the Scholars of New England," come
closest of any of his inclusions to being set pieces. But what one
feels for the most part is a regret for the exclusions. One takes un-
willingly the absence of the opening poem of *Chills and Fever,*
"Agitato ma non troppo," since, as its title suggests, it establishes
this poet's prevailing tone. And even if no serious themes are omitted,
several of the gayest passages have been sacrificed, perhaps on the
ground that they tended to get out of hand. But a signal loss is
involved in "In Mr. Minnit's House," wherein some of the liveliest
Skeltonics of our period also presented the kind of compressed drama
over which Ransom possesses such great command. In fact, as the
reader considers further, he becomes aware that several of the poems
left out could take their stand with the best work in any representative
modern anthology. "Amphibious Crocodile" may not have the exact
control of "Philomela," but it is rich in its social observation of the
American abroad. "Persistent Explorer" is hardly second to "Man
Without Sense of Direction" in its portrayal of the divided sensibility,
and "Morning" is one of Ransom's sharpest contrasts between free
imagination and fixed reason.

What this last paragraph amounts to is a cumbersome way of noting
that once Ransom established his style, he rarely fell below it. It is
also a plea for a collected rather than a selected edition of his two
mature books. For what catches the reader's attention on nearly every
page is an extraordinary gift of language, turns of phrase that correspond to perceptions distinct from anyone else's:

> Tawny are the leaves turned but they still hold,
> And it is harvest; what shall this land produce?

> A meager hill of kernels, a runnel of juice;
> Declension looks from our land, it is old.
> Therefore let us assemble, dry, grey, spare,
> And mild as yellow air.

This opening stanza of "Antique Harvesters" is among his best-known instances of what we mean, the full signature of a matured style. The "antique" in the title, underscored by the localization of the scene, in the epigraph, on "the bank sinister" of both the Ohio and the Mississippi, sets up the peculiar tone, the kind of contemplative detachment which may be gained through the deliberately archaic. But the archaisms are not merely literary: in the "runnel" from the "meager" hill we hear the old-fashioned country expression, the Elizabethan or seventeenth-century usage that was brought to this country by the first settlers and that has disappeared now except from remote rural and mountain areas, especially in the South. But the particular countryman whom Ransom has devised as the speaking voice or *persona* of this poem is learned to the point of that odd and wryly pedantic use of "declension." He can also fall naturally into the elaborate courtly phrases of an older public speech: "Therefore let us assemble."

All these means of characterization by language are developed and enriched through the remainder of the poem, but their striking effectiveness is due to Ransom's ability to pack so many of them into a single stanza. He has given us his locale, even to the very look of the Southern autumn with its "tawny" leaves and "mild yellow air." He has given us essential traits of the older cultural South with the thoroughness that only the most accurate and efficient words can command. He has thereby prepared the way to give us also, in three lines, the quintessential expression of his devotion to his region, his distillation of the heroic element in its history:

> We pluck the spindling ears and gather the corn.
> One spot has special yield? "On this spot stood
> Heroes and drenched it with their only blood."

How Ransom's sense of proportion has enabled him to avoid sentimentalization of that history—unlike some of the extremists in the Southern Agrarian school that followed him—could make an essay in itself. But my concern here remains primarily with his language. That is not to imply that his metrical gifts are negligible, though they are less varied. His usual iambic has considerable variations from the pentameter norm. But his irregularities are seldom casual or haphazard; they are designed to bring out what is essentially a speaking rather than a singing voice. Among the attributes that establish him as an artist secure within his limits is the care with which he has made certain revisions. Perhaps the most interesting case is that of "Vaunting Oak," one of his most moving accounts of love's perishability. In reconsidering it, he seems to have felt that it needed tightening up, for he cut out two stanzas. What was far more exacting, he decided to introduce the interlinking rhymes of *terza rima.* The result is very instructive, since such a change—to use some of his own favorite critical terms—inevitably involved the interplay between texture and structure. The middle stanzas are those in which the girl turns to the great oak in the hopeful thought that here at least is a witness to endurance:

First Version

And she exulted—being given to crying,
"Heart, Heart, love is so firm an entity,
It must not go the way of the hot rose dying"—

For the venerable oak, delivered of his pangs,
Put forth his flames of green with profuse joying
And testified to her with innumerable tongues.

And what but she fetch me up to the steep place
Where the oak vaunted? A meadow of many songs
Had to be traversed; and a quick populace

Of daisies, and yellow kinds; and here she knew,
Who had sorely been instructed of much decease,
Better than brag in this distraught purlieu.

Revision

And exulted, wrapped in a phantasy of good:
"Be the great oak for its long winterings
Our love's symbol, better than the summer's brood."

Then the venerable oak, delivered of his pangs,
Put forth profuse his green banners of peace
And testified to her with innumerable tongues.

And what but she fetch me up to the steep place
Where the oak vaunted? A flat where birdsong flew
Had to be traversed; and a quick populace

Of daisies, and yellow kinds; and here she knew,
Who had been instructed of much mortality,
Better than brag in this distraught purlieu.

To make the necessary alterations in the rhyme-words Ransom felt
his way back into the meaning of the poem, and strengthened it
ponderably. A girl "given to crying" is a fairly stock figure; she becomes more complexly alive and appealing when her illusion is phrased
positively as "a phantasy of good." The omission of the usual rose
for a more direct apostrophe to the oak is also a shift from a negative
to a positive symbol; and "peace" rather than "joying" is clearly a
more appropriate attribute for the old tree. Though the other two
changes here are slighter in their effect, they still bring out some of
Ransom's special qualities. "A flat where birdsong flew" contains his
distinctive mixture of colloquial and oblique, as the more conventional earlier phrase did not. The barer statement that results from
the omission of "sorely" may strengthen the drama by not overstating
it, and the greater weight of "mortality" over "decease" may also
contribute to the same effect.

There are several comparable changes in the rest of the poem,
and perhaps the only loss in flavor through a new rhyme-word is
after the girl's lover has evoked "a hollow tone" by rapping on the
tree's trunk. He originally grieved that "the old gentleman" is
largely "cadaver," but that yielded to how he "holds gallantly" in
appearance. The burden of the final stanza is, of course, the falseness
of that appearance, how the "dolorous cry" of the dying tree out-
sounds even "the tears of a girl remembering her dread." The earliest
version of that final line—not in *Chills and Fever*, but in the selection issued in England by Robert Graves—said "discovering." The
deepening of the girl's emotional awareness that is suggested by "remembering" foreshadows the dominant effect of the later changes.

Thus by examining even such slight details we can perceive the
central element in Ransom's conception of poetry, how a poem must
be an act of knowing. Each of his poems is designed to afford us
a singularly whole experience. His inclusive concern with both feeling
and thought has caused him to be referred to as a metaphysical poet,
but his style would appear to have developed independent of the
revival of interest in the seventeenth century, and, unlike Eliot, he did
not borrow any devices directly from Donne. The nearest equivalent
to Ransom's irony is from a more immediate background, in Hardy's

Satires of Circumstance. But Ransom's method is all his own, and can be apprehended only through a whole poem. In the preface to his selections he said that he had arranged them as near to the order of their composition as he could remember, and one surprise to the reader from that arrangement is that "Dead Boy" comes almost at the beginning. For this poem displays all the aspects of his skill in their full development. By choosing the very kind of theme upon which the nineteenth century spilled out its worst sentimental excesses, it is as though he deliberately set out to demonstrate his complete break with the Southern romantic past:

> The little cousin is dead, by foul subtraction,
> A green bough from Virginia's aged tree,
> And none of the county kin like the transaction,
> Nor some of the world of outer dark, like me.
>
> A boy not beautiful, nor good, nor clever,
> A black cloud full of storms too hot for keeping,
> A sword beneath his mother's heart—yet never
> Woman bewept her babe as this is weeping.
>
> A pig with a pasty face, so I had said,
> Squealing for cookies, kinned by poor pretense
> With a noble house. But the little man quite dead,
> I see the forebears' antique lineaments.
>
> The elder men have strode by the box of death
> To the wide flag porch, and muttering low send round
> The bruit of the day. O friendly waste of breath!
> Their hearts are hurt with a deep dynastic wound.
>
> He was pale and little, the foolish neighbors say;
> The first-fruits, saith the Preacher, the Lord hath taken;
> But this was the old tree's late branch wrenched away,
> Grieving the sapless limbs, the shorn and shaken.

The diction works upon us in the ways we have already noted, but here the occasional elaborate-pedantic words are introduced into the very first rhyme for a shock of wit that makes us aware at once through the odd dryness that we are faced with no conventionally moist poem on the death of a little cousin. The unobtrusive thoroughness with which Ransom presents a whole way of life and its milieu can be sampled through the deft off-setting of "the county kin" against all the rest of the world as "outer dark." The usages and

values of the Virginia forebears are re-enacted in this dynastic cere-
monial, and the saturation of these values in the language of the
Bible extends far beyond the words of the Preacher. Phrase after
phrase from "the green bough" through "outer dark," the "cloud full
of storms," the "sword beneath his mother's heart," to the "late
branch wrenched away" are either direct or indirect allusions to the
rich King James version.

The prevalence of that source in traditional country speech accounts
for the mingling in that speech of the simple and the archaic, a mingling which Ransom seems consciously to emulate even in phrases
which have no direct connection with the Scriptures. Such mingling
gives rise in particular to the quiet compelling eloquence of the fourth
stanza where the simple "box of death" is suddenly more forceful than
the expected "coffin" could be; and where the archaic unfamiliar
"bruit" is by its very unfamiliarity made to release its full store, not
only of the "rumors" of the day, but of the very breath and sound
of the old men voicing them. But lest Ransom's combination of
the homely and the learned be made to sound too deliberate, we
must remember how his diction is always being spiced by the easily
colloquial: "a pig with a pasty face," "squealing for cookies."

These few notes on the contrasting and combining elements in
Ransom's language can lead directly into a description of his poetic
method, for it also is one of combination through contrast. That is
what is meant by speaking of it, as Cleanth Brooks has, as a method
of inclusion. In this poem, as we have noted, any expectation of
sentiment is undercut in the opening line, and in the first half of
both the second and the third stanzas the case is stated against the
grief before the grief is described. We are thereby given two views
of a situation, the difference, we might say, between what the
situation is felt to be and what it really amounts to when seen by
the eye of detached common sense. But that latter rational stance, this
poem is also saying, is never adequate to the grasp of human values.
That is why Ransom is always counterpointing the difference between
reason and imagination. Reason alone can merely point to the contrast between a situation experienced from without and from within.
And as the poem advances to its end, it is the doubting neighbors, not
the involved kinsfolk, who are "foolish." Yet the objective view also
remains: despite the natural anguish, this boy would not have measured up to much in the world; the older vitality of this heritage is
gone.

Ransom's irony became more devastating in some of his poems dealing with the suffering of lovers, for there he was not balancing one view against another to bring out the partial validity of both. He was writing of the tragic limitations of "desperate men and women." In one of his latest poems, the haunted "Prelude to an Evening," he pushed his expression of frustrated anguish about as far as it could go. That may be why, in his subsequent criticism, he went out of his way to take exception to a poetic method depending too exclusively upon irony and choosing its themes, never from "human aspirations triumphant," but always from "efforts that turned out indecisively, or brought up in the sands." It is as though he were bidding farewell to his own kind of poetry, and it may be regretted that he has not found another way of expressing other aspects of the concrete "beauty of the body" which he has always known to be the source of re-invigoration for the too abstract mind. But that regret must not betray us into the error described at the beginning, the error of underestimating the value of the integrated accomplishment. Ransom has not been deluded into the anxious striving to be a poet for the career's sake. He has said what he was compelled to say in a form uniquely his own. He has not attempted to live up to any extraneous expectations, nor watered down his accomplishment by diluted sequels. He has produced some of the best minor poems in our language.

PORTRAIT OF THE CRITIC–POET AS EQUILIBRIST

Donald A. Stauffer

There is something central and unassuming in the gentleman from Ohio.* It is not the location that matters, it is the gentleman. We know his connection with the South, and his connection with England, and his connection with the Atlantic seaboard. Ohio seems an accident, but there, with imperturbable stability, he is. He would think as he does, write as he does, have the same influence, if he were a resident of Trieste or Nottingham. A cartoonist, making a literary-critical map of the United States, would undoubtedly draw in the suave, white-haired, self-contained figure of Mr. Ransom sitting on his hill at Kenyon. This geographical region would allow the artist considerable room to outline a portrait, and justice would compel a good-sized figure if he wanted to sketch the state of our criticism and poetry in fair proportions.

There is a story of an Indian who, when asked if he was lost, said: "Injun not lost. Teepee lost. Injun here." Mr. Ransom resembles the Indian, and American letters can use him as a *point de repère,* of which we have far fewer than we need. In the present chaotic state of literary theory and practice, Mr. Ransom remains collectedly himself, and Gambier may be the closest approximation we have (with the exception of Ripton, Vermont) to a Sabine farm. From gentle habit he resists all temptations—whether those temptations lie

*This essay originally appeared in *Sewanee Review,* LVI (Summer, 1948) , 426–34.

in the too easily flowing pen, or the money that gushes from popular words, or the autopsies which academicians frequently perform upon literature, or the latest intellectual fashions. Mr. Ransom admirably preserves his balance. That this firmness springs from conviction rather than laziness is evident in his long performance of one of the most arduous, unrewarding, and necessary jobs in the field of literature: the editing of a thoughtful literary quarterly.

The focus on Mr. Ransom as a conservator does not imply that he stands still. He moves gracefully, but not until he knows where he is going. And he streamlines his luggage. For a critic whose prime interest is the metaphysics of aesthetics, he almost miraculously avoids swollen systems of thought and even phrases in technical jargon such as I have been guilty of in this sentence. He simplifies, constantly striving for that elegance so dear to mathematicians. This does not mean that his thought is easy; it pays a far greater compliment in suggesting that his thought is as easy as he can make it. Philosophy is in a parlous state today; the philosophers are so shoved off balance by the successes of science and the pressures of sociology that they seem to have lost trust in their own approach. They could do worse than cast a glance in the direction of Mr. Ransom, whose respect for philosophy at least equals his respect for literature. And is it not the second of English poets who says: "How charming is divine philosophy"? For the selective precision of his philosophical approach to literary criticism, Mr. Ransom deserves an order of merit. Tentatively he sets up his gyroscope in chaos.

But his criticism has gained some of the attention it warrants. His poetry has seldom been rightly valued. Perhaps there is too little of it. Let us count that a virtue for our purposes, and suggest that his three volumes *Poems About God, Chills and Fever,* and *Two Gentlemen in Bonds,* coupled with the rigorous exclusions and revisions in *Selected Poems,* offer excellent material to help a young poet learn his art. Inspiration cannot be taught, but craftsmanship can.

The poems show stability and richness. They stand still; they are like objects; they may be scrutinized, for they are solid, and sometimes you can see some of the strokes that make them. They are rich and seemly, as if their annals could neither be brief nor ignoble, as if back of them were a great store of legend. They pay their own tributes to a rich past, though usually the tributes are more veiled than in Ransom's refingering of a Hopkinsian theme in his poem "Of Margaret." The young poet will find that Ransom increases one's respect for tradition, and requires some knowledge of past art if he is to be savored fully. In his "Survey of Literature" Ransom writes of the older poets that

> What these men had to eat and drink
> Is what we say and what we think.

But it is more than that. His poetry, with its suave glints and re-flections, continually tempts the reader into those profitless compari-sons: How is the wit of Donne and the Metaphysicals blended with the chiseled grace of Ronsard and the Pléiade? What twentieth-century device of rhythm, rhyme, or diction does Ransom not show himself aware of, or prescient of, in poems that remain unmistakably his own? How can the spirit of ballads and nursery rhymes and of the French Parnassians be held in equilibrium in a single poem? In his later verse, how does Ransom balance bitter philosophical subtleties with the brash gallops and clangings of Skelton, Lindsay, and Dun-bar? Are "tiny attent auricles" Tennysonian? Is not "diuturnity" a Marvellous word? Could such a phrase as "the nautical technicalities" have occurred in a poem—it is Ransom's "Good Ships" but it is also "Prufrock" and "Portrait of a Lady" and much of Auden—written before the last quarter-century?

But our hypothetical and eager student may get down to profitable studies without going outside the poems. He may observe how richness and stability are infused into the earlier poems through medi-eval diction. Few people today would dare introduce into their poems (and Ransom himself has moved to other modes in his later verse) such words as thole, halidom, lissome, wight, ogive, malfeasance, richly dight, "a godly liege," or "his thick chevelure." This goes deep-er than mere surface diction: it even dictates archaic pronunciations for such words as "wound." It is no mere copying of Chaucer, "swilling soup from his saucer," no last afterglow of nineteenth-century medievalism. In Ransom's poems this diction is an appropriate sei-zure, drawn from "chivalry's quaint page," at once mocking and monu-mental.

The bright-eyed student will go on to technical studies. He will find new forms and uses of the sonnet—where novelty always seems impossible to achieve *again*—in "The Tall Girl," "Good Ships," "Part-ing at Dawn" (there's another echo, ironical!), and in the beautiful lyrically patterned "Piazza Piece." He can discover Wilfred Owen and Dante crossed (I think before MacLeish tried it) in "Vaunting

Oak." He may look at a late poem such as the "Address to the
Scholars of New England" if he wants to see how the static principle
of the sestina may be modified in new stanzas, or how long experience with alliteration and assonance and their partial ghosts may
hold a poem together. The sound of a poem is just as important in
"To Margaret," the static principle in "Painted Head," and both
are late poems. And he will learn tricks which, if he cannot copy
them, may at least show him how poetic structures are made. Who
else, except possibly De la Mare, would have thought of writing a
poem like Ransom's "Judith of Bethulia" in which each six-line
stanza rises at the end of the fifth line to a question?

One of the best ways of learning how to write poetry is to find
out, through the help of stuffed owls, what it is *not*. Our diligent
student may look up *Poems About God* and figure out why Mr.
Ransom the critic (after all, we have *Two* Gentlemen in Bonds)
did not include in his *Selected Poems* any piece from that earliest
volume of Ransom the poet. In his later volumes also, Ransom knows
how to excise lines and stanzas that do not pay their way, or even
to recast an entire poem, such as "Vaunting Oak."

Now the industrious apprentice should be so fired with respect
for a difficult craft that he will watch Ransom's changes. If I may
use a parallel from Horace again (the last parallel, I promise), Ransom does better than allow a poem nine years to mellow. He does not
publish until the poem is good, and his later changes are meticulous
improvements that offer an education in poetic taste. Sometimes he is
almost three times as careful as Horace. After meditating for twenty-
one years, he will delete a single comma ("Winter Remembered").
Sometimes, as in "Miriam Tazewell," he will rip out a string of commas in the first stanza, excise later ones, soften a semicolon to a comma, and change the next-to-the-last line, which in the original version—

The principle of the beast was low and masculine!—

must finally have seemed at once not in key with the imagery and
too direct in its plucking out the secrets of his heroine. His well-
known "Bells for John Whiteside's Daughter" makes three changes:
in punctuation, one for a clearer meaning and one for flow; in
syntax (a Yeatsian trick in revision and composition), the omission
of an ugly weak connective "that."

The changes, many of them minuscule, are usually toward greater
control, austerity, dignity, chiseled form. "Rigour" turns to "rigor"

(page 43 in *Selected Poems*); "on little pink feet" becomes "across the world" (43); "I would not weep, and" tightens to "I, not to weep then," (56). In a single poem ("Spectral Lovers"), the early sentiment and poetic diction of "asunder," "Her thrilling," "the very moon," "Two clad in the shapes of angels, being," "Trailing a glory of" might be all right in De la Mare or Wylie or Teasdale. In the later version they become Ransom, *seriatim*, as "apart," "Scarcely her," "the moon," "Two tall and wandering, like," and "White in the season's." The revision of the poignant elegy "Dead Boy," though only six changes are made and all seem minor, increases its marmorean beauty.

The revisions are impeccable. I regret only one: that in "Armageddon" Ransom felt compelled to give up his sensible pun "Impastor" and turn poor Antichrist into "Impostor."

Surely this is a small study of minutiae. But if form and content are inseparable, then structures may be understood more fully if some attention is paid to fine textures. Ransom does not do much with interweaving between poems. Each can stand alone, although "intertexture" slides in occasionally, as when "Parting, Without a Sequel" refers back to the "Vaunting Oak," or the late and famous "The Equilibrists" does over the "Spectral Lovers." But read them all and they seem to make one work. If, as Yeats believed, each artist has some symbol or set of symbols that is the image of his secret life, what is Ransom's? Is it the perilous and beautiful idea of equilibrium, the dangerous and precise starting-point of warm and cold, the flames and ice in their nice orbit? Is it the severed head of "Judith of Bethulia" and "Painted Head," that as "officious tower" clashes with body in "The Equilibrists," so that bone and flesh, logic and aesthetic, lonely brainwork and the world's body eventually become the antipodes for even his critical thought? Is it the Old Man, whether playing with children, or a rheumy wraith, or a gentleman in a dustcoat or grim in his little black coat as the sleazy beetle? Or did Ransom find an objective correlative in the old Southern manor, with its tombstones, its stability, its decay, its pride, reserve, and sense of the past?—so that, smoking his cigar, he saw himself in the token and

> went with courage shaken
> To dip, alas, into some unseemlier world.

Or is this irony?

For the poems are held to each other by mastering moods, and Ransom is adept at irony. Sometimes the irony seems hidden, or takes on its own peculiar quality of bland detached humor. Who is being laughted at—Thomas Gray? or Borden's Milk? Poetic diction? or realism?—when Ransom writes

> Now the air trembles to the sorrowing Moo
> Of twenty blameless ladies of the mead.

And how are humor and irony to be blended with pathos in his many elegies and eclogues? That is Ransom's secret. Although we can find key words such as "grey," "little," and "prim," his own quaintness cannot be imitated. Here again we have the equilibrium: the heart can clang while the gaunt tower of the head observes.

The ambiguity of attitude is a part of the style and structure. It is not that Ransom is afraid of saying something. He might be had up before a Congressional investigating committee for the anti-Americanism of "Philomela." Or war posters might be made out of his grim tributes to courage in "Captain Carpenter," "Puncture," and "Dog." Rather, it is that Ransom knows, as all good poets do, that saying too much too directly is not saying enough. And he may be left with his open secret.

One final word on the small things of technique, since they may be the bases of the large things of criticism. I am aware that Mr. Ransom and some of his followers hold that the aesthetic judgment is not a moral judgment, and that logical structures become possibilities for poems because of irrelevant textures. As to the first tenet, is it not true that critics who are also poets frequently build their general criticism upon their own poetic practices? Ransom would agree with Auden that art is a *fait accompli*, which seeks to bring nothing about. Ransom's poems, almost without exception, are limited to retrospection. Their subjects do not move; their emotions are over. They take "the little man quite dead," or the spectral lovers, or the old debates of body and soul among the Pilgrims and Plato and Plotinus and figures from the Old and New Testaments, or a survey of literature, or old men, old mansions. If we meet a "Tall Girl" she is tugged by the Queens of Hell and the Queen of Heaven. If we meet "Blue Girls" they are told that their beauty will fail and that it has not been long since a blear-eyed lady with a terrible tongue "was lovelier than any of you." These elegiac and ruminative subjects, on which judgments have been passed and which, as objects or people, do not move about or develop, are the stern stone which Ransom can chisel. Yet a necrological criticism based on a particular practice may not apply to, say, Shakespeare or Shelley.

As for irrelevant texture: Ransom is so loving a craftsman that he must be fully aware of the pull which technique may exert in shaping or even warping the original thought of a poem. James Sutherland in *The Medium of Poetry* has established clearly enough how the search for a word necessary to the formal pattern of a poem may often seem to create a new image, an unsought idea, an unexpected freshness. These discoveries, demanded by the texture of the verse, may seem irrelevant to the logic of the argument. When Ransom writes the line "By the summer's flare and winter's flaw," the final word may have been chosen in part for its double alliteration. But the texture here actually intensifies the balanced structure of the thought; and indeed a word cannot seem "inevitable" unless both logical and formally aesthetic expectations are more than satisfied. When, in his fantastic medieval tourney "Armageddon," Ransom writes of Christ "Brooding upon his frugal breviary," the first word, through both assonance and double alliteration, may govern the choice of the last two and make for a rich texture. But the line "Brooding upon his fruity Bremerhaven" would not do. It is as rich both in sound and in imagery, and if irrelevance were in itself a virtue, it is a better line. In his practice Ransom is the equal of Hopkins in finding words that hit right both for sound and sense, and is superior to Hopkins in his respect for decorum. In his theory he may go too far in the separation of texture and structure. What a poem needs is not the irrelevant word but the relevant word, whether it is expected or unexpected. If Mr. Ransom the critic is at fault here, perhaps he has been led astray by the technical brilliance and the complex integrity of Ransom the poet.

THE FUGITIVE PARTICULAR:
JOHN CROWE RANSOM, CRITIC

Morgan Blum

We cannot base our final judgment of any serious critic upon his conclusions alone.* Often an inferior mind, as the result of accident or direct influence or the spirit of an age, will arrive at the same position that the superior intelligence reached only after some heroic journey of the spirit. (How many little men in the nineteenth century—none of them fit to brush Coleridge's intellectual boots—came to base their aesthetic judgments upon some quality which they called the "Imagination" and which on clear days could be observed to bear a certain resemblance to Coleridge's famous definition.) It is only when we look at the marshaling of the facts, at the structure of the argument, at the detailed understanding of the human heart and the human predicament, that we can begin to separate the sheep from the goats.

When dealing with criticism, the method of historical scholarship has been, not infrequently, the lumping of sheep and goat. A particular critic's conclusions are presented as evidence, and judgment— for example, guilty of being a Neo-Classicist, or a Precursor of Romanticism—passed. In the process, whatever *unique* value the critic happens to possess is negated, and he becomes an undistinguished and indistinguishable unit in the battle of historical forces. Certainly he can no longer be freshly evaluated. Worse than that, his

*This essay originally appeared in *Western Review*, XIV (Winter, 1950), 85–102.

critical method, which—as a systematic approach, a developed and coherent terminology—might have reasonably been expected to become a point of departure for later generations, is available now only for autopsy and civil interment. If we are to outwit these tactics of mortification, it is particularly important that the living critic—and particularly the living critic whom we want to remain alive—be studied for his unique contribution, *in his own terms and out of the detailed structure of his own dialectic.*

Viewed as a historical scholar might view it, Mr. Ransom's criticism becomes simply another defense of modernist-metaphysical poetry; Graves's Registration has provided the proper marker. But viewed as an object deserving of study in its own right, his criticism—*The World's Body,** in particular—begins to reveal its tremendous vitality and rightness. The scrupulous discrimination of terms, the constant awareness of the relation of literature to the rest of life, the closeness and precision of argument, all begin to emerge almost as functions of the prose's own precision. The great danger in judging criticism of this authority lies in the temptation to premature evaluation. The benefits that are potential in it will be elicited not by the act of praise, but only by discovering the object as in itself it really is.

I. Analysis: The Object in Itself

Mr. Ransom, as I have already suggested, is interested in furthering the public reception of a poetry which is defined most generally in historical terms—a poetry whose appearances and disappearances depend directly upon whatever happens to be the spirit of each age. As a critic of conscious historical sophistication, he has refused to commit himself in anything like absolute terms to the defense of such a poetry. He has instead derived his basic argument from a historical definition of that poetry's audience: modern man. He is explicit in his preface to *The World's Body:*

I was concerned with urging that it is not a pre-scientific poetry but a post-scientific one to which we must now give our consent. . . . a poetry

---

*The book on which this analysis is almost entirely based. Mr. Ransom's other criticism generally rests on the structure described in this book. The chief departures result less from a change in the method itself than from some extrinsic occasion—usually an editorial controversy or the need to answer some "new" aesthetic position—where the nature of the antagonist suggests an extravagant or vehement answer.

which would not deny what we in our strange generation actually are: men who have aged in these pure intellectual disciplines and cannot play innocent without feeling very foolish. The expense of poetry is greater than we will pay if it is something to engage in without our faculties. I could not discover that this mortification was required.

Although in the body of Mr. Ransom's work the audience is not always readily apparent as a term of critical import—in his practical criticism its immediate significance is often negligible—it remains always functional as the pivotal point from which his practical criticism springs, and furnishes the basic terms of his dialectic.* These terms are, I would suggest, "pre-scientific," "post-scientific," and—by obvious implication—"scientific." The ultimate poetic good is "post-scientific," but it can be approached most profitably if we think of its natural development in time and consider first things first—in the immediate instance, pre-scientific poetry. This phrase is commonly used throughout the essays as a basis for condemnation; but the terminology involved varies considerably, and "childish," "feminine," "physical," and "non-intellectual" are all employed to denote variant aspects of the same general malady. Here is one aspect: "The kind of poetry which interests us is not the act of a child or that eternal youth which is in some women, but the act of an adult mind. . . ." It is evident from this passage that maturity is one of the essentials of good poetry, and, therefore, of "post-scientific" poetry; but it is not necessarily its exclusive property and might presumably characterize a scientific poetry, which would possess its own peculiar forms of limitation. The question of maturity (or masculinity or intellectuality) is one that Ransom constantly poses in his practical criticism, as in the following instance where Miss Millay's verse happens to be its immediate object.

Is the experience comprehensive or "expressive" of the whole personality? (The reviewer's masculine and contemporary personality, not Miss Millay's

*The value of Mr. Ransom's historical aesthetic might be emphasized by comparison with the critical naiveté of those who have affirmed the eternal supremacy of a particular mode of poetry—whether neo-classical, romantic, or metaphysical—and who, as Ransom points out, forget "that poetry is an event in time." The immediate superiority of a temporal mode of poetry is necessarily contingent upon temporal factors, although the audience, if the most obvious of these, is not the only one. In a period such as the nineteenth century, for example, where self-expression rather than communication is of dominant interest, it may well be the poet, and not his readers, whose historical definition furnishes the central basis for a critical systemization of tastes. Some such device would seem to be fundamental in the criticism of both Wordsworth and Coleridge.

which may have to be assumed as perfectly expressing itself.) Is it up to his mental age or general level of experience? And is there any positive nonsense in it? The last question concerns the competence of the poet to carry out her intention consistently, whatever the limits of the intention. For the devoted critic must maintain that poetry on whatever level must make as consistent sense as prose, and he does not like being committed in it to nonsense.

In the case of Miss Millay, Ransom puts these questions with rigor and consistency. He observes the inconsistent identification of the mythical and astronomical qualities of the Moon in her "Endymion" sonnet and his verdict is "positive nonsense." He defines the "limitation of Miss Millay":

If I must express this in a word, I still feel obliged to say it is her lack of intellectual interest. . . . I used a conventional symbol when I phrased this lack of hers: a deficiency in masculinity. It is true that some male poets are about as deficient; not necessarily that they are undeveloped intellectually, but that they conceive of poetry as a sentimental or feminine exercise, themselves as under a strange compulsion to practice it.

He cites two examples of her earlier work, the latter a singularly lush bit from "Renascence," and comments, "It is with something of a feeling of guilt that the *intellectual male* [italics mine] participates in them."

I have emphasized Ransom's essay on Miss Millay as the convenient locus of his attack on the effeminacy of pre-scientific verse, since his theme there—"The Poet as Woman"—allows for its fullest and most explicit treatment; but the principle involved is a constantly recurring one. In "A Poem Nearly Anonymous," he compares the austerity and control, the "aesthetic distance," that govern Milton's grief in "Lycidas" to the ingenuous heartbreak that informs so many modern elegies. Milton's method, the critic observes succinctly, permits the artist to bear "the character of a qualified spokesman and a male."

It is to the final section of pre-scientific verse—variously defined as "imagistic," "physical," or "pure" poetry—that the basic term is most explicitly applied. It is a poetry of childhood, but childhood in a strict and limited sense—a poetry that revels in images not because it knows nothing better but because it knows nothing else. Ransom suggests the natural history of this fixation: "The child is occupied mostly with things, but it is because he is still unfurnished with systematic ideas, not because he is a ripe citizen by nature and comes along already trailing clouds of glory. Images are clouds of glory for the man who has discovered that ideas are a sort of darkness." To discover this darkness in idea it is necessary first to know and master idea, and it is to the intermediate period that this activity is relegated and to that period that scientific poetry belongs. It is a poetry that applies itself to "improving or idealizing the world," to the abstraction from, and utilization of, things rather than to things for their own sake and in their own right; it is a "Platonic" poetry. But the distinction can be made in Mr. Ransom's own terms:

Platonic [i.e., scientific] Poetry is allegory, a discourse in things, but on the understanding that they are translatable at every point into ideas. (The usual ideas are those that constitute our popular causes, patriotic, religious, moral or social.) Or Platonic Poetry is the elaboration of ideas as such, but in proceeding introduces for ornament some physical properties after the style of Physical Poetry; which is rhetoric.

Thus Platonic Poetry introduces objects as illustrations or documents in proof of a positive thesis (one of "our popular causes"), and consequently negates their value as natural compounds in perceptual experience. Ransom quotes as a convenient example Pippa's song and comments: ". . . a piece of transparent homiletics; for in it six pretty, co-ordinate images are marched, like six little lambs to the slaughter, to a colon and a powerful text."

But the Platonic poet may find that all is not right with the world, that the infinite particularity and contingency of the objects which constitute the world's body cannot be subsumed under the thesis that governs his particular cause; and such a failure involves him in a negative Platonism ("Romantic Irony") where, if he only could, he would shatter this body to bits and remould it nearer to the heart's desire. The way of Platonism is thus the way of science; it entails an absorbing interest in ideas and a healthy disrespect for things, which are for it only utilities and never self-sufficient ends. It is the precise contrary of the way of art. Mr. Ransom hammers at this point so constantly that it is necessary to cite at length his most explicit statement of this relationship.

This contemplation [of objects] may take one of two routes; and first, that of science. I study the object to see how I may wring out of it my physical satisfaction the next time; or even how I may discover for the sake of a next time the physical satisfaction which it contains, but not too transparently; analyzing and classifying, "experimenting," bringing it together under the system of control which I intend as a scientist to have over the world of objects. It is superfluous to observe that I, the modern scientist, am in this case spiritually just as poor as was my ancestor the caveman. My intention is simply to have bigger and quicker satisfactions. . . . But I may contemplate also, under another form entirely, the form of art. And that is when I am impelled neither to lay hands on the object immediately, nor to ticket it for tomorrow's outrage, but am in such a marvellous state of innocence that I would know it for its own sake and conceive it as having its own existence; this is the knowledge, or it ought to be, which Schopenhauer praised as "knowledge without desire." The features which the object discloses then are not those which have their meaning for a science, for a set of practical values. They are those which render the body of the object, and constitute a knowledge so radical that the scientist as a scientist can scarcely understand it, and puzzles to see it rendered, richly and wastefully, in the poem, or the painting. The knowledge attained there, and recorded, is a new kind of knowledge, the world in which it is set is a new world.

The application of this doctrine in Mr. Ransom's practical criticism develops in two distinct ways to correspond with two distinct types of scientific poetry. The one type—represented by Pippa's homiletics—is not properly poetry but an ornamented prose where there exist not "real images but illustrations." The second type is a "poetry by assemblage." Mr. Ransom describes it briefly: "Now some poetry, so-called, is not even lemonade [a mixture, but an unnatural and arbitrary one], for the ingredients have not been mixed, much less compounded [as in the case of a compound that exists in nature, such as salt]. Lumps of morality and image lie side by side and are tasted in succession." Lord Tennyson's "Bugle Song" would be a case in point.

But what of the final period of poetry, where post-scientific man "has discovered that ideas are a sort of darkness"? The answer is implied in the terms themselves: it is a recapitulation and a uniting of the two contraries of the temporarily divided mind of the past. In the original pre-scientific era, art was impossible for it was without the formative assistance of ideas.

Adam [pre-scientific man], in the absence of technical thought-processes, was incapable of a distinguished aesthetic experience. No percept without a concept, sharp percepts mean sharp concepts, rich percepts mean a multiplicity of concepts; and lacking the latter he could not have had the former, and his integral or uniting experience could not have been like the work of art, but must have resembled that of the uninformed child. . . . The brilliant effect we admire in a poem is the result of compounding many prose effects, and technical or specific ones. The business of poetry, in fact, is to take the technical prose effect, which is hard, and soften and dissolve it in a total experience.

It must be remembered, however, that Adam was not faced with the danger of the technical effects' taking exclusive possession of his mind. And that is the real danger in a period when ideas, with their imperatives of utility and efficiency, become the dominant force. The mind that they possess exclusively can be expected to seek a return in ideas from anything, including poetry, with results that are not uniformly happy. Mr. Ransom suggests some of the least happy:

The definition which some writers have given to art is: the reference of the idea to the image. The implication is that the act is not for the purpose of honest comparison so much as for the purpose of proving the idea by the image. But in the event the idea is not disproved so much as it is made to look ineffective and therefore foolish. The ideas will not cover the objects on which they are imposed, they are too attenuated and thread-like; for ideas have extension and objects have intension; but extension is thin while intension is thick.

It is here that the post-scientific mind enters. For it can return to the objects of original affection but with the multiplied and heightened perceptions that an exposure to conceptual science has created. The actual metaphors that Ransom employs in defining the peculiar and apparently illogical fascination that a remembered object holds for us are significant. He mentions the man who, having progressed from early poverty to a position of affluence in industry (in *God Without Thunder* Ransom defines industry as applied science) , returns for emotional satisfaction to objects of no remarkable utility—to the old oaken bucket and the scenes of his childhood. Or the metaphor may involve a Sherman's march through Georgia where everything that cannot be of immediate use is destroyed. "But when it goes into camp for a day the aesthetic self, which has had very little part in directing so urgent a march, steals back upon the route, and here or there finds a place to stop, to make its peace with the violated region, and to enjoy the country." In view of this incessant employment of the metaphor of a return, it is not surprising that memory is a basic term in Ransom's critical method, since only memory attaches itself to those elements of experience which are not of immediate importance in the efficient satisfaction of the animal desires. And it is these elements, stored as images in the memory, that invoke other and still other images until "the past takes form again." Thus memory functions as a revulsive force that turns us toward art and toward aesthetic experience in general. "It is the dream, the recollection, which compels us to poetry, and to deliberate aesthetic experience. It can hardly be argued, I think, that the arts are constituted automatically out of original images and arise in some early age of innocence. . . . Art is based on second love, not first love. In it we make a return to something . . . we had willfully alienated." It is clear from this that the "early age of innocence" and the period of willful alienation is each in itself inadequate. A later statement—". . . the specific poems, the ones that we cherish as perfect creations . . . are dramatizing the past"—reveals additional reasons for their inadequacy. For the past cannot be "dramatized" unless inutilities (i.e., inutile for the scientist) are treated in themselves and for themselves, and density of detail (see Mr. Ransom's comparison of *Murder in the Cathedral* with *Samson Agonistes*, in *The World's Body*, 167 ff.) is fundamental in the composition of drama. But science which, as science, must take all experience at its lowest and most naturalistic definition, cannot profitably recall "images in their panoply of circumstance and with their morning freshness upon them."

But though the pre-scientific and scientific periods are alike inadequate, if necessary, stages in the individual's aesthetic development, the two, synthesized through the agency of memory in the final and post-scientific age, form the basis for art. Ransom is precise.

Rebels, Utopians, in the recklessly efficient societies, appeal to an age of innocence as prior to all efficiency; but what they really mean is an age when sensibility and efficiency were equal, and married, and had the prescriptive respect of husband and wife for one another. They deceive themselves in thinking that happiness obtained best before the cruel husband appeared at all, or when he was but an infant; it could not have been marriage, with the husband lacking, or between children whose sexual distinctiveness was not yet realized.

Or he may express the advantages of such a marriage in briefer terms that are equally precise. "Or, man distinguishes himself from woman by intellect, but he should keep it feminized."

It should be evident from this that there is a dialectical relationship between the three central terms of discourse quite as fundamental as their historical relation. In it, "pre-scientific" and "scientific" are basic contraries, with "post-scientific" representing their union upon a higher level. (They might presumably be united upon a lower level as well, with "poetry by assemblage" where "lumps of morality and image lie side by side" as a possible instance. But Mr. Ransom is not very explicit here, and the concept does not seem fundamental to his argument.) As is so common in three-term dialectic, this relationship is susceptible of subtle variation; by the momentary exclusion of one of the contraries, its fellow may function as the immediate contrary of "post-scientific." It should be obvious, moreover, from what has already been said that Mr. Ransom's criticism falls within the form-content mode. This involves a dual approach on the part of the critic, who must examine the prose object which the poem celebrates and the form in which that celebration is cast. It would seem valuable to consider this relationship in terms of the two contraries which must be united within the artistic experience. This is most effectively approached through a lengthy passage which it seems relevant to quote in its entirety.

The critic should regard the poem as nothing short of a desperate ontological or metaphysical manoeuvre. The poet himself, in the agony of composition, has something like this sense of his labors. The poet perpetuates in his poem an order of existence which in actual life is constantly crumbling beneath his touch. His poem celebrates the object which is real, individual, and qualitatively infinite. He knows that his practical interests will reduce this living object to a mere utility, and that his sciences will disintegrate it for their convenience into their respective abstracts. The poet wishes to defend his object's existence against its enemies, and the critic wishes to know what he is doing, and how. The critic should find in the poem a total poetic or individual object which tends to be universalized, but is not permitted to suffer this fate. His identification of the poetic object is in terms of the universal or commonplace object to which it tends, and of the tissue, or totality of connotation, which holds it secure. How does he make out the universal object? It is the prose object, which any forthright prosy reader can discover to him by an immediate paraphrase; it is a kind of story, character, thing, scene, or moral principle. And where is the tissue that keeps it from coming out of the poetic object? That is, for the laws of the prose logic, its superfluity; and I think I would even say, its irrelevance.

A poet is said to be distinguishable in terms of his style. It is a comprehensive word, and probably means: the general character of his irrelevances, or tissues. All his technical devices contribute to it, elaborating or individualizing the universal, the core-object; likewise all his material detail. For each poem even, ideally, there is distinguishable a logical object or universal, but at the same time a tissue of irrelevance from which it does not really emerge.

What is involved here is the integrity of the object that the agency of memory has left rich and individual and perceptually significant. Once it is perceived in all its thickness, a body of words adequate to maintain that thickness and individuality and to resist the universalization that is prose becomes necessary. And it is this "tissue of irrelevance," the sums of poetic technique involved in the adult poem, that furnishes such a form. "The poet requires a technique for escaping techniques," if the object he celebrates is to retain its body against the incessant ingressions of an abstracting science.

This dual function of techniques—to exploit and to obstruct exploitation—is closely interwoven in Mr. Ransom's concept of the nature and function of organized societies. The established society perpetuates two types of forms or techniques: work-forms and play-forms. The work-forms serve the ends of utility and permit the most efficient satisfaction of animal desires. But the play-forms, serving the aesthetic self, have as their precise objective the hindrance of efficiency at those moments when hindrance seems desirable. Mr. Ransom illustrates the aesthetic forms by the use of a triangle, with the natural man at one angle, the objective of his immediate desire at another, and one of the play-forms at the third. The man as an animal with a desire that demands immediate satisfaction marches directly upon the adjacent angle where his objective rests and ruthlessly purges his desire and with it the object that gave it rise. But the man may also have an aesthetic self and the dignity that this implies. In that instance, he will approach his object by the longer route around the triangle through the specific means that a wise society has constituted for that purpose; and by the singularly inefficient act of ritualistic contemplation, by the very austerity of his restraint, he perpetuates and glorifies his object and places it out of the power of the efficient self to destroy at the exhaustion of its immediate utility. It has now achieved the "dignity of a particular," and no longer can another of its universal kind serve as a substitute. If it is the woman he loves, he can approach her through an aristocratic code of manners; if it is the object he is to immortalize in a poem, he has his traditional art-forms. Ransom is particularly explicit in the case of these last. "Given an object and a poet burning to utter himself upon it, he must take into account a third item, the form into which he must cast his utterance. (If we like we may call it the *body* which he must give to his passion.) It delays and hinders him." But what are these technical or formal devices? Mr. Ransom nowhere gives a complete list; but there are many partial ones, and no impertinence would seem to be involved in a synthesis of these. The device that he refers to most frequently is "character," and its function is fundamental in his method of analysis. "The poet does not speak in his own but in an assumed character. . . . This was enough to release him from his actual or prose self and to induce poetic experience." Or he may apply the principle precisely, as in the case of "Lycidas." "Milton as a Greek shepherd was delivered from being Milton the scrivener's son, the Master of Arts from Cambridge, the handsome and finicky man, and that was the point." The aesthetic tenet that both of these statements maintain is wholly coherent with, and wholly relevant to, his major thesis. The poet who is dramatizing the past must constantly particularize his object if it is to resist prose universalization. The device of the "costume" incessantly reinforces the fact that a specific person stands in a specific relationship to that object, and emphasizes the point that all statements of that object's nature are not those of the universalized prose self that speaks in science or philosophy, but are referable only to the individualized point of view that a particularized character would bring to bear upon a particularized situation.

The function of meter—the second technical device whose importance Ransom stresses—is similar to that of character. It partakes of the nature of the mask and frees the sensibility from the bondage of the "juridical or prose self."

The poet within is released by the adoption of a tongue [metre] whose principle is novel, and wholly irrelevant to the virtues of prose discourse. We require the foreign language. There is a paradox that holds good up to a point, I think, within the experience of any poet: the more accurate the metres, the freer and more incalculable the discourse. . . . The metre is the guarantee of an eternal "play" or looseness in its [poetry's] substance.

The third and final technical device that is functional in constructing the "tissue of irrelevance" necessary for the maintenance of the object's integrity and individuality would be—to provide my own phrase in place of the one Mr. Ransom fails to provide—poetic diction. Mr. Ransom does furnish us with its definition: "any systematic usage [in poetry] which does not hold good for prose is a poetic device." Among his list of such usages are three items that fall clearly under the head of diction: inversions, solecisms, and tropes. To one variety of trope, the conceit, he gives chief attention and it deserves extended consideration here. We may begin with his definition: "A conceit originates in a metaphor; and in fact the conceit is but a metaphor if the metaphor is meant; that is, if it is developed so literally that it must be meant, or predicated so boldly that nothing else can be meant. Perhaps this will do for a definition." Or another name for the conceit would be "miraculism," which "informs a poetry [i.e. the metaphysical] which is the most original and exciting and intellectually perhaps the most seasoned that we know in our literature." And miracle describes this technique accurately, for the unswerving and literal statement of a correspondence that has no scientific justification is precisely the form of the historic miracle. The function of the conceit, when correctly practiced, is to enhance the object in all its particularity and its "morning freshness." But if the metaphor is not explored, if it is not literalized, the effect is exactly contrary to the intention. Ransom cites such an instance and adds an apt commentary.

> Thou young Dawn
> Turn all thy dew to splendour . . .

But splendour is not the correlative of dew, it has the flat tone of a Platonic idea, while physically it scarcely means more than dew with sunshine upon it. The seventeenth century would have said: "Turn thy dew, which is water, into fire, and accomplish the transmutation of the elements." *

But there is a further distinction suggested in Mr. Ransom's comparison of two fairly analogous conceits.

*For what the metaphysical poet actually did say, see Marvell's "On a Drop of Dew."

> The red rose cries, "She is near, she is near";
> And the white rose weeps, "She is late";
> The larkspur listens, "I hear, I hear";
> And the lily whispers, "I wait."

And this is a technical conceit. But it is too complicated for this author, having a plurality of images which do not sustain themselves individually. The flowers stand for the lover's thoughts, and have been prepared for carefully in an earlier stanza, but their distinctness is too arbitrary, and these are like a school-girl's made-up metaphors. The passage will not compare with one on a very similar situation by Mr. Humbert Wolfe:

> "I know her little foot," gray carpet said:
> "Who but I should know her light tread,"
> "She shall come in," answered the open door,
> "And not," said the room, "go out any more."

Wolfe's conceit works and Tennyson's does not, and though Wolfe's performance seems not very daring or important, and only pleasant, he employs the technique of the conceit correctly, he knows that the miracle must have a basis of verisimilitude.

Thus "a basis of verisimilitude" and "literalness" function as the fundamental criteria of the conceit. Their place in the total pattern is clear, a pattern that holds equally for all the formal devices. On the pre-scientific side, the thickness of the object must be preserved, and therefore "literalness"; on the scientific side, "poetry on whatever level must make as consistent sense as prose," and therefore "a basis of verisimilitude."

In summary, it should be said that the basic critical method of *The World's Body*, although its emphasis is almost exclusively poetic, affords its author a machinery of approach to an amazingly wide variety of problems, both literary and non-literary, that are not questions of utility. With a few purely practical alterations, it can damn the Platonism in a Shelley's poetry or a Santayana's philosophy; it can judge the inadequacy of a religion or a metric with equal facility. For the objects upon which it works are the variables; what is constant is the distinguishing of form and content, and the application to each of this question: Does it involve a compounding upon a higher level of science and pre-science; is it post-scientific?

Thus Mr. Ransom falls into the long tradition of form-content critics, a line which traces at least as far back as the *Phaedrus* (I do not know that Mr. Ransom will be wholly happy at having Plato's skeleton unearthed from the family vault) and which would include, among others, Horace, Vida, Jonson, Boileau, and Dryden. His relationship to this group becomes more explicit if we substitute nature for pre-science and art for science in his argument. This shift need not occasion any great wrenching of meaning, but the principle of studying a writer in his own terms is not one to be violated with impunity. Such substitutions are particularly unwise in the treatment of a critic who, like Mr. Ransom, offers a dialectic frame so closely integrated that the careless alteration of a term can do structural as well as local harm.

II. Evaluation

This study has thus far been largely analytic, and evaluation, which is quite as fundamentally a part of the critical act, has for the most part been neglected—for the most part, since the very fact of intensive analysis implies a deserving object and constitutes its own tribute. Indeed it would be particularly difficult to recall any sizable group of contemporary critics whose terminology is sufficiently scrupulous or whose aesthetic is at once sufficiently subtle and precise to evoke like tribute. But when that has been said, it has only been said that Mr. Ransom has devised a promising lantern for the illumination of specific texts, the proper goal of literary criticism. The fact of illumination remains undemonstrated.

Mr. Ransom has bent his lantern's rays on a wide variety of literary types; but to only two has he given any considerable attention, and it is on the basis of these that he may most fairly be judged. It is in his comments on the first—we may call it lyric poetry, but Mr. Ransom in his unconscious Platonism makes no precise Aristotelian distinctions—that the critic is most helpful. He is constantly close to his text, constantly aware of the claims of the poem in its objective existence as prior to any peculiar psychological phenomena that exposure to it may occasion in the critic's personality. His essay on Miss Millay is the perfect act of critical justice; his extended note on "Lycidas" illuminates not only the text at hand but also the complex psychic process we call creation. And he is so often right that any adverse comments will sound like pure cavilling. But certain of his rare critical aberrations are fundamental to his method and invite moralization.

There is, for example, a statement anent Miss Millay's "Endymion" sonnet. "The *by deathless lips adored* is pure obstruction, though it is to be expected that something pretty will turn up in a romantic poem." Now the poet's phrase is curiously bad on several levels; it is difficult to discover in a competent twentieth-century poet so awkward a commitment to inversion in the name of rhyme; "adored" is singularly imprecise in its application to lips; and the choice of lips as the agent of adoration seems to have no very high appropriateness. But my immediate objection is Mr. Ransom's "pure obstruction." *Deathless* is not precisely obstruction; it is fundamental to the movement of a poem which celebrates a goddess' love for a mortal and the ironic fact of insufficiency inherent in instances where the lover, like love, is undying. The poem, insofar as it possesses a coherent movement, proceeds by the basic opposition of death and love's resolution to immortality and irresolution; and in such a progression "deathless lips" becomes a necessary parallel for "mortal Endymion" and "earthen you" if the resolution of the poem—

> Whereof she wanders mad, being all unfit
> For mortal love, that might not die of it.

—is to have any appropriateness.

I have given a great deal of space to a minor critical misstep; but as I have suggested earlier, it merits moralization. What is involved, I think, is this. Mr. Ransom, who is distinguished among contemporary critics in the scrupulous attention he accords imagery (I need parentheses here to include a similar tribute to Mr. R. P. Blackmur and to the later and more valuable portion of Mr. Allen Tate's critical writing), tends to isolate that imagery from the total structure of the unit poem.

I should like now to cite one more instance in support of the above statement because it introduces an important variation upon the same error. It occurs when Mr. Ransom examines the tomorrow-and-tomorrow soliloquy in an effort to define the extent of its metaphysicality or, more precisely, to decide whether it, like a Donne lyric, commits "the feelings in the case to their determination within the elected figure." He observes the imagery-patterns with their magnificent linkage of light, darkness, and shadow; and he concludes that the connection between image and image exists psychologically, in the mind of the speaker, and is therefore sub-logical and apart from the metaphysical tradition with its logical exploration of metaphor.

I hasten to add that Mr. Ransom implies no condemnation here: he recognizes quite clearly that complete metaphysical poems "would be destructive of any drama into which they might be admitted." This position, as far as it goes, would seem sound (Actually, he appears to misinterpret "To the last syllable of recorded time"; this, however, is incidental to his basic argument). But it contains an essential omission which implies an equally essential critical failing. What I am suggesting in this: a metaphysical lyric is a self-contained formal unit. As such, its essential movement of metaphor (or imagery) would be functional in establishing whatever formal unity it might possess (this statement holds for every metaphysical lyric I have analyzed); and if that unity were so perfectly realized that the analyst could say, "Here there is nothing that can be added, nothing that can be taken away or altered without disturbing the perfect whole I have observed,"—that coherence would then imply a corresponding coherence in the imagery. But, as Mr. Ransom realizes, the soliloquy is only material within a formal unit and wholly without a formal self-sufficiency of its own. The question of whether or not its basic metaphor is logical in its immediate realization is, therefore, an informal one and not a proper analogue to the question of metaphor that is regularly pertinent in the analysis of a Donne lyric. But if this question is one of only incidental significance, the question Mr. Ransom fails to ask is all-important and fairly comparable to the one he puts to Donne. To what extent is the curious patterning of light, darkness, and shadow that characterizes this soliloquy materially vital to the structure of the total work? Or, more explicitly, what relation does it bear to the witches as symbols of the world of darkness and to the false visions they construct to light the protagonist to that sin whose wages are to be dusty death? The precise answer to this question is unimportant here, but Mr. Ransom's failure to raise it is sufficiently characteristic to define a problem. Why should a critic who devotes such constant and intelligent attention to poetic detail fail to relate that detail in some functional sense to the total aesthetic unit?*

*I have suppressed certain other strictures that I might have advanced against the essay "Shakespeare at Sonnets." Mr. Arthur Mizener (in the *Southern Review*) and Mr. Cleanth Brooks (in *The Well Wrought Urn*) have indicated effectively some of these. I would like to add for present purposes one general qualification. These defects do not proceed from Mr. Ransom's method, but from a misuse of that method. Specifically, they proceed from erecting the results of a presumably limited and inaccurate inductive investigation into prescriptive or normative

The second field of study that engages Mr. Ransom's interest is the philosophic criticism of literature and, more especially, its practitioners; and here his lapses are not occasional but frequent and, I am afraid, fundamental to his method. A distinction, however, had best be observed at once. Mr. Ransom is singularly adept at probing the weaknesses in the critics he considers: the inadequacies of their understanding of the creative process or the aesthetic moment, the impertinences in their value-theories or critical practice. But he is by no means so adept at unearthing their strengths, and the reason for this should be clear. What he constantly does is approach each critic through his own dialectic (a subtle and meticulous one, it is true), and consequently through a terminology and set of questions that may not always have the most immediate relevance. The practical result is that, all too often, the critical system under examination becomes something other and, not surprisingly, something lesser than the thing it was.

In support of these general statements, I should like to consider specifically Ransom's remarks on Aristotle, which are extended and typical. The following is the first of significance: "Aristotle laid down two fundamental propositions. . . . First, that art in form is a mimesis or imitation of reality; and, second, that at least one variety of art, or tragedy, has for its function the catharsis, or elimination from the mind by purging, of the emotions of pity and terror." The first of these propositions is innocent enough and accurate; the second is scarcely innocent, and, what is equally to the point, not Aristotelian. This becomes obvious later when he gives definition to the rather ambiguous "has for its function" by lumping tragedy and certain kinds of music together as art-forms "justified by their cathartic action." It is, of course, Aristotle who bases his justification of Phrygian music upon its cathartic action. That, however, is in the *Politics,* where the question of the place of music in education for the state raises, inevitably, the problem of the final, or telic, cause of the lyric. In the portion of the *Poetics* that we have, no such problem arises. The

---

standards. Thus, Mr. Ransom, basing his conclusions upon what is, in fact, an important but incidental effect in a number of sonnets, says that the rhyme scheme in the standard English sonnet is "directive" and establishes a "requirement" for the structure of the sonnet. Similarly, Mr. Ransom seizes upon a type of metaphor that is common in Donne and establishes it as a norm against which characteristic metaphors in the Shakespearean sonnet are to be judged. But as Mr. Brooks and Mr. Mizener have pointed out, this is a difference in kind rather than a difference in quality. It provides an inadequate basis for judgments of good and bad.

questions asked there concern poetry as a making art, its formal and material causes, and no extrinsic end for tragedy is considered. Aristotle himself observes on no less than two occasions in the *Poetics* that the end and first principle of tragedy is plot (or the ordering of the incidents), and Aristotle—we have Mr. Ransom's authority here—is explicit. What status does this leave Mr. Ransom's view of the tragic catharsis? As far as the *Poetics* is concerned, it seems rather beside the point. Tragedy can have but one formal principle; and since this is given by the ordering of the incidents, the catharsis must be left with another role. In the *Poetics* it would appear to be that of the differentia which specifies tragedy within its genus. As such, it separates those forms which give an effect distinctive with tragedy from those which do not. If it has another function, Aristotle fails to record it.

But it is not this mistake, vital as it happens to be, that characterizes Ransom's interpretation of Aristotle. Rather it is his basic position, and it is this that almost certainly accounts for his readiness to unearth from the *Poetics* a political end for tragedy.

Aristotle comes into Mr. Ransom's dialectic very much on the side of science. As a scientist, he cannot possibly respect poetry for itself; he can accept it only because it purges certain passions which would otherwise interfere with the maximum efficiency that the young Athenians were to bring to their daily tasks. For Aristotle, Mr. Ransom continues, had no interest in the play-forms of and for themselves, and it was only when they permitted a more complete realization of the work-forms that he would tolerate them.

Mr. Ransom proceeds to demonstrate this. He remarks the objectivity, the lack of warmth with which Aristotle regards the poetic forms, and concludes that he was "a rationalist, of low aesthetic and religious [another play-form] interest" whose purpose it was "to intensify the esthetic moment in order to minimize it and localize it and clear the way for the scientific moment." "Lack of warmth" forms a fragile base for so towering a structure. Only a stylistic device or historic accident, it implies no criticism graver than the observation that Aristotle is other than the wine-tasters, the connoisseurs, the George Saintsbury's of literary criticism; and of these we have quite enough for practical purposes. I should like to suggest what I cannot demonstrate here: that Mr. Ransom's treatment of Aristotle is typical of the quality of attention he ordinarily accords his fellow-guildsmen. He is all too likely to negate whatever unique value each critic has by reducing him to his own terminology and to a dialectical myth which is rich and suggestive and off the point.

One vexing question still remains. We have already observed how subtly and how fully this same myth has served to illuminate all types of poets from the post-scientific Milton to the pre-scientific Millay. Why, then, has it so often served to obscure critical writings? I can discern no theoretical basis for an answer, but Mr. Ransom's practice suggests that the respect which he tenders poetry is sufficiently greater to account for much of the disparity. The analysis of criticism is, after all, largely a work-form.

THE ACHIEVEMENT OF JOHN CROWE RANSOM

Vivienne Koch

When one reads Ransom's first volume of poetry, *Poems About God* (1919), all of which the author has wisely suppressed in later collections, the friendly critic could wish to let sleeping dogs lie.* Still, the poet was in his twenty-ninth year when they were written; they were published in his thirty-first year; and the poems can in no sense be considered juvenilia, although their role in Ransom's poetic career might merit such a designation. The scheme of the poems, the young poet tells us in a deprecatory introduction, grew out of his recognition that his first poems all used the word "God," and that since this was the most poetic of all terms possible, he "went to work to treat rather systematically of the occasions in which this term was in use with *common American men.*" The curious Whitmanism suggested by the italicized words was an attachment never again to appear in Ransom's writings, but the notion that God was the most poetic of all possible terms was one which was to continue to disturb him. His final disposition of the problem eleven years later in a prose study, *God Without Thunder,* was, as the title suggests, a pragmatic compromise.

In reality, *Poems About God* is not so studiously schematized as the introduction would suggest. When "God" does not appear in a

*This essay originally appeared in *Sewanee Review,* LXVIII (Spring, 1950) , 227–61.

poem, the word "Christian" does—to keep the frame of reference straight. However, the poems are hardly devotional. It is just possible that there was a deliberate irony in the very *absence* of a religious tone in contexts where "God" occurred.

All of the *Poems About God* are Emersonian in their sense of aspiration and Frostian in their feeling for the detail of country life. This was the time of Frost's great popularity in America. *A Boy's Will*, published in 1915, had been followed by *Mountain Interval* and *North of Boston*. Ransom's predilection for homely domestic scenes, for a rather refined colloquialism, as well as the bantering humor with which these materials are employed, all suggest a close study of the New England poet. "Grace" is a Southern version of "Death of the Hired Man." Its skillful realism, especially in the brutal incongruity of the anti-poetic effects surrounding the hired man's death, makes an honest and fairly interesting narrative. Unlike Frost, however, Ransom rarely bothers to employ a dramatic frame. Most of the *Poems About God* are "I" poems, and transparently autobiographical. There are Southern people, the poet's parents, a Southern reverence for women (with the exception of "drabs . . . fondled for pay"), a great deal of talk about eating, some pretty country scenery, and a surprisingly adolescent sense of sin—mostly in relation to sex.

But, even in this inauspicious and heavily descriptive collection, there are foreshadowings of Ransom's later interest. "Overtures," a sentimental and conventional love poem, employs the archaic setting which Ransom was later to use successively as dramatic framework, while "The Wicked Swimmer" anticipates his exploitation of an antique vocabulary for supporting an archaic milieu. But it is in "The School," a blank-verse confessional, that Ransom intimates his awareness of a conflict which was to become a dominant strain in his poetic investigations:

> Equipped with Grecian thoughts, how could I live
> Among my father's folk? My father's house
> Was narrow and his fields were nauseous.
> I kicked his clods for being common dirt,
> Worthy a world which never could be Greek;
> Cursed the paternity that planted me
> One green leaf in a wilderness of autumn.

This conflict between the classically-trained man and his inimical environment is dealt with in "Philomela," four or five years later; but the nuances of irony, of detached self-appraisal which enrich the latter poem, could never have been predicted from the rough romantic rebelliousness of "The School." Later, this conflict was to split into two versions of it: the conflict between the mythic past and the de-valued present; and the same conflict, reduced to social scale, between the Old South and the new industrial South. But although this may account for many of the preliminary paces in Ransom's prose, and, surely, in some of his poetry, it does not explain his most interesting work. Robert Penn Warren considers this conflict the key to Ransom's poetry, which he describes as "peculiarly whole" and "systematic" and which "refers to a center which is precise, and has been objectively formulated by the poet himself, although not in relation to his poetry." Although Warren himself does not produce a satisfactory definition of that center, he says of it: "It is to be defined in terms of that sensibility whose decay Ransom, along with other critics, has bewailed. . . . To an astonishing degree, in far more than a majority of cases, the hero or heroine of the poems is a sufferer from that complaint of 'dissociation of sensibility.' "

As a matter of fact, on a purely quantitative count of those poems which Ransom has selected for preservation in his *Selected Poems* (1945), the majority of the heroes or heroines, while they may suffer from a "dissociation of sensibility," do not suffer this condition because of the myths of nineteenth-century science "like evolution" and "vitalism" which they have uncritically accepted and which, according to Mr. Warren, are at the roots of their disorder. On the contrary, the split in sensibility reflects human problems which have always given rise to conflict, and probably always will. Such poems—to be numbered among Ransom's best—as "Miriam Tazewell," "Bells for John Whiteside's Daughter," "Lady Lost," "Blue Girls," "Old Man Playing with Children," "Janet Waking," "Winter Remembered," "Parting at Dawn," "Vaunting Oak," "Her Eyes," "Parting, Without a Sequel," "The Equilibrists," "Prelude to an Evening," "Of Margaret," "Spectral Lovers," "Emily Hardcastle, Spinster" and others derive their irony very incidentally, if at all, from the "dissociation of sensibility" produced by an invading and hostile science. That a few of Ransom's poems—such as "Philomela," "Captain Carpenter," "Address to the Scholars of New England," "Adventure This Side Pluralism," "Plea in Mitigation," "Blackberry Winter," "Prometheus

118   VIVIENNE KOCH

in Straits," * and "Amphibious Crocodile" **—do, indeed, reflect such
a conflict, either directly or obliquely, is undeniable. But with Ransom, as with other critics who are also poets, we do a disservice to
his poems if we read his critical values into them too naively.

When in 1924 Ransom's second volume of poems, *Chills and Fever*,
appeared, the little introductory poem professed an attitude which
implied a break with popular poetic values. Looking backward, it
seems a fairly commonplace repudiation of the postwar temper, a
repudiation of romantic agony in favor of romantic irony and one
which Pound had made almost a decade before in "Hugh Selwyn
Mauberly." Robert Penn Warren, approving the irony of Ransom's
introductory lines,

> I will be brief
> Assuredly I have a grief
> And I am shaken; but not as a leaf.

says that "the pure emotional cry is only a fragmentary expression of
the experience of which the complete sensibility is capable." In effect,
he implies that the experience most representative of what the "complete sensibility is capable" is irony, a judgment I must take issue
with. It is one which Ransom himself, in his critical guise, would
question. For irony is a special instrument or special attitude (depending on its usage) relevant to special situations in human experience.
It can be an inclusive attitude and a complex one, but that it represents the experience of the "complete sensibility" more adequately than
other "effects" is hardly proved by mere assertion. Mr. Ransom, in an
impatient but acute admonition to Cleanth Brooks, says of Mr.
Brooks's stress on irony in his *Modern Poetry and the Tradition:*

My belief is that opposites can never be said to be reconciled merely because
they have been got into the same complex of affective experience to create
a kind of "tension"; that if there is a resolution at all it must be a logical
resolution; that when there is no resolution we have a poem without structural unity; and that this is precisely the intention of irony, which therefore
is something very special and ought to be occasional. . . . We should not so
much be in favor of tragedy and irony as not to think it good policy to require them in all our poems, for fear we might bring them into bad fame.

*It surely is of some significance that Ransom has eliminated the last four poems
named (all in *Chills and Fever*) from *Selected Poems*.
**Originally printed in *The Fugitive*, December, 1925. Not reprinted in the *Se-
lected Poems*.

This is clear enough, and should make the critics pause before affixing the familiar label of "irony" on Ransom's poems. For the irony in them appears to be impure, a mixed effect, and is often colored by other equally powerful emotive intentions. Ransom's views on irony were formulated almost two decades after the publication of *Chills and Fever,* supposedly the exhibition gallery of the "new and complete" sensibility. An examination of the book on its own terms and without any *post hoc* interpolations is necessary.

To look for a connection between the Ransom of *Poems About God* and the author of *Chills and Fever* at first glance appears as paradoxical as the shift in focus hinted by the title. What had happened to Ransom in the intervening years is perhaps for the biographer rather than the critic to reconstruct. One guesses that back from the wars, and once more in his proper university setting, Ransom began an assiduous course of reading directed largely to the seventeenth-century metaphysicals and their Cavalier descendants. In addition, in the stimulating company of the young Fugitives, Ransom's knowledge of what contemporary poets were doing undoubtedly took on new energy and breadth. More, the fact that *The Fugitive* emphasized its connections with tradition undoubtedly compelled Ransom to engage in a systematic revaluation of his own poetic resources.

The results of this revaluation are so radical in *Chills and Fever* that we are tempted to diagnose a complete split in poetic personality. But more careful reading points to an equally interesting, although less dramatic, explanation. We find the themes of *Poems About God* present in *Chills and Fever* but translated to a different level of discourse, and purged of their former sentimentality by an objective and careful scrutiny of the intellect. We discover, for example, that the love poems have taken on control and sophistication because of two devices, both of which lend aesthetic distance to the occasions of love: an increasing reliance on archaic diction, and an imagery appropriate to such diction. Both elements contribute to "situation."

Archaic language ("perdure," "polls," "frore," "woody grot," etc.) is also found in poems where the cast is colloquial and contemporary. This feature presages the more cunning Ransom whose courtly turns of speech and syntax operate as humorous reminders of the distance between the situation and the values against which it is judged. But sometimes, as in "Fall of Leaf," where the lovers are seen against an arty medieval setting—St. Gregory's Tomb, charms, woodman, Holy Rood, and Sweet Saint Margret's Sisterhood—the result is a contrived "period" supernaturalism, which in its laborious exactitude reminds one of a De Mille pageant film.

More positively, some period pieces serve as five-finger exercises for Ransom's then increasing virtuosity. "Number Five," a ballad written in a curious amalgam of "literary" Irish and Cockney speech, suggests such practicing. But there is no drama in the balladry; some dramatic props are merely noted. In "Winter's Tale," another story of a timorous lover (Mr. Ransom's lovers are invariably timorous, just as his ladies are invariably rejecting. This would seem to be the wry remainder of the courtly and "ideal" relations between the sexes in the ante-bellum South), Drury, set against a fake medieval setting, takes instruction from his cats' behavior and goes to court Jenny. Here, the frankness of the artifice cooperates successfully with the dryly humorous tone of the fable, and the poet establishes a credible distance from other timorous lovers, closer to him in time, who like Drury might take advice from the animals.

Perhaps the loveliest assimilation of a remote diction to a perennially moving human situation is seen in the nicely modulated metaphysical tone of "In Process of a Noble Alliance." A rejecting lady is consigned by the poet to her proper element:

> Reduce this lady into marble quickly
>
> . . . . . .
>
> And crown her queen of the House of No Love:
> Ye harping the springe that catches the dove.

Another theme announced in *Poems About God* is now managed differently. The "tragedy" is objectified in the framework of a mock-heroic narrative such as "Captain Carpenter" or "Boris of Britain." Other frames are provided in ordering experience of a more homely, domestic nature. Where, in *Poems About God*, Ransom's rustic observations in first person notations savored of a naive identification with his materials, that is to say of rusticity, he now invents individually appropriate dramatic situations by which to explore these data. The social types, still Southern, have, for the most part, shifted from the country to the town. There are still the local idiots and the local lovers, but genteel old-maid types like Emily Hardcastle, Miriam Tazewell, or Miss Euphemia suggest town-folk rather than country people. The plethora of rejecting and ultimately rejected ladies in Ransom's poems seems to be a special sort of blight inherited from Southern society. The historian of fashions in writing, to say nothing of the sociologist, might note that the province of the old maid in the literature of recent years has shifted from New England to the South.

Now the country terrain is no longer merely catalogued but instead is involved in the dramatic circumstance. In "Conrad Sits in Twilight" * Conrad's particular malaise of age and purposelessness is tied in with the physical defects of the region. The localism of the following stanza is honest and not sentimental, because as a spiritual autumn is on Conrad "teasing," so (although the "so" is precisely what Ransom suppresses in all his poems) :

> Autumn days in our section
> Are the most used up thing on earth
> (Or in the waters under the earth)
> Having no more color nor predilection
> Than cornstalks too wet for the fire,
> A ribbon rotting on the byre,
> A man's face as weathered as straw
> By the summer's flare and winter's flaw.

The theme of culture-versus-impoverished-environment which was directly stated in *Poems About God* is now enriched by a further participation in conflicts which are in themselves dramatic. For example, in two poems the poet appears in the conventional but nevertheless disguised shapes of the bard and the unacknowledged king. "Adventure This Side Pluralism," a long, erudite, and witty poem, which Ransom unfortunately has not seen fit to reprint, depicts the paradox of a pluralistic religious scene in which the various creeds, while fighting for their "truths," forget their common descent and source and do one another in to death. The subject is detached from the poet's own feeling about it by the simple license of "I rent my smooth locks and spoke." In "Tom, Tom, the Piper's Son," Tom, a lonely man, "Yet privy to great dreams, and secret in vainglory," is variously appraised by others as an "ambulant worm," "a changeling . . . a Prince." The pathos of Tom's failure, that is to say the pathos of the poet's isolation from what he would command by

---

*Reprinted in the *Selected Poems* as "Conrad in Twilight."

love, is partly controlled by the transparent mask and so is kept from disintegrating into self-pity.

In at least two other poems, the poet's plight is given a more domesticated disguise. In "Plea in Mitigation," a humble and charming apologia *pro sua vita,* the fable tells of a doomed scholar whose fate was "to love unusual gods," so that he feels an outcast in his own community, with the sole possibility of social connection invested in the form of friendship. In the closing stanza, the third-person fiction is thrown off and the scholar-poet speaks directly:

> And if an alien hideously at feud
> With those my generation, I have reason
> To think to solve the fester of my treason:
> A seven of friends exceeds much multitude.*

In "Nocturne," a dualism of knowledge and experience as it causes a minor social crisis in the life of a young scholar is scored by a parody on the Prufrockian agony:

> Our man shall cast few capers in his dark seer-sucker coat,
> His grave eye subduing the outrageous red tie at his throat,
> Considering if he should carry his dutiful flesh to the ball,
> Rather than upon his book, which is flat; and metaphysical.

In Ransom's best poems, as we shall see, the objective fable is less transparent, and this tighter structural logic enriches meaning.

But in *Chills and Fever* Ransom begins to take possession of another order of the fabulous. This is the fable of childhood, childhood viewed as innocence, as a necessary condition to knowledge which corrupts, and which is difficult and tragic in its essence. The ultimate, permissive grace given to this kind of knowledge is most luminous in later poems like "Dead Boy" and "Janet Waking." Here, the clearest exposition is in the much-admired "Bells for John Whiteside's Daughter." But this delicately-turned elegy, suffused with an affectionate humor by the poet's intrusion into the child's own universe of geese and grass, in the end reckons death as an incongruous visitor:

> There was such speed in her little body,
> And such lightness in her footfall,
> It is no wonder her brown study
> Astonishes us all.

*At that time the Fugitive group numbered exactly seven.

Robert Penn Warren points out that it is the words "astonishes" and "vexed" which are pivotal to the pathos of the poem. I should add to this the colloquial term "brown study," which is domestic and yet foreign to the nature of childhood, which is all "speed" and "lightness." The repetition in the last stanza of "brown study" in conjunction with the key word "vexed" clinches the unwillingness of the narrator to accept the "little lady" as departed:

> In one house we are sternly stopped
> To say we are vexed at her brown study,
> Lying so primly propped.

In "The First Travels of Max" we have a fable of childhood in which death is apprehended not as fact, but as an essential aspect of all knowledge. The fable, although possessed of a fairy-tale ingenuity, exhibits the faults together with the virtues of Ransom's more perceptibly "worked" structures. Here, as in some of the mock-heroic structures, notably that of the well-known and I think over-rated "Captain Carpenter," one feels that Ransom allows the frame (which is only "logical" structure) to claim too much for the total meaning. Max travels the downward path to wisdom through a "degenerate" forest where he meets an obscene Red Witch, whose evil nature is somewhat arbitrarily symbolized by a "wide bosom yellow as butter." The atmosphere of an obscure but immanent evil is adroitly built up, but the purpose for it never becomes clear. In the last stanza we are returned to a Max miraculously restored to his rightful sphere. The humorously pedantic tone in which this is reported ("Max is more firmly domiciliated.") leaves us with a conventionalized picture of innocence and order as the children play under their nurse's supervision. It means, I suppose, that the terrors of childhood are not visible to the casual eyes of adults. But for all its deft detail, the poem seems ill-adapted to this end. For terror leaves its mark and Max's travels should be seen upon him (at least by the poet, who, after all, has seen all the rest) even as he plays against the deceptively green and candid lawns.

I shall now discuss a group of poems from *Chills and Fever*, among which are some of Ransom's best, and which he has included among the poems he wishes to preserve. In *The New Criticism* (1941) Ransom provides a useful map to the reading of these poems, although there he considers only the *principle* of reading. Referring to I. A. Richards' use of the terms "tone" and "intention" as "not quite decisive," Ransom stresses the concept of "Dramatic Situation" (an inconclusive term for the connections between tone and style, tone and manners, and tone and person addressed) as "almost" the first head under which one should try to understand a poem. Most poems, Ransom soundly reminds us, inferentially represent a particular speaker. From this he is led to conclude that lyric poetry derives from dramatic dialogue. Now, the dramatic situation in most of the poems I shall discuss derives from the presence of a speaker-poet. The tone of the narration is usually that of an ironic detachment from its occasion. But there are times when the narrator is himself involved with the subject of his narrative by the intimacy of his vantage-point. A study of how this works in his poems may lead us to a slight re-weighing of the role of inferential speaker in Ransom's criticism.

"Miriam Tazewell" and "Dead Boy" both employ an affectionate address by which the narrator qualifies his relationship to the subjects from whose values he keeps apart. Such quizzical intimacy permits the poet a close rendering of his people, for unlike Wallace Stevens', almost all of Ransom's poems are about people. Sometimes, however, as in "Parting at Dawn" and "Spectral Lovers," the poet, while involving himself in the lover's stratagems, takes a juridical view of their disposition. Still, in poems as dissimilar as the fine Metaphysical-via-Frost lyric, "Winter Remembered," and "Philomela," a satire on the death of myth reminiscent of "Sweeney Among the Nightingales," the dramatic necessities involve the poet at once as narrator, subject, and protagonist. It would seem, then, that it is the particular way in which the factors of tone, style, manner, and persons addressed are blended which determines the atmosphere of the poem, rather than the mere presence of a given inferential speaker.

The rich possibilities in such combinations are demonstrated by the well-known "Dead Boy." The tone hovers perilously between irony and sorrow, or irony and nostalgia. The irony is complex: it is directed against the narrator himself, "Nor some of the world of outer dark, like me"; against the subject, the little cousin, "A boy not beautiful, nor good, nor clever,/ . . . A pig with a pasty face, so I had said . . ."; and against the narrator's own judgment of the relationship of the dead boy to the equally dead Virginia past, ". . . But the little man quite dead,/I see the forbears' antique lineaments." This fusion of the elegiac and the satiric is illumined by the final stanza, where the narrator abandons his role as participant and becomes the Olympian commentator:

> He was pale and little, the foolish neighbors say:
> The first fruits, saith the Preacher, the Lord hath taken;
> But this was the old tree's late branch wrenched away,
> Grieving the sapless limbs, the shorn and shaken.

"Miriam Tazewell" is a poem showing Ransom's hand as distinctly in its light rhyme and half-rhyme effects and feminine endings (devices carried over from the early light verse) as it does in its subject, the extravagant actions of an elderly Southern maiden when her lawn is "deflowered" by a storm. In the second stanza the third-person narrative shifts to direct address:

> And the sun, Miriam, ascended his dominion,
> The storm was withered against his empyrean.

The intrusion of the poet is neither explained nor repeated. The poem continues in the casual voice of a society reporter:

> Suppers and cards were calendared, and some bridals,
> And the birds demurely sang in the bitten poplars.

The last stanza does not resume direct address, but again brings the narrator close to his subject by his use of her name:

> To Miriam Tazewell the whole world was villain
> To prosper when the fragile babes were fallen,
> And not to unstop her own storm and be maudlin
> For weeks she went untidy, she went sullen.

The third line of this stanza, as I have given it, is a substitution made in the *Selected Poems* for the original "The principle of the beast was low and masculine," and is a telling example of Ransom's exactitude. For the new line not only drastically alters the "logical structure" of the poem, but also subtly transforms the "texture" by rounding out the tempest metaphor and extending it from the natural universe to Miriam's inner life. The line changes a mild satire of physical negation to a satiric tragedy of spiritual frustration, two unequal aspects of human deprivation. The poem has been translated from the realm of domestic comedy to that of domestic tragedy. The universe (the weather at odds with Miriam's flowers) is like Miriam's split self, and when the storm, like a violent lover, "deflowers" Miriam's protected garden, it is a traumatic event.

"Spectral Lovers" is another poem whose "trimming and revising" in the *Selected Poems* illustrates Ransom's method. It is less successful than the similar "Equilibrists," commonly thought to be one of Ransom's best metaphysical poems. Both poems deal with renunciatory lovers, but with this difference: in the first, it is the lover who decides that "This is the marble fortress not to be conquered," while in the later poem the decision against consummation is mutual. It is the lovers' predicament to discover "Honor among thieves, Honor between lovers." In both poems the lady's body is conceived in traditional terms as respectively a city and a field, to be taken. The poet participates as narrator and commentator in both poems. In "Spectral Lovers" he assumes the first person, a daring stratagem, in the last stanza:

> They passed me once in April, in the mist.
> No other season is it when one walks and discovers
> Two tall and wandering, like spectral lovers,
> White in the season's moon-gold and amethyst,
> Who touch their quick fingers fluttering like a bird
> Whose songs shall never be heard.

Still, this venture of the poet into the *situ* of the dramatic action is rewarding: he is the spectator who vouches for the authenticity of the event he has reported; at the same time, he introduces the interesting possibility, supported by the last two lines of the first stanza, that he is really regarding his own past. The shock of this recognition creates an additional dramatic and emotive dimension at the very close of the poem. The half-wry little complaint of the first stanza is now hinted to be the intimate experience of the narrator:

> Why should two lovers go frozen apart in fear?
> And yet they were, they were.

There is not only renunciation, but the somewhat rueful judgment of it. There is not only the lost past, but a conscious present which is critical of it.

Other revisions in "Spectral Lovers" are worth examining. Changes are heaviest in the first three and the last of its seven stanzas. An interesting substitution in stanza one is:

> Else angels lost in each other and fallen to earth.

for:

> Else two immaculate angels fallen on earth.

The extra syllable of the later version permits the spondaic variation of "each other" and thus relieves the regularity of the metrical pattern. The substitution of "lost in each other" for "immaculate" enriches the denotative content of the line. The idea of loss, the real theme of the poem, is thus established early; the original adjective, "immaculate," was a contradiction in sense to "fallen on earth." The logical structure of the poem has been strengthened by the change.

Larger alterations in stanzas two and three must be considered for different reasons. The original version of two reads:

> Over the shredding of an April blossom
> Scarcely her fingers touched him, quick with care
> Of many delicate postures she cast a snare.
> But for all the red heart beating in the pale bosom
> Her face of cunningly tinctured ivory
> Was hard with agony.

In the final version the changes commence with line three:

> Yet of evasions even she made a snare.
> The heart was bold that clanged within her bosom,
> The moment perfect, the time stopped for them,
> Still her face turned from him.

Two kinds of alteration have been made: substitutions of "structure" or "paraphrasable core," and substitutions of "texture" or "local excitement." The elimination of the romantic décor of "red heart," "pale bosom," "tinctured ivory," and "hard agony" is sound. I do not favor the overstatement of "clanged" but it strengthens the total meaning. The replacement of the description of the lady's face by the information, "The moment perfect, the time stopped for them," which

is completed by the anti-climactic "Still her face turned from him,"
emphasizes the "determinate" meaning of the poem. Similarly, the
more abstract rendering of line three, as "Yet of evasions even she
made a snare," underlines the negative quality of the relationship.
In short, the revisions go toward producing a more generalized experience of unfulfilled love. The gestures and features of the lovers
are refined into the airy tracery of their essences, an appropriate condition for spectral persons. Still, where it is judicious to do so, Ransom
willingly eliminates the general in favor of the particular.

Only two other changes require comment. The pathetic fallacy in
the second line of stanza three, "Passionate being the essences of the
field," is now more quietly reported as "And the stealthy emanations
of the field." In the concluding stanza, the phonetically awkward
syntax of "Two clad in the shapes of angels, being lovers" becomes
the more melodic "Two tall and wandering, like spectral lovers." The
last change makes for concreteness, but of a kind suitable to specters.
The modification also serves to revalue and echo the theme of loss
stated in stanza one. I have ignored certain aspects of this poem, such
as the "local excitement" created by the little fable of the knight's
wishful and symbolic beheading of the field-flowers, in an effort to reconstruct the motive for the changes. The best restatement of "Spectral Lovers" occurs in "The Equilibrists," which I shall examine later
in this study.

Two poems bearing Ransom's curious signature, the more visibly
in that they are not wholly successful, are "Old Mansion" and "The
Tall Girl." Although unlike in subject, both poems fail for the same
reason—the over-elaboration of "structure." This defect is important
to understand for it is a risk which all of Ransom's poems undergo,
although one which the best survive. Making the structure top-heavy
is an emphasis which derives from Ransom's own critical bias, one
first formulated in his earliest critical work, *God Without Thunder*,
where he pleaded a similarity for the functions of poetry and myth.
Both poetry and myth are a form of "appreciative knowledge," a
term Ransom owes to Kant's "Formal knowledge, knowledge of objects or events for their own sake." Appreciative knowledge is to be
distinguished from scientific knowledge which concerns itself with objects or events in terms of their immediate practical value. According
to Ransom,

The myth of an object is its proper name, private, unique, untranslatable, over-
flowing, of a demonic energy that cannot be reduced to the poverty of the class

concept. The myth of an event is a story which invests the natural with a supernatural background and with a more than historical history. . . . *Myth resorts to the supernatural in order to restore the fulness of the natural.*

The myth-maker "seeks to restore the individual image, or else to go back and seek fresh experience."

Dr. Gordon Mills in a thoughtful study of Ransom's critical position* points out that his belief that the combination of extension and intension creates the "very great God" is correlative to his belief that poetry is created through the combination of texture and structure. Dr. Mills notes that Ransom nowhere defines myth satisfactorily, but nevertheless appears to agree that since all appreciative knowledge is myth, and since all myth is knowledge of particulars for their own sake, "the red chair" or "the old oak" when used specifically are myths. This seems to me nonsense. "Myth," like some other terms in Ransom's ambitious critical system, strives for such high-order abstractness (fighting the scientists with their own weapons!) that it tends to abrogate the very function it would claim for myth—its *superior* knowledge of reality, as opposed to the inferior kind provided by science. If knowledge of particularity for its own sake is "myth"—"the red chair," "the green lawn," etc.—then the myth-maker at certain levels would seem to have a commonplace function indeed, as a mere transcriber of particulars. This is a role I do not believe Ransom would urge for him.

I am tempted to transpose the syntax of Ransom's "Religion is an institution existing for the sake of its ritual," to his critical scheme: "A poem is a structure existing for the sake of its texture." In Ransom's own poetry, this aim is not always realized. Often, the structure is too overbearing and subdues the texture. In "The Tall Girl" and "Old Mansion" this is precisely what happens. The machinery of the structure is too elaborate for the thinness of the texture. In "The Tall Girl" Ransom relies on an arbitrary supernaturalism: the Queens of Hell with "lissome necks" try to seduce the "tall girl with long tread" to their errant ways, while "the Queen of Heaven . . ./In the likeness, I hear, of a plain motherly woman" decides to best the Hell Queens and warns the girl, "This will come to no good!" The poem leaves one uncommitted. The diabolism of the Hell-Heaven opposition seems too much infernal machinery to set up for the little sonnet. We are unconvinced of the tall girl's danger. The texture of the poem supplies no note of jeopardy with the exception of the Hell Queen's

Myth and Ontology in the Thought of John Crowe Ransom.

suggestion that they walk "by the windows where the young men are working." Perhaps the girl's gold hair is meant to be a symbol of her vulnerability. But then why must we have the Queens of Hell to test it? And why must a kindly old woman become the Queen of Heaven? Surely, Ransom himself would agree that we should reserve our "myths" for rare occasions, lest they fall in disfavor for ill-usage.

In "Old Mansion" the element of the supernatural is not quite so flagrantly imported. The narrator intrudes upon the aged eminence of a Southern manor house where "Decay was the tone of brick and shingle," and knocks upon the door,

> To beg their dole of a look, in simple charity,
> Or crumbs of legend dropping from their great store.

But he is dismissed by a servant who says the old mistress is ill. As the speaker leaves, he notes

> How lovingly from my foreign weed the feather curled
> On the languid air; . . .

The narrator takes this to be a token of his own attraction to the crumbling house (the house of the past). The tone of his narration is wryly appraising, an effect achieved by connectives like "emphatically," and by pedantic circumlocutions appropriate to the "tired historian." But we are left with the uncomfortable feeling that the poet is claiming too much for his house of the past. The old manor is not only the repository of a certain not "ignoble" history, but seems as well to stand for the house of life:

> . . . "Your mansion, long and richly inhabited,
> Its exits and entrances suiting the children of men,
> Will not be for ever thus, O man, exhibited,
> And one had best hurry to enter it if one can."

Later, the house appears as the house of Death:

> The old mistress was ill, and sent my dismissal
> By one even more wrappered and lean and dark
> Than that warped concierge and imperturbable vassal
> Who bids you begone from her master's Gothic park.

I like the last two lines: they are good lines; they add "local excitement" to the determinate meaning of the stanza. Still, if the lean dark servant of lines one and two is meant to be a minion of the house of Death, what could that "Gothic Park" stand for and who could be that "warped concierge and imperturbable vassal"? Surely the Gothic Park is the domain of Death from which the live wayfarer is excluded. Why need the servant of line two be "even more" wrappered and lean and dark than Death's concierge? One reluctantly concludes that here, as in "The Tall Girl," the supernatural has got imported into the poem because Ransom *believes* he needs it to adequately "represent the fullness of the natural." The result in "Old Mansion" is a conflict in structure which spuriously thickens the texture. The ambiguity of the house symbol is not a legitimate ambiguity; it clogs rather than opens up new areas of meaning. We feel we have been needlessly mystified with parlor prestidigitations.

When Ransom writes his very best poems (and he has written a few of the best poems of his time) he becomes more careless of the supernatural in representing "the fullness of the natural." In these poems the myth of the poem is personal and immediate, a genuine function of its structure compounded with its texture. I shall consider first "Lady Lost," then "Janet Waking," "Blue Girls," and finally "Antique Harvesters," Ransom's most distinguished long poem.

"Lady Lost," like "Janet Waking," fashions a personal myth out of the particulars of domesticity in a way which is special to Ransom. The distinctive effect of both poems is pathos, a pathos all the more poignant for its repression by the light, fanciful tone taken toward the object of pathos. In the first poem, a lost bird assumes the stature of a lost lady; in the second, a dead hen assumes the guise of Death.

The gossamer metaphor of "Lady Lost" is falsified by paraphrase. A lady-bird flies to the poet's bird-bath, knocks on the window-pane to be let in from the rain, and looks to him as if she would cry. The last two stanzas present the poet's response to her entreaty:

> So I will go out into the park and say
> "Who has lost a delicate brown-eyed lady
> In the West End section? Or has anybody
> Injured some fine woman in some dark way
> Last night, or yesterday?
>
> "Let the owner come and claim possession,
> No questions will be asked. But stroke her gently

With loving words and she will evidently
Return to her full soft-haired white-breasted fashion
And her right home and her right passion."

The delicate charm of this poem derives from the propriety with which the metaphor is sustained from beginning to end. But it is the correctness of the poet's attitude toward the lady-bird which, after all, is the *sine qua non* making the metaphor credible. And this attitude is possible only in a society where chivalric values toward women still have some sanction.

In an essay, "Forms and Citizens," in *The World's Body* (1938), Ransom says in a passage reminiscent of Baudelaire's "Dandyisme" (as the latter derived it from Joseph de Maistre): "A natural affiliation binds together the gentleman, the religious man and the artist—punctilious characters, all of them, in their formalism." And discussing Eliot's program, he offers as substitute: "In manners, aristocratic; in religion, ritualistic; in art, traditional." I hardly think this program explains "Lady Lost." On the other hand, it is doubtful whether the special gallantry of the conception could have been possible to one who did not at least give service to the notion of punctiliousness in manners. For it is the full measure of gentlemanliness which not only restores the lost lady to her rightful owner, but also takes responsibility for instructing him in how to treat her rightly. In this poem the dramatic fable, slight, intimate, and original, does not rely on a supernatural machinery to blow up the event into "the fullness of the natural." The relationships are simple to start with: the poet is appealed to as a protector; the lady-bird is in need of help. The relationships, I suppose I need not add, are human ones. It is only in the last phrase "and her right passion" that there is the hint of the least ambiguity in the connection between the two. Has the lady left home on this tempestuous night and deliberately sought protection from one who is not entitled to give it? The attractive fluidity of the prosodic frame (four cinquains rhyming abbaa, and a preponderance of run-on lines from two to four lines in length) provides a quaint counterpoint to the measured colloquialism of the diction. The result is a curious blend of lyric and dramatic qualities. I cannot think of any poet writing in English besides Ransom who could have managed just this tone of a warmly personal, yet almost ritual, gallantry.

"Janet Waking," like "Lady Lost," creates a pathetic dimension.

But the pathos is more intense. The incongruity between Janet's universe of grass and hens, and the universe of death in which she "would not be instructed . . ." is a paradox basic to the human condition and not merely to the experience of little girls with dead hens. The convention of the poem is that the narrator is the father, guardian, or grown-up friend of Janet. He is clearly moved by her inability to accept the death of Chucky, yet by the distance he keeps from expressing it he controls his own predicament. The measure of this control is communicated by his manners toward Chucky:

> It was a transmogrifying bee
> Came droning down on Chucky's old bald head
> And sat and put the poison. It scarcely bled,
> But how exceedingly
>
> And purply did the knot
> Swell with the venom and communicate
> Its rigor! Now the poor comb stood up straight
> But Chucky did not.

Chucky's death is rightly viewed by the adult narrator as part of the give and take of a "natural" universe. While the inexorability of this exchange is humorously understated, its brutality is acknowledged in the short "But Chucky did not." The final stanza completes the evaluation: it becomes clear that the narrator accepts the significance of Chucky's death on Janet's terms, terms which are fraught with poignance for all of us:

> And weeping fast as she had breath
> Janet implored us, "Wake her from her sleep."
> And would not be instructed in how deep
> Was the forgetful kingdom of death.

As in "Lady Lost" the structure of the poem is simple. There is no supernatural machinery. The relationship between Janet and the hen is right because it is a human one; the relationship between the narrator and the hen is right, because he sees her as part of a larger scheme of which her mortality is a sign; finally, the relationship between the narrator and Janet is right, because while he does not accept her evaluation, he understands it.

"Blue Girls," written on one of the oldest poetic themes imaginable, the Horatian *carpe diem,* with an admonitory ending added, is likely to be one of the chief poems by which Ransom's name will continue to be admired. It is clearly obligated to the tradition of the Cavalier descendants of the metaphysicals, more nearly to Herrick, perhaps, than to Carew. The metaphysical conceit, which Ransom can assimilate successfully, is absent. Instead, the pure lyricism of Cavalier song is adapted to the more colloquial rhetoric of the metaphysicals. The superiority of "Blue Girls" to hundreds of other graceful poems on the same subject lies precisely in the purity and elegance of the language working *against* the affectionate address. The poet addresses the blue girls not as a lover, who would seduce them into spending their beauty, but as an older, more knowledgeable person. He urges as a disinterested yet concerned observer:

> Practise your beauty, blue girls, before it fail;
> And I will cry with my loud lips and publish
> Beauty which all our power shall never establish,
> It is so frail.
>
> For I could tell you a story which is true;
> I know a lady with a terrible tongue,
> Blear eyes fallen from blue,
> All her perfections tarnished—yet it is not long
> Since she was lovelier than any of you.

The meticulous usage of the verbs "practise" and "publish," the direct address, the testimony from personal experience, the coincidental factor that the tarnished beauty's eyes were blue (the blue girls are so by virtue of their skirts)—in short, the hint of a personal motive on the speaker's part toward the lady who not long since "was lovelier than any of you": all this, when combined with the detail of the "terrible tongue" (as drastic a detail for beauty's degradation as are worms and winding sheets), makes "Blue Girls" one of Ransom's most telling fables.

The structure of "Blue Girls" is one of simple antithesis. The bitter example in the last stanza collides with the proclaimed graces of the blue girls in the first three. At the same time, there is a cumulative progression. The last stanza climaxes the warnings the poet can offer the blue girls, whom he had begun to admonish even in the first:

> Go listen to your teachers old and contrary
> Without believing a word.

Here again the myth of the poem is a human one. The recognition of man's inability to stay the hand of time in "Beauty which all our power shall never establish" is lifted from the realm of commonplace by the rich ambiguity of the verb. "Establish" is here intended as "erect" or "set up" and also as "demonstrate" or "prove." While facing up to this human inadequacy, the poet does not resort to the supernatural in representing "the fullness of the natural" (the blue girls). The line of relationship between the girls' untested beauty and the poet's superior experience of beauty which is dimmed is, again, a human one.

When we examine "Antique Harvesters," along with "Blue Girls" the most widely anthologized of Ransom's poems, we find a greater machinery of structure operating to combine with the "local excitements" (texture) of the poem. I do not agree with Robert Penn Warren that Ransom's is a poetry "purged of merely local excitement." In Ransom's best poems, such as "Antique Harvesters," there is a perfect interpenetration of structure and texture. The intricacy of this "compounding" is best understood if we part the paraphrasable core from the local excitements.

The logical structure of "Antique Harvesters" is introduced by a setting which serves as footnote to the title: "Scene: Of the Mississippi the bank sinister, and of the Ohio the bank sinister." At harvest time, in an old land, "dry, grey and spare" men assemble to gather corn. They are old men who remember the heroes who died here, but the young men want none of their "sable memories." The poet (a privileged rhetorician) steps forth from the group and evokes certain images of the past such as the fox hunt. He urges the harvesters to "garner for the Lady" so that they may prove themselves men and know their "Lady's image." "The sons of the fathers" must not forsake her if they are told they can prosper better elsewhere. It is true that while their Lady ages, she has not stooped. If we talk of death, let us recognize that in the mortal scheme all life is fragile and dependent on God's vitality.

But merely to extract the "paraphrasable core" is, as always, to slander the poem. First, it is important to recognize the rhetorical tone of the whole. Questions and the answers to them occur in four of the eight stanzas. The rhetoric shifts from a forensic tone in the first four stanzas to a hortatory style in the next three and, in the last, to a note of invocation and prayer. From the beginning there is an ambiguity regarding the poet's role in this situation. He flatly reports setting and action; then, oracularly, he both asks and divines questions. He announces, at the end of stanza two, in an impersonal construction, that the past has greater vitality than is thought. Yet in stanza three, he again identifies himself with the group as their spokesman, using the collective "we." He reports fragments of the old men's talk about the heroic past. This past is the past of the South for the echoes of it are like "echoes from the horn/of the hunter. . . ." Hunting as a symbol for the Old South needs no comment. But (and here the poet dissociates himself from the group and is again omniscient) only the old men nourish these echoes with love. Then, interrupting the progress of the harvest, there is introduced a beautiful description of a hunt, one presented with such immediacy as to confuse us about its past-ness. Or, perhaps, it is a real hunt, repeating the gracious movement of the past-in-present.*

> Here come the hunters, keepers of a rite;
> The horn, the hounds, the lank mares coursing by
> Straddled with archetypes of chivalry;
> And the fox, lovely ritualist, in flight
> Offering his unearthly ghost to quarry;
> And the fields, themselves to harry.

It is worth remarking how closely the notion of the hunt as ritual corresponds to Ransom's idea of religion as "existing for the sake of the ritual." The fox is a "lovely ritualist." The hunters exist for the sake of the rite. And, as the fox offers himself to "quarry" in the service of the rite, so in the same scheme of intertwining sacrifice "the fields, themselves to harry." The aristocratic past is a formal system of "degree" and interdependent responsibilities. But the concrete quality of this past as represented in the hunt is never openly articulated with the rest of the poem. As if a dream were to be brushed aside, the poet continues:

> Resume, harvesters. The treasure is full bronze
> Which you will garner for the Lady. . . .

*I am indebted for this alternate reading of the hunt symbol to Mr. Allen Tate.

In the next stanza the imagery hardens into a frieze-like cast:

> Bare the arm, dainty youths, bend the knees
> Under bronze burdens. And by an autumn tone
> As by a grey, as by a green, you will have known
> Your famous Lady's image; for so have these;

The Lady is the South, past and present. Her vaguely religious appellation suggests the prayer-like adoration implicit in the total conception of the poem.* The Lady's aspects are inexhaustible, the poet implies; she can be known under more than one mode. She can be known as well in her old age (by "an autumn tone") as in her innocent youth ("as by a green") or in her gallant maturity ("grey," the color of the Confederate uniforms). The visual composition of this stanza presents the youths in a ritualistic formalism of movement: by working the soil, they perform an act of homage. It is a way of knowing their sources, as the fathers have known them.

The seventh stanza urges the young men to reject those who would have them forsake the South, and also appears to make a somewhat adventitious reference to Ransom's sociological distinction between the new culturally impoverished South and the old aristocratic, agrarian South to which he asks the legitimate heirs to return.

The last stanza, a tender invocation of fealty to the South, achieves a poignant authority managed partly by the antique endings of the verbs ("ageth," "Hath," "wearieth") as well as by the syntax of the last two lines in which earth's dependence on God's will is equated with the heirs' dependence upon the Lady's. The proposition is put in proverbial form and the syntax legislates for our acceptance of it:

> True, it is said of our Lady, she ageth.
> But see, if you peep shrewdly, she hath not stooped;
> Take no thought of her servitors that have drooped,
> For we are nothing; and if one talk of death—
> Why, the ribs of the earth subsist frail as a breath
> If but God wearieth.

*In connection with Ransom's almost mystical faith in the Old South, a faith for which he has constructed an elaborate rationale (see *I'll Take My Stand* and *Who Owns America*, two symposia to which he contributed), a sentence from *God Without Thunder* seems apropos: "It is well to believe a good many things without having to conduct a continuous epistemological discussion about them."

"Antique Harvesters" shows Ransom triumphing on purely poetic grounds over his own critical notions concerning poetry and
belief. His latest formulation of this problem is to be found in *The
New Criticism*. "I should say," he writes, "that old science (with
gods, demons, and Ptolemaic spheres) was poetico-science, which was
available to poetry and that modern science is pure science, which
is not . . . good poets are not like the romantic ones, repeating
what they would like to believe but cannot any longer believe. . . ."
But questions concerning the relationship of poetry and belief do
not usually stem from the conflict Ransom has described. That is
to say, the conflict is not so much between what the poet would
like to and *cannot* believe, although this sometimes happens; when
it does, the question is interior to the poet's psychology and *anterior*
to his poetry. It is rarely a question of poetry *versus* belief. The
real question is what the reader *cannot* and the poet *would like*
him to believe. An example of this would be Pound's Gesellian
economics employed as *deus ex machina* in the Cantos. Or, to bring
the case home, Ransom's faith in the superiority of a return to
an aristocratic, agrarian economy in the South as opposed to the
possible offerings of pluralistic socio-economic structures. The fact
that "Antique Harvesters" is a moving experience even for one who,
like myself, does not share Ransom's belief in the practicality of
the South's return to a regional economy, proves that a poem can
triumph over its "ideas." Ransom is repeating what he wishes to
believe, believes, and, because he is a good poet, can temporarily
persuade the reader to believe. This amounts to "a willing suspen-
sion of disbelief" on the reader's part. For *the duration of the poem*
the poet's version of this experience is entirely congenial to the
same reader who would reject Ransom's statement of it in his prose.*
In short, we can consider "Antique Harvesters" as a conquest of

---

*I trust this brief discussion of the problem of poetry and belief will not be
taken to be my final view of this troublesome question. In spite of the critical intelligence which has been devoted to this problem in the last two decades, a satisfactory resolution has not been proposed. Ransom, in an essay on T. S. Eliot in
The New Criticism, takes Eliot to task for waiving the problem of belief in poetry:
"I incline to think that the problem exists in poetry as in religion, and is very
nearly the same problem. . . . I can see no necessity for waiving the intellectual
standards on behalf of poets." But Ransom fails to provide an exposition of his
inclination. For example, he merely affirms, without proving, that Dante's beliefs are
"substantively better grounded" than Shelley's. A non-Catholic atheist might argue
this point, while conceding the superiority of Dante's poetry. I do not think, in
the long run, Ransom has been very helpful.

structure by texture. As an aesthetic experience, the poem operates to refute Ransom's critical propositions on the connections of poetry and belief.

The five poems written since 1927 which Ransom has included in *Selected Poems* are slender evidence on which to generalize his present direction, unless we take the smallness of the number as evidence of a thinning poetic stock. In subject matter they have little connection. At least two of them have a somewhat concocted look; they are good "occasional" poems. "Address to the Scholars of New England," delivered as the Harvard Phi Beta Kappa Poem in June, 1939, is interesting for its autobiographical witness to the impact of New England myths on the early development of the poet:

> Scared by the holy megrims of those Pilgrims,
> I thought the unhumbled and outcast and cold
> Were rich Heirs travelling incognito,
> Bred too fine for the country's sweet produce
> And but affecting that dog's life of pilgrims.

"What Ducks Require" is a heightening of Ransom's early impulse toward humorous verse into a complexly "clever" style, while preserving the original lightness. The poem is interesting less for its logical structure (a salute to the adventurousness of ducks) than for linguistic innovations which it shares with other late poems I shall discuss.

"Of Margaret" is a charming act of elegiac fealty to "that far-away time of gentleness" when Margaret "whose generations were of the head" gave the world her maiden pageant. It is closer than any of the late poems to Ransom's early poetic diction and, indeed, to one of his early poetic themes—praise for the dead virgin. The poet is appreciably mellower toward his subject than in some of the related early poems such as "Emily Hardcastle, Spinster."

"Prelude to an Evening" and "Painted Head" testify to Ransom's close reading of the "moderns," of whom he had once made the interesting distinction that they wrote two kinds of poetry, which he designated "thin, pure" poetry and "rich, obscure" poetry. Both poems fall in the second category. They suggest an especially close study of the work of Wallace Stevens whom, oddly enough, Ransom had classified among those who wrote thin, pure poetry. Another obligation is to E. E. Cummings, a "romantic" whose poetics would seem,

at first glance, to be the antithesis of Ransom's courtly and somewhat finicky muse. From Cummings Ransom has taken the odd dis-
posal of adverbs, the attaching of negative prefixes to adjectives and
nouns, the compounding of nouns, and a general telescoping of syntax.* Ransom has also developed a respect for free verse (although
no doubt he would be the last man to say so) for, in spite of the
fact that he arranges his lines into stanzas which look like quatrains,
they are unrhymed and follow no traditional metrical scheme. There
is an echo of Stevens in such decorative pastel images as:

> You in your peignoir, dainty at your orange-cup,

and in the phonetic iteration of such word-play as:

> That dreamed and undreamt become each other,

while the "idea" of "Painted Head" is a Stevens leit-motif:

> . . . Beauty is of body.
> The flesh shallowly on a head
> In a rock-garden needing body's love
> And best bodiness to colorify.

Further, one guesses that Ransom has been attentive to some of the
innovations of the Surrealists (or their Elizabethan models) in the
denser imagery and phonetic power of passages like

> For cry, cock-crow, or the iron bell
> Can crack the sleep-sense of outrage.

The result of Ransom's innovations is a poetry of greater ambiguity. But it would be wrong to assign this effect merely to the
technical strategy, when, in fact, the whole "tenor" ** of the poems

---

*While all of these practices have long since passed into common use among the
moderns, Cummings, by virtue of his persistent emphasis, may be thought of as
the source of most of them.
**A term Ransom takes over with qualifications from I. A. Richards. Its weak-
ness, incidentally, is to be seen in a discussion (in *The New Criticism*) in which
Ransom takes issue with Richards on Denham's "Cooper Hill." Ransom and
Richards, both well-equipped readers, make diametrically opposite assignments of
those aspects of the poem which are its "tenor" and those which are its "vehicle"
(importation of foreign content.) Terms which evince such resistance to use in
a simple poem seem of questionable value when the critic contends with "obscure"
ones.

reveals a different approach to the "paraphrasable core" than does Ransom's early work. "Prelude to an Evening" builds up to a fine, rich sense of an unnamed evil which pervades the world of two adults from the nether world of their submerged selves. And the hinted-at sinister doom of the elders in the last stanza begins to infect the world of the "warm children":

> You like a waning moon, and I accusing
> Our too banded Eumenides,
> You shall make Noes but wanderingly,
> Smoothing the heads of the hungry children.

"Painted Head," while indebted to Ransom's early "metaphysical" body-mind dualism, nevertheless now allows body to triumph in the contest. Stanza one proclaims the status of the head and shows the influence of Cummings' diction:*

> By dark severance the apparition head
> Smiles from the air a capital on no
> Column of a Platonic perhaps head
> On a canvas sky depending from nothing;

Stanzas five and six develop this essential anti-Platonism into a Stevens-like consideration of the paradoxical but inevitable opposition of the imagination and the "actual." There are some autobiographic penitences to be sensed here as well:

> So that the extravagant device of art
> Unhoused by abstraction this once head
> Was capital irony by a loving hand
> Who knew the treason of a head like this;
>
> Makes repentance in an unlovely head
> For having vinegarly traduced the flesh
> Till, the hurt flesh recusing, the hard egg
> Is shrunk to its own deathlike surface;

Finally, let me comment on the quality of Ransom's poetic vision. The totality of Ransom's tone, like the totality of Eliot's, suggests a poetry of failure. Irony, in both Ransom and Eliot, is an instrument

*The metrical variations which Ransom works on the iambic base of these "free verse" lines are ingenious.

for the assimilation and the ordering of failure into an endurable scheme of existence. Ransom's irony, professedly derived from the seventeenth-century metaphysicals, and especially from Donne, has, nevertheless, a distinctly personal cast. One way to get at it might be to say that Ransom has the irony without the passion of Donne. Or, to approach it another way, Ransom would appear to have made an eighteenth-century neo-classical addition to his metaphysical sources. One measure of Ransom's great distance from Donne and Marvell is to be seen in his love poems. In the best of Donne and Marvell the convention is for the narrator to be the lover. This method is adopted by Ransom in very few poems, for he seems to be more *outside* the experience of love, and judges it, as I have pointed out, like an omniscient spectator even in those poems where he permits himself a first-person involvement. While history has made the situation favorable for such a role, this rigorous elimination of the poet's "personality" is something which Ransom deliberately sought. His essay on "Lycidas" suggests such an objective. The goal of the poet, he urges, should be a perfect anonymity. Milton's poetry breaks down, he asserts, precisely at those points where we come too close to the man himself. Paradoxically enough, Ransom in his own poems has not been able to fully eradicate "personality," although doing everything poetically possible to inhibit it. For while he has successfully eliminated passion, he has nevertheless left the distinctive mark of an odd, intense, and fine wit on everything he has touched.

We must face, then, the fact that Ransom's generous wish for "a totality of experience" in poetry breaks down in his own practice to mean a totality of experience relevant to this particular "structure." And it is precisely at this point that the critical misunderstandings of Ransom's significance enter. For while Ransom's "structures" are, on the whole, quite narrow segments of "reality," his experience of them is not. His poetry, it seems to me, represents the triumph of an original sensibility over an essentially small stock of "ideas" or "structures."

THE IRONY OF JOHN CROWE RANSOM

G. R. Wasserman

All irony is a form of contrast between appearance and reality; the elements which are essential to it are an ironic will (in nature a god; in fiction the author), a spectator, and a victim.* Ironic effect is the secret intimacy enjoyed by the will and the spectator at the expense of the latter, or, in other words, the awareness of the discrepancy between reality and its false appearance in the mind of a victim.

Originally, the term designated the manner of speaking of a stock character of Greek comedy, the *eiron*, who, though a seeming fool, regularly triumphed over his antagonist, the *alazon*, by his skill in dissembling his knowledge. A similar irony of manner may be seen in Socratic irony, though here the deception is not directed at an individual victim, but applied to dialectical ends; Socrates' ignorance was an indirect way of arriving at the truth, a skepticism of every dogma that was not proven to rest upon first principles. From verbal irony and the irony of manner, ironic contrast was introduced into the structure of a dramatic plot by making an audience aware of elements in the situation of which a character was ignorant. Words and actions were thereby made to have a peculiar effect derivative from the contrast between the spectator's knowledge and the character's ignorance.

*This essay originally appeared in *University of Kansas City Review*, XXIII (Winter, 1956), 151–60.

In none of these historical forms of irony does an author constitute one of the essential elements of the contrast. In both the primitive Eironeia and the Socratic dialogue, the deception is practiced by a dramatic character; and in the Greek tragedy, the ironic will is invested in a God or Fate who arbitrarily prepares for the sudden disillusionment of a character. Moreover, the objectivity of the classical tragedian was assured by a stable and ordered structure of ideas. The classical ironist spoke for neither the gods nor man. He did not need to, for classical irony was vitally connected with the Greek moral view of life; it was a way of asserting the golden mean, of reconciling the gods and man without committing the author to either party.

But the modern ironist cannot count on a universally acceptable explanation of experience. Objectivity thus becomes a pose for being critical or satirical. Like satire, irony carries with it the standards of judgment and norms of conduct by which contrasts may be perceived; it includes the explanation of the irreconcilable elements which compose it—even when that explanation is merely an awareness that the elements are irreconcilable. That awareness implies, of course, that the ironist is himself a victim; it means not only (if the poet has any integrity in his work) that he cannot flee from his knowledge to assert his own explanation of experience, but also that he cannot, like the satirist, remain perfectly objective to apply his knowledge as an irrevocable standard of judgment. He cannot, humanely, criticize, without qualification, those who are not aware that God and man are irreconcilably opposed. In order, then, to describe the irony of a modern author and to judge the validity of the positive values he has to offer, one must determine the degree to which, under the pose of objectivity, his view of the world passively—if not actively—involves him in that irony. One must, further, apply that distinction—suggested in Henry James's Prefaces—between an "applied irony" that is "a campaign, of a sort, on behalf of something better . . . that blessedly, as is assumed, *might* be" and an "operative irony" which "implies and projects the possible other case—the case rich and edifying where the actuality is pretentious and vain," but which is "the 'moral' sense of a work of art" dependent upon "the amount of felt life concerned in producing it."

In general, the development of Ransom's irony may be described as a modification of "applied irony" or satiric objectivity, a modulation from his early ironic models—Hardy's *Satires of Circumstance*—

to a more personally realized view of the ironic contrasts in the world. I refer to the progress which extends from *Poems About God* to *Two Gentlemen in Bonds*. Ransom's latest work—poems like "Prelude to an Evening" and "Painted Head"—may be considered as the fruit of this development: commentaries of ironic inclusiveness, but expressed in a more impersonal and direct manner.

The irony of Ransom's earliest volume, *Poems About God*, is of this "circumstantial," or satirical, sort. The poet, in his own or an assumed voice, comments upon the irony of Fate: Nature, or common sense, persuades us to believe that events are in the main forseeable, that we shall find what we seek, that we need not expect our sense of the probable to be violated. But actually, the poet says, what happens is the unexpected, the unlooked for. "Under the Locusts," for instance, begins with the question: "What do old men say,/Sitting out of the sun?" Fate shares her knowledge with the experienced, who look about at the uncomprehending, and answer: "Dick's a sturdy little lad," but "Agues and rheumatic pains/Will fiddle on his bones." The poet simply records, in climactic sequence, the surprises which are apparent to a removed and knowing observer.

In the poem called "Grace," one finds perhaps the most interesting specimen of Ransom's early irony, for it presents, in primitive form, the essential character of his later irony. The poem relates the humiliating and mean death of a pious hired man. Like "Under the Locusts," its irony is external, between God and man; the poet simply observes, and records the contrast between desert—a gracious death—and the reward which actually constituted God's Grace—a miserable one:

> Who is it beams the merriest
> At killing a man, the laughing one?
> You are the one I nominate,
> God of the rivers of Babylon.

The verbal ironies of the poet are, in fact, more bitterly satiric here than in any of the other poems in the volume: the poet thinks "how he was saved/One day while ploughing in the corn"; and remembers the hired man's hymn, " 'There did I bury my sin and pride'," to scoff, "Sinful pride of a hired man!/Out of a hired woman born!"

> I thought of the prayers the fool had prayed
> To his God, and I was seeing red,
> When all of a sudden he gave a heave
> And then with shuddering—vomited!
> And God, who had just received full thanks
> For all his kindly daily bread,
> Now called it back again—perhaps
> To see that his birds of the air were fed.

But in making this irony deeper by thus emphasizing and widening the contrasts between desert and reward, the poet himself becomes involved in the situation. The irony is made less pure, the scorn of the hired man ameliorated. The objective observation of the willful acts of an unpredictable God leads the poet to an awareness of his own vulnerability, and to his open rebellion against them:

> If silence from the dead, I swore,
> There shall be cursing from the quick!
> But I began to vomit too,
> Cursing and vomit ever so thick;
> The dead lay down, and I did too,
> Two ashy idiots: take your pick!
> A little lower than angels he made us,
> (Hear his excellent rhetoric),
> A credit we were to him, half of us dead,
> The other half of us lying sick.

The sickness of the poet is not a detail which emphasizes his disgusted scorn of the hired man, but one which signifies that he too is a victim of God's will. The differences between "Grace" and Ransom's more mature work are obvious when one compares the ironic death of the hired man with those by "chills and fever," or—at the worst—by "foul subtraction," in the following poems. Nevertheless, the personal element in "Grace," Ransom's awareness of human limitations in general—his own as well as that of the protagonist of the poem—is a feature which distinguishes the "operative irony" of his later poems from the "applied" and more completely objective irony of his early "satires of circumstance."

The problem of the dissociated sensibility, which Robert Penn Warren has isolated as the chief concern of Ransom's poetry, has its expression, in the poems in *Chills and Fever* and *Two Gentle-men in Bonds,* in two general forms: as elegies and poems which show the perilous nature of life and beauty, and as poems about lovers which show the fragility of love. Throughout these poems there are conflicts, paradoxes which the heroes and heroines believe they can resolve, or struggle to make compatible, but which are actually irreconcilably and forever opposed. It is this contrast between wish and fulfilment, the ideal and the actual, which provides the materials of Ransom's irony. One thinks, for instance, of the "Spectral Lovers" who "go frozen asunder in fear," of the "Equilibrists," who "rigid as two painful stars" in "their torture of equilibrium," burn "with fierce love always to come near," yet are kept apart by "Honor." There is the "young Adam" of "Nocturne" who might, "if he had the heart and the head," for a furious bacchanal, lay aside his book, "flat and metaphysical"; and Miriam Tazewell, who, when she heard "the tempest bursting," went, "with heart full of the flowers," to weeping. And there are the innocents: children like the one who "would not be instructed in how deep / Was the forgetful kingdom of death"; and adults, like those in "Eclogue," who conclude that their innocence was a "dream," and might as well be "beneath ground as above."

In these poems, and in others, Ransom is first of all an objective spectator; and, abstracted from their contexts, these fragments are difficult to read without some suspicion of intended mockery. But in almost every poem, Ransom has a special sympathy for his deluded characters. That is because there is no solution to the problem in the poems; and insofar as the elements of the situation are irreconcilable, Ransom is subject to the same yearning and defeat as his characters.

"Blackberry Winter," the subject of which is the poet's inability to perform his nature, deals with Ransom's own predicament, and also indicates his knowledge of, and feelings for, the characters in all of his poems. The modern poet's insufficiency is attributed to the influence of science upon the world, and upon the poet himself. The life ("the breath of a girl" and "the music in the warrior's chambered ear") which once inspired poetry has been killed off by the abstractions and mechanizations of science: "I have listened, there is no one breathing here,/And all of the wars have dwindled since Troy fell." The poet is left with only the "Daughter of Heaven," who is "cold," and whose house is "garnished":

148 G. R. WASSERMAN

I have seen her often, she stood all night on the hill,
Fiercely the pale youth clambered to her, till—
Hoarsely, the rooster awakened him, footing the mould.

That is the irony which warrants the disillusioned tone of the
first stanza, and which, with its own rhetorical ironies—the "cigars"–
"stars" rhyme, and the use of "steam" (bodiless and vacuous) for
"smoke"—sets the tone of the poem:

If the lady hath any loveliness, let it die,
For being drunken with the steam of Cuban cigars,
I find no pungence in the odour of stars,
And all my music goes out of me on a sigh.

The first line of this stanza is in part directed against "the pale
youth"; it is the objective ironist applying the standard of judgment to the poet. But that cannot be the last word of a poet who
would still ply his own muse—even though it is out of season:

But still would I sing to my maidenly apple tree,
Before she has borne me a single apple of red;
The pictures of silver and apples of gold are dead;
But one more ripeneth yet maybe.

The opening line of the poem is also, then, the voice of a responsible poet, the expression of a personal attitude which warrants
the qualification of disillusion and futility.

To the degree that this poem is "personal," the modification of
the objectivity of the irony is accomplished at the expense of the
"pale youth," by the contrast between the vanity of his fierce efforts to clamber up the hill, and Ransom's own humble resignation
in the last stanza:

But still I will haunt beneath my apple-tree,
Heedful again to star-looks and wind-words,
Anxious for the flash of whether eyes or swords,
And hoping a little, a little, that either may be.

Nevertheless, the poet's purpose is not self-elevation; he is speaking for poets in general. And that is the principle I wish to establish. Ransom has a special sympathy for his deluded characters.
The fact that he knows they are deluded and they do not does

not make him satiric because it is only by perceiving their delusion that he realizes, by its inevitability, the vanity of his own efforts. The very elements which make the situations of Ransom's poems susceptible to objective and ironic mockery allow the softening of its effect with personal feeling.

The manner by which this complex attitude is maintained in "Blackberry Winter"—a shift in voice or point of view, or the telescoping of the objective observer into a knowing participator—is typical of Ransom's ironic method in other poems. "Janet Waking," a kind of mock tragedy with pathetic overtones, illustrates its more customary form in a dramatic poem. This work is constructed of two interrelated ironies: the incongruous juxtaposition of the serious and the trivial (the poet's exaggerated interest in the death of a little girl's pet hen); and that implied by the contrast between the title, "Janet Waking" (to reality), and her mistaken interpretation of that reality. The poet is removed from the situation, objectively recording the discrepancies—even when they produce an inappropriate joke ("the poor comb stood up straight/But Chucky did not").

In achieving this distance, or objectivity, Ransom becomes aware of deeper ironies in the situation. Chucky's death represents Janet's first encounter with reality. She had slept "beautifully" in innocence, "till it was deeply morning." Her refusal to be "instructed," then, is seen as the universal quandary of all men confronted by the irrational circumstances of nature. Ransom's revision of the second line of the third stanza ("Running across the world upon the grass") — originally "Running on little pink feet upon the grass"—suggests this effort to secure a more distanced and objective view, to warrant a more comprehensive and universal application of the irony.

But as the irony of the situation grows deeper, as the discrepancy between the action and the standard of judgment which the poet, until now, has set beside it widens, the tone of the poem changes:

> So there was Janet
> Kneeling on the wet grass, crying her brown hen
> (Translated far beyond the daughters of men)
> To rise and walk upon it.

The irony of the parenthesis, evoking both the heroic glory and the religious solemnity of death, carries on the mocking exaggeration of the poet; but Janet's prayer for a miracle (notice that she is "kneeling"), suspended as it is before and after these ironic echoes, indicates the inadequacy of orthodox norms. She turned to "us"— the poet's first and only personal reference in the poem—and "implored": " 'Wake her from her sleep.' "

My double quotes, here, are significant. Ransom distinguishes nicely between his mockery and his sympathy! Janet has not deluded herself into believing that her experience is all a bad dream; she simply cannot fathom the fact of death, "And would not be instructed in how deep/Was the forgetful kingdom of death." The lines have become infused with the poet's personal feeling. The phrase, "forgetful kingdom of death," is not an accusation of the fraility of human love and faithfulness, but the expression of comforting solace. What had seemed, then, to be the objective reporting of a disinterested and amused spectator, is actually the controlled expression of a sympathizer.

The conflicts in Ransom's poems, then, are variations on the struggle between the human and the non-human forces in life. And, as a responsible human being himself, Ransom cannot, as a rule, help siding with the human forces, even though he realizes that their efforts are futile and frequently laughable, and that the rational and irrational are irreconcilable in existence. Nevertheless, his patience with some of these efforts is occasionally tried—particularly in the instance of a character who, unlike Janet, willfully distorts the circumstances of reality in order to assert his own explanation of experience.

"Miriam Tazewell" will serve as an example of the rather perilous tension to which Ransom's irony may be put—perilous, because the balance of Ransom's feelings for the character tends to fall on the common-sense or actual side rather than on the ideal side. The subject of the poem is the ironic effect of the discrepancy between an ideal world and the natural world, between Miriam's romantic dream of a universal feeling of pity for her storm-ruined garden, and the actual callousness of "the regular stars . . . busily on their courses":

> When Miriam Tazewell heard the tempest bursting,
> And his wrathy whips across the sky drawn crackling,
> She stuffed her ears for fright like a young thing,
> And with heart full of the flowers, went to weeping.

Here the foolishly romantic attempt of Miriam to make the real
world conform to her ideal is emphasized by the satiric phrases,
"like a young thing," and "heart full of the flowers." In the second
stanza, the poet politely reproves her by explaining that such dis-
asters are only the ways of the world. But in addressing Miriam
directly by name, he does so with a remarkable softening of tone:

> But the earth shook dry his old back in good season,
> He had weathered storms that drenched him deep as this one,
> And the sun, Miriam, ascended to his dominion,
> The storm was withered against his empyrean.

The direct address of Miriam is a reinforcement of the poet's
point of view. We have a sense of assurance that he feels responsible
for her, that he is quietly reasoning with her to be resigned to the
situation. But of course Miriam does not hear him; they are not
even talking together. The name is spoken out of hearing distance,
further removed, indeed, from the entire situation of Miriam's garden. There is the sense that the poet has been able to secure a more
exterior point of view in order to gain a wider perspective. The
situation becomes more transparent, revealing a deeper irony than
that resulting from the mere contrast between Miriam's expectation
and fulfillment. We see by the terms in which the affairs of the
world are recounted—terms of her own romantic interpretation of
the world—that she is in part the cause of her excessive grief: she
is incensed that "some bridals" were calendared, and that "the birds
demurely sang in the bitten poplars." To Miriam, the world is not
merely callous; it has become wanton. The deflowering of her lawn
by the storm is the deflowering of her innocence by experience:

> To Miriam Tazewell the whole world was villain,
> To prosper when the fragile babes were fallen;
> The principle of the beast was low and masculine!
> For weeks she went untidy, she went sullen.

Miriam is a romantic ironist; she attempts to escape the realities
of the world by willful self-deception. But Ransom does not express
his criticism of her by means of unmasked irony. Instead, he man-
ages the gentle reproof of the second stanza which sincerely ac-
knowledges the hardness of the real world; and, moreover, begins

the calendar of worldly affairs in the poem with an item the tone of which causes one almost to forgive Miriam her self-indulgence:

The spring transpired in that year with no flowers.

It is this softening property of Ransom's irony, the modification of his objective and knowing attitude toward characters and situations in the poems, that I particularly wish to point out in this essay, for, although the personal quality of Ransom's poetry has frequently been recognized, it has usually been considered as a function of the poetry which opposes the irony, rather than as a function of the irony itself. Ransom's critics have emphasized the affinity of his irony to metaphysical wit, its ability of stiffening "soft" subjects rather than softening stiff ones. The attention given to Ransom's poems on the death of children is indicative of this tendency. It is of course true that a part of the irony of "Bells for John Whiteside's Daughter" and "Dead Boy" depends upon the contrast between the stock response to the subject and Ransom's attitude toward it. The latter poem, for instance, begins with an objective view of "a boy not beautiful, nor good, nor clever,"

A black cloud full of storms too hot for keeping,
A sword beneath his mother's heart . . .

But the poet's attitude toward the boy is not left at that; nor, I maintain, is it modified merely by the rhetoric of the poem. The awareness of an irony that is deeper than the contrasts between certain words is inevitable—as I have already indicated—to Ransom's peculiar position as ironist. The poet's attitude is qualified and humanized by the boy's relationship to something for which the poet feels a more tender, although controlled, nostalgia, "a noble house":

The first-fruits, saith the Preacher, the Lord hath taken;
But this was the old tree's late branch wrenched away.

And supporting the modification of this irony—the irony dependent upon the contrast between "first-fruits" and "late branch"—is the shift in point of view implied in the first line of the third stanza ("A pig with a pasty face, so I had said"), from that implied in the opening stanza:

The little cousin is dead, by foul subtraction,
A green bough from Virginia's aged tree,
And none of the county kin like the transaction,
Nor some of the world of outer dark, like me.

It is the closeness of his attention, his objectivity, in the third stanza, which undercuts the sentimentality of the situation and criticizes the "muttering low" of the "elder men" on "the wide flag porch" as "friendly waste of breath." But it is the distancing of the first stanza which permits him safely to subject this irony to his personal feeling, to reconsider, in a sense, not "the elder men" as "foolish," but those outside "neighbors" for whom the boy was "pale and little," and finally to extend to the former one note of sincere, but controlled, sympathy: "Their hearts are hurt with a deep dynastic wound."

The effect of the irony in the poems just mentioned—modified as it is by structural factors like the manipulation of point of view—does more, then, than make us aware of the irreconcilable contrasts which are opposed in them. Because we are able to see both sides of the situation, we are made to feel some sympathy for the effort of reconciliation, however impossible it is of attainment. By balancing one view against the other, we see the partial validity of both. That is one way by which irony arrives at truth. Another way is by making the reader ironically aware of human limitations by indicating the inadequacy of an apparent reconciliation of opposed elements in a conflict. Here, we may suspect, Ransom might be less sympathetic with his characters, for in resigning themselves to an inadequate reconciliation of both extremes of their predicament, they have in fact ceased to struggle to attain either of them:

Ah, the strict lovers, they are ruined now!
I cried in anger.

This is the poet's remonstrance to "The Equilibrists," the lovers who have tried to resolve the conflicts between the intellect and emotion, head (the "grey doves from the officious tower" which cry "Honor") and body (the "lilies," "beseeching him to take"). Their resolution is, however, "their torture of equilibrium . . . rigid as two stars, and twirled":

> They burned with fierce love always to come near,
> But Honor beat them back and kept them clear.

One might describe this ironic triumph in the terms with which William James referred to Santayana's dualistic philosophy—a "perfection of rottenness." Yet the poet's anger subsides; he becomes resigned to the lovers' dilemma. "Man" has this decision to make:

> Would you ascend to Heaven and bodiless dwell?
> Or take your bodies honorless to Hell?
>
> In Heaven . . .?
> Your male and female tissue sweetly shaped
> Sublimed away, and furious blood escaped.
>
> Great lovers lie in Hell . . .
> . . . . .
> Stuprate, they rend each other when they kiss;
> The pieces kiss again—no end to this.

The only alternative which is logically possible—the integration of thought and feeling—is, in the lovers' existence, impossible. Thus, the poet's epitaph for their tomb:

> Equilibrists lie here; stranger, tread light;
> . . . . .
> Let them lie perilous and beautiful.

I have cited here only a few examples of Ransom's characteristic irony, and spoken specifically of only one means—the manipulation of point of view—by which that irony is achieved in the poems. In each instance, however, the ironic contrast implicit in the subject of the poem, or the poet's vision of the tension existing in this contrast, is to some extent modified by the personal feeling of the poet. Ransom's awareness of his own complicity, as a citizen, in the predicament with which, as a poet, he is concerned—the awareness to which Robert Penn Warren referred as the "ethical center" which kept Ransom from becoming enamored of the effect of irony as a means of escape from reality—keeps him also from that positive, or practical, purpose of objective irony, satire. Rather, the "ethical center" is the reference of the poems' insights.

In effect, then, Ransom's irony bears a resemblance to Socratic irony; it accepts human limitations in order to arrive at truth.

In this respect too, it bears a resemblance to that form of irony with which the name of Friedrich Schlegel is associated. Schlegelian irony—to distinguish this concept from the German variants of "romantic irony" and from Tate's special sense of that term—designates the objectivity of a literary work which nevertheless reveals the subjective qualities of its writer. It is the most objective work, according to Schlegel, which most adequately reveals the essential subjective qualities of the author—his creative power and his breadth of wisdom. Such an author is at once creator and observer.

Because the development of this concept may throw some light on the distinction I wish to make here, I shall briefly summarize Alfred Lussky's discussion of if.* Schlegel early advocated imitation of the Greeks as the only means of creating literature of any importance. His study led him to the belief that nothing but "complete objectivity" characterized all Greek literature, or was responsible for its perfection. Objectivity became for him the standard of all great literary art. Schlegel, therefore, felt that he could not approve of modern poetry because of its lack of objectivity. The most persistent quality which he found in this poetry, the most typically modern trait, he termed *das Interessante,* a quality which Mr. Lussky defines as that of the "author's immanence" in his production, and which Schlegel condemned for its lack of objectivity. As the antithesis of "objective," however, *interessante* is not to be identified with "subjective." Schlegel considered Shakespeare the greatest writer since the Greeks and the chief representative of the moderns because he revealed to the greatest extent *das Interessante.* Yet from a certain point of view, he could also regard him as objective as the Greeks. The dilemma to which these observations logically led was solved by an analogical argument from religion. Schlegel formulated the proportion: as God is to His creation, so the great modern artist is to his literary creation; both creations are perfectly objective, their creators being both utterly detached from their productions; yet, both creations are also self-revelations of their creators. The concept of irony in the reasoning consists in this: what appears as complete objectivity on the part of the artist toward his creation, is in fact a vehicle for the purpose of revealing his personality. There is thus a contrast between appearance and reality.

*Alfred Lussky, *Tieck's Romantic Irony* (Chapel Hill, 1932), 45–92. *See also* Georg Brandes, *Main Currents in Nineteenth Century Literature,* II, 71–72. I am indebted to Professor Austin Warren for the suggestion that Ransom's irony is similar to Schlegelian irony.

JOHN RANSOM'S CRUELL BATTLE

Louis D. Rubin, Jr.

To expect Allen Tate's and Robert Penn Warren's poems to be much influenced by Ransom's is like expecting two nightmares to be influenced by a daydream," Randall Jarrell has written.* The opinion represents a rather widespread attitude toward Ransom's poetry. Critics recognize the firmness in the poetry, but they tend to dwell on the gentility. For Robert Lowell, Ransom's best poems "have the magic, which Matthew Arnold esteemed and called *Celtic*, and which, whatever it is, art must never lack, if it desires to delight." Delmore Schwartz refers to Ransom's "mockery and playfulness." For Isabel Gamble, Ransom's "imaginary kingdom, like that of another civilized man, E. M. Forster, is Love." Cleanth Brooks notes his "teasing whimsy," his "good-humored self-deprecation." Marshall McLuhan remarks his "light poise."

All these attributes are true, and yet there is the danger that Mr. Ransom is being turned into a Good Grey Poet, in whose presence one treads lightly. Insofar as this attitude involves a proper recognition of the urbanity and hard-wrought decorum of Ransom's poetry, it is appropriate. But insofar as it engenders an attitude of sentimentality and fond reverence, it impedes a proper awareness of the essential quality in Ransom that makes the poems so peculiarly effective. The characterization of Ransom as being essentially a poet

---

*This essay originally appeared in *Shenandoah*, IX (Winter, 1958), 23–35.

of sweetness and light is misleading. It obscures the underlying mood of the poems: terror and savagery, running throughout his poetry, sending a chill along the reader's backbone. Masked by urbanity, accented by the seeming contradiction of whimsical irony, its very elusive, teasing status makes it all the more frightening and effective.

Throughout the poems of John Crowe Ransom is the theme of death—savage, cruel, terrible. There is an imagery of violence, mocking the gentleness and playfulness. Take the early poem entitled "Miriam Tazewell," for example. An old maid "with heart full of the flowers" goes out into her garden after a storm. She walks forth

> . . . with skirts kilted
> To see in the strong sun her lawn deflowered,
> Her tulip, iris, peony strung and pelted,
> Pots of geranium spilled and the stalks naked.

The gentleness of this poem consists of being playfully mocking while the old maid confronts what to her is utter violence and destruction. "For weeks she went untidy, she went sullen," we are informed. It is a small death; we are amused; but it is not a pretty poem.

The deaths are not always so minor. Much of the imagery is bloody and barbarous. In "Necrological" the friar, after having "scourged his limbs," observes the bodies on a battlefield:

> Not all were white; some gory and fabulous
> Whom the sword had pierced and then the grey wolf eaten;
> But the brother reasoned that heroes' flesh was thus,
> Flesh falls, and the postured bones lie weather-beaten.

Nearby a dead horse and rider lie: "the great beast had spilled there his little brain,/And the little groin of the knight was spilled by a stone." The friar sits "lost in a vast surmise" at the carnage, "And so still that he likened himself unto those dead/Whom the kites of Heaven solicited with sweet cries."

A slaughter is also in prospect in "Armageddon":

> His trump recalls his own to right opinions,
> With scourge they mortify their carnal selves,

With stone they whet the ax-heads on the helves
And seek the Prince Beelzebub and minions.

Similarly "Judith of Bethulia" waylays the invader in his tent, after
which the hosts of the Lord

. . . smote them hiding in our vineyards, barns, annexes
And now their white bones clutter the holes of foxes,
And the chieftain's head, with grinning sockets, and
    varnished—
Is it hung in the sky, with a hideous epitaphy?
No, the woman keeps the trophy.

Another battle poem, "Puncture," describes a wounded soldier with
a gash "which bled upon the ground." "But they must have struck your
side," a comrade expostulates; "It must be looked at/And mended."
"No, it's an old puncture . . ./Which takes to bleeding sometimes,"
the soldier says; "Go work on the corpses if you wish,/Prop their heads
up again, wrap their bones in,/For they were good pious men."

The idea of death coming to little children is a theme of several Ransom poems. In "Dead Boy" the family gathers about the
corpse of a dead child, "the little man quite dead." The frequently
anthologized "Bells for John Whiteside's Daughter" depicts a little
girl "lying so primly propped." In "Janet Waking" it is not the
child who dies, but a pet chicken.

It scarcely bled,
But how exceedingly

And purply did the knot
Swell with the venom and communicate
Its rigor! Now the poor comb stood up straight
But Chucky did not.

Ransom can show horror and despair lurking in such domestic
situations just as easily as on a battlefield. In "Two in August" he
remarks of a husband and wife who have quarreled that it "is not
well understood,/. . . why two entities grown almost one/Should rend
and murder trying to get undone,/With individual tigers in their
blood." Ladies of loveliness and grace are reminded in "Blue Girls"
of "a lady with a terrible tongue,/Blear eyes fallen from blue,/All her

perfections tarnished. . . ." Then there are the two feuding women who confront each other at a tea, where they exchange only freezing formalities. Ransom likens them to ships: "So seaworthy one felt they could not sink;/Still there was a tremor shook them, I should think,/ Beautiful timbers fit for storm and sport/And unto miserly merchant hulks converted" ("Good Ships"). Lovers in "The Equilibrists" are reminded of Heaven where "no marriage is,/No white flesh to your lecheries,/Your male and female tissue sweetly shaped/Sublimed away, and furious blood escaped." Great lovers, however, "lie in Hell, the stubborn ones/Infatuate of the flesh upon the bones;/Stuprate, they rend each other when they kiss,/The pieces kiss again, no end to this." Finally there is the happy family circle of "Prelude to an Evening," with its picture of the man come home from the office:

> Do not enforce the tired wolf
> Dragging his infected wound homeward
> To sit tonight with the warm children
> Naming the pretty kings of France.

Ransom spies out the misery in any situation and comments upon it. Human endeavor may mask its distresses in politeness, but the agony is there all the same. In "Address to the Scholars of New England" he summarizes the ideally platonic New England cultural flowering, where

> Perfect was the witch floundering in water,
> The blasphemer that spraddled in the stocks,
> The woman branded with her sin, the whales
> Of ocean taken with a psalmer's sword,
> The British tea infusing the bay's water.

In the poem "Dog" he presents a pleasant rustic scene in which a small dog taunts a bull into helpless rage, whereupon along comes the farmer whose "stick and stone and curse rain upon the brute/That pipped his bull of gentle pedigree." The dog sulks to his kennel, wherein may be discerned "two red eyes that stare like coals." In another country poem three theological villagers boast of the prowess of their pets. One brags of a hound: "Bring your bristled village curs/ To try his fang and tooth, sweet sirs!/He will rend them, he is savage,/ Thinking nothing but to ravage. . . ." Another owns an elephant: "Pile his burden to the skies,/Loose a pestilence of flies,/Foot him in the quick morass" . . . the elephant will not be daunted. The third has a lamb:

> Have ye a lion, ounce, or scourge,
> Or any beast of dainty gorge?
> Agnus lays his tender youth
> Between the very enemy's mouth,
> And though he sniff his delicate meat
> He may not bruise that flesh nor eat,
> He may not rend him limb from limb
> If Agnus do but bleat on him.

One of Ransom's most savage poems is that entitled "Painted Head," which has to do with the perils of Platonic cerebration as compared with the Aristotelian notion of wholeness. Ransom sweetly depicts his Platonist adversaries as resembling a head severed from the body. This is their punishment for their intellectual sins, and they must now make

> . . . repentance in an unlovely head
> For having vinegarly traduced the flesh
> Till, the hurt flesh recusing, the hard egg
> Is shrunken to its own deathlike surface.

All of this—and there is much more of it—seems to me far removed from the picture of a good grey poet making pleasant little ironies about life. Rather the true picture is of an artist appalled by and obsessed with the unhappiness of the human situation, who uses gentility and decorum in order to heighten the incongruity of the savage reality imbedded in the civilized patterns.

It is not enough merely to point out that both these elements exist in Ransom's poems. They are not only there; they are masterfully played off against each other to achieve the utmost poetic effect. Ransom works with consummate skill upon his reader's sensibility, first stating the violent motif, then denying it as it were with his language, then stating it again, only to seem to take it all back, and so on. The result is a precarious balance, a hovering effect that intensifies the suspense.

Precisely how this is achieved can be demonstrated by an examination of a well-known Ransom poem, "Captain Carpenter." The Captain, we note at once, is a man of gentility and courtliness. He rises up of a morning, he puts on his pistols, he goes riding out in the best chivalric fashion. The opening lines seem merrily archaic:

> Captain Carpenter rose up in his prime
> Put on his pistols and went riding out
> But had got wellnigh nowhere at that time
> Till he fell in with ladies in a rout.

There is a ballad flavor to the lines; we expect something pleasingly whimsical. Instead, however,

> It was a pretty lady and all her train
> That played with him so sweetly but before
> An hour she'd taken a sword with all her main
> And twined him of his nose for evermore.

The last two lines mar the pleasant soiree. In tones of the utmost courtliness, Ransom informs us that the so gentle lady has "twined him of his nose for evermore." The language is so quaint, so informal, yet the deed described is anything but quaint. Is it all a comedy, a fantasy? We read on to see:

> Captain Carpenter mounted up one day
> And rode straightway into a stranger rogue
> That looked unchristian but be that as may
> The Captain did not wait upon prologue.
>
> But drew upon him out of his great heart
> The other swung against him with a club
> And cracked his two legs at the shinny part
> And let him roll and stick like any tub.

Here again the good captain's knightly demeanor is abused. His stout and chivalric sword is up against the unglamorous, prosaic club of the stranger, who instead of meeting the captain in approved cavalier combat swings at him and fractures both his legs, so that the dignified captain rolls and sticks "like any tub." This time the violence is stronger, something less like jolly good fun.

Next the captain attempts to take on the witch-wife of Satan as all good knights would be expected to do:

Their strokes and counters whistled in the wind
I wish he had delivered half his blows
But where she should have made off like a hind
The bitch bit off his arms at the elbows.

The doughty captain again falls into the fray in gentlemanly fashion, but instead of routing the wicked witch, who by all the laws of romance should have fled, he has his arms severed at the elbows by "the bitch." Ransom's word choice is particularly clever here. Previously he had termed Satan's wife a she-wolf, so that in calling her "the bitch" he plays both upon the literal and the colloquial meanings of the word. The modern reader instinctively makes the colloquial reading first, of course, yet the literal meaning is in strict usage as well. Not only in the word play, but in the diction of the entire stanza Ransom apparently denies the violence its full horror by using the archaic vocabulary, yet the cumulative effect renders it the more sinister.

The same technique is repeated in the stanza that follows:

And Captain Carpenter parted with his ears
To a black devil that used him in this wise
O Jesus ere his threescore and ten years
Another had plucked out his sweet blue eyes.

The amputation of the Captain's ears by a black devil—a Moor? a Negro? the archaic texture varies the classical and Southern colloquial readings most skillfully—is pictured in a particularly blood-less fashion: "parted with his ears" . . . "used him in this wise." The abrupt realism of the verb phrase "plucked out" is almost denied by the absurdity of the adjectives: "sweet blue eyes."

The poem moves toward its climax with the tension being built up between the quaint, storybook diction and the savage reality of the events chronicled. Finally the captain, armless, legs broken, blind, minus ears and sweet blue eyes, staggers out to sound still another challenge: "I heard him asking in the grimmest tone/If any enemy yet there was to fight"; whereupon "the neatest knave that ever was seen/Stepping in perfume from his lady's bower" straightaway "put on his merry mien" and attacked the Captain once more.

I would not knock old fellows in the dust
But there lay Captain Carpenter on his back

His weapons were the old heart in his bust
And a blade shook between rotten teeth alack.

The rogue in scarlet and gray soon knew his mind
He wished to get his trophy and depart;
With gentle apology and touch refined
He pierced him and produced the captain's heart.

Now even the verb is remotely visual or gory; the heart is merely "produced." In attitude of purest chivalry and in language of impeccable taste, Captain Carpenter's heart is cut out. "God's mercy rest on Captain Carpenter now," Ransom eulogizes; ". . . an honest gentleman/Citizen husband soldier and scholar enow. . . ." "But God's deep curses follow after those," he continues, "that shore him of his goodly nose and ears, . . ." Only in the last stanza is the decorum breached, and the poem made to state in unequivocally realistic terms what has happened:

The curse of hell upon the sleek upstart
Who got the Captain finally on his back
And took the red red vitals of his heart
And made the kites to whet their beaks clack clack.

Never is Ransom's mastery of his idiom more strikingly demonstrated than in that final stanza. He still retains the trappings of the antique diction, the ballad form: "The curse of hell upon," "the red red vitals," "made the kites to whet their beaks." But now the words are at the same time proper and bloody, dramatizing the action in visual images. The previous tension produced by the contradiction between the bloodless language and the violent content has been resolved, in words that retain their consistent archaic tone and yet at the last commit the poem definitely on the side of the savagery. The last line, with its harsh, onomatopoeic conclusion, is a triumph of meaningful form, ringing down the curtain on the tragedy of Captain Carpenter, in pure jangling cacophonous snapping.

At the last, then, the quaint formality of the poem's tone has served to intensify and climax the impact of the horror depicted therein. The terror is made possible by the decorum. Ironically the poet maintains his distance to the last, staying aloof in diction from his subject matter, yet committing the poem. Ransom's use of the archaic ballad form, at the end when his words finally picture as well as state the full terror of the action, provides an effective counterpoint of formality to a most startling and unrestrained incident.

A more colloquial, subjective diction could scarcely have made the story of Captain Carpenter's "cruell battle" so terrifying. It was the mannered objectivity of the narration that provided a structural rigidity, a contained medium upon which the gory tale could be displayed to best effect. Thus the ironic, detached gentility of John Ransom's style, far from masking or gentling the blood-and-guts content, only emphasizes it. The total effect of "Captain Carpenter" is not one of a daydream, a gentle reverie. It is rather an urbane contemplation of uncivilized, savage aspects of human experience.

The violence of Ransom's poetry brings inevitably to mind the violence in the work of other of his Southern contemporaries. One finds it in Tate's and Warren's poetry as well, but with a significant difference. Terror, horror, blood, and gore run through the poems of all three men. The difference is in the use made of such things. With Tate and with Warren the elements of violence are directly stated, for shock effect, in violent images. A passage from Tate's "Ode to the Confederate Dead" illustrates this:

> What shall we say who count our days and bow
> Our heads with a commemorial woe
> In the ribboned coats of grim felicity,
> What shall we say to the bones, unclean,
> Whose verdurous anonymity will grow?
> The ragged arms, the ragged heads and eyes
> Lost in these acres of the insane green?

These are powerful, arresting lines, and the violence is skillfully used for its shock value. The suppressed force of the image of the man bowing his head in grim felicity, followed by the explosive suddenness of "bones, unclean," brings the reader up sharply, and it is succeeded by the vividness of the ragged arms, heads, and eyes and capped by the adjective "insane," which in the context is devastating in its very abstraction.

With Ransom, however, the violence is masked, made to contrast at all times with resilient irony and gentility. It is never directly and baldly experienced; instead Ransom plays masterfully upon the reader's sensibilities with a violence accompanied by the denial of violence. The result is the precarious balance, the hovering effect that tends to exaggerate both the violence and the gentility without ever quite committing itself to one or the other.

I am not attempting to maintain that the presence of violent elements in Ransom's poetry should be surprising. One encounters it in all the modern Southern writers. The Southerners, as Herbert Marshall McLuhan has noted, exhibit in their work an acute awareness of evil, and an utter unwillingness to gloss over or ignore it. It is rendered the more startling because it is a personal, experienced violence, not an abstract, meaningless viciousness. Erupting as it does out of a strong social pattern, its sudden appearance is so much the more startling, direct. One of the most horrifying scenes in Faulkner's *Absalom, Absalom!*, for example, is that in which Sutpen engages for pleasure in fisticuffs with his slaves. The horror is immeasurably enhanced by the fact that it is *Sutpen,* the lord of Sutpen's Hundred, gentleman and would-be founder of a dynasty, who does this. And it is not simply that he fights; he fights with his *Negro Slaves.* Nothing could be more directly contrary to the social patterns of the community in which he resides. His family, his chronicler, and the reader are appalled. The violence comes to mock and shatter a formalized social design.

But Faulkner is Faulkner, and Ransom is Ransom; what is there that would lead this urbane, gentle professor, born of a ministerial family in Tennessee, to begin in his thirties to write poetry so full of violence and blood?

That part of a writer's attitude which can be attributed to environment and history might, I think, provide part of the solution. For like his fellow writers of the Southern literary renascence, he was during his "formative years" witness to a change from one way of life to another. Around him the South, which had been rural and agrarian and a place of belief in the so-called traditional values, was changing in the twentieth century into the New South, with vastly different standards of value. The old concepts were being challenged by modernity. At Vanderbilt University Ransom came as a student into contact with the New South represented by the busy business community of Nashville, and with the philosophy of Progress as exemplified by such men as James A. Kirkland and Edwin Mims. Here, for the minister's son from Tennessee, was an intellectual climate not only different from but even at loggerheads with that of the rural Tennessee from which he came. Afterwards came a stay in England, as a Rhodes Scholar. And then the First World War, and the idealism and belief in progress and goodness was confronted with trench warfare. The shock of the war, the subsequent upsurge of materialism and "Progress" in the South; above all, change, and the conflict of loyalties and beliefs— Ransom too experienced these, just as his fellow Southern writers of the renascence did.

"Mad Ireland hurt you into poetry," W. H. Auden has remarked of William Butler Yeats, and one is inclined to say the same of the twentieth-century South and the writers it produced. Whatever it was, suddenly the young Southern poets and novelists began producing their stories and poems in undreamed-of profusion, and through their work the strain of violence, erupting in an otherwise tranquil social pattern, runs continually.

John Ransom was a product of those times, and he was older by a few years than his fellow Nashville poets, and perhaps the change seemed sharpest of all to him as he looked around him in the Nashville of the early 1920's.

At any rate, there is in Ransom's work this precarious set-to of violence and order, savagery and courtliness. The urbane diction contrasts with the bloody happenings.

Perhaps the poem entitled "Armageddon" may help to explain it all. Ransom describes the meeting of Christ and Antichrist on the plain. Instead of doing battle, they greet each other most courteously, loath to fight: "Originally they were one brotherhood;/There stood the white pavilion on the hill." They attempt to settle their dispute in honorable truce, and each accommodates the other in fellowship. They feast, and drink together:

> At wassail Antichrist would pitch the strain
> For unison of all the retinue;
> Christ beat the time, and hummed a stave or two,
> But did not say the words, which were profane.
>
> . . . .
>
> And so the Wolf said Brother to the Lamb,
> The True Heir keeping with the poor Impostor,
> The rubric and the holy paternoster
> Were jangled strangely with the dithyramb.

It is inevitable in reading "Armageddon" that one thinks of Ransom's book *God Without Thunder*. This work assailed the modern-day corruption and watering-down of God into an amiable Yea-Saying abstraction. Science in particular was held responsible for the glorification of the New Testament God of Love and the dwindling away of the Old Testament God of Wrath. God, Ransom contended, had been civilized into a meaningless love symbol. What was needed, he contended, was a return to a God of thunder and awe and fear, the worship of Whom would cast man into his old position of essential dependence upon and humility before the inscrutability of nature. The intellectual God-abstraction of modern times, he declared, was the product of a wrong relationship of man to nature.

Thus "Armageddon" shows Christ become tamed and urbane, forgetting his old Revelatory mission at the place of settlement with Antichrist, turning instead to intellectual hair-splitting, good fellowship, vapid tolerance, and the like. Christ becomes a modern, in other words.

Finally, however, one old grey-beard is so distressed that he protests to Christ, whereupon Christ realizes what has been going on:

> Christ shed unmannerly his devil's pelf,
> Took ashes from the hearth and smeared himself,
> Called for his smock and jennet as before.
>
> His trump recalls his own to right opinions,
> With scourge they mortify their carnal selves,
> With stone they whet the ax-heads on the helves
> And seek the Prince Beelzebub and minions.

Christ and his followers thus reject the amiable tolerance of sin and the spineless pleasantries of modernity, and renew their faith in the Old Testament God of Wrath. Confronted with this, Antichrist's hosts "made songs of innocence and no bloodshed." The prospect of fighting and blood disturbs Antichrist: " 'These Armageddons weary me much,' he said."

Thus "Armageddon" is a poem of modernity sampled and finally rejected, and of a return to old fundamentals. It is an affirmation of the need for belief in the traditional verities, in the hard consciousness of good and evil hidden by the moderns under a civilized veneer of tolerance and pleasantries.

It is this theme that seems to underlie all Ransom's poetry. The poems are those of a modern man, written in a style both learned and amiable, who has become aware of the savagery and violence of life hitherto glossed over by his urbane intellectual contemporaries. Far from the gentle daydream, the poems are those of a nightmare indeed—modern man confronting evil. Randall Jarrell writes of Ransom that "he has written poems that are perfectly realized and occasionally almost perfect—poems that the hypothetical generations of the future will be reading page by page with Wyatt, Campion, Marvell, and Mother Goose." Perhaps unwittingly, Jarrell has given us the clue; here indeed is some of that curious mixture of childlike nonsense fantasy and curious horror that one finds in the Mother Goose book. It is with the clear eye of the child that Ransom views experience. He does not gloss over its undesirable aspects with a sophisticated veneer. And yet his verse is sophisticated, urbane, on the surface at least. It is an odd interplay of one upon the other, a poetry of antitheses. The excitement comes from the tension growing out of the gentleness and the horror working on each other. Like his own Captain Carpenter, Ransom the poet confronts with chivalric decorum the savagery beneath the artificialities of our time. With poise, with irony, with wit, the urbane modern looks steadily at the yawning precipice below.

JOHN CROWE RANSOM AS ECONOMIST

Kelsie B. Harder

Three years ago, there was published a little volume called *Poems and Essays*, by John Crowe Ransom (Vintage Press paperbacks).* And this is my basis for an examination of Mr. Ransom as an economist.

The poems are good ones, ironic, modern only in the sense that they are in traditional meters and treat traditional themes, a trifle better, it seems to me, than Mr. Randall Jarrell's judgment that they are "doggerel." Anyway, the poems are not recent ones, and so far as I can determine they are not revisions; the commas haven't been moved. One critic said that Mr. Ransom would reflect on and contemplate a verse twenty years, and then decide that a comma is needed. The comma then is meticulously inserted, as if with a sort of ritual.

Really, no one can accuse Mr. Ransom of haste. I like to think of this slow, careful, contemplative way of Ransom's as a lingering Southern habit: no need to rush! There'll be time for revisions of revisions. This may sound quaint in this year of sputniks and social engineers, but the method does the job eventually in a workmanlike, humane way, even if to some minds it is anachronistic, stubborn, culture-lagging, and so on to more extreme vulgarisms. I have a suspicion, however, that a comma is just about as important to a *good* poet as a fancy differential equation is to an average statistician working on a set in marginal probability.

*This essay originally appeared in *Modern Age*, II (Fall, 1958) , 389-93.

The essays are well-selected ("by the author," says the blurb) prose continuations of the aesthetic ideas first presented in the poems. The commas are not so important here. These essays move with dignity through the chaos of modern critics' night where sailing is not always smooth and where towers of dark purple prose obscure the beautiful aesthetic path. Admittedly, these essays lend credence to the belief that Mr. Ransom is a giant among critics. I hesitate to say that he is a New Critic, except in the sense that he is a contemporary critic. Ransom is credited with tagging some new critics as new, and as tagging a certain type of intellectual exercise and exegesis as new criticism. We are all acquainted with that. But what we sometimes do not realize is that Ransom's tag is not necessarily a license, even though the two are synonymous in Midland dialects. Ransom's use of "new" is ironic, and his irony backfired, for he has been included by the popular critical mind in the group of "new" critics.

Ransom's critical method, if I may be pardoned for using "method" in its neologistic sense, is an old one, one that says, "Let's read the poem, not about it and its author." The statement is heard more and more in pedagogic circles. Certainly his critical method has spawned (the figure is unfair, but manifestly true) many imitators among the younger apostles of the critical creed. This is well and good. Needless to say, many of us have taken second looks at poems after being provoked by an explication by such students of the caliber of Brooks, Warren, and Tate. We have been the better for it. We have learned that a good poem is more than a document, more than a fragment of a philosophical scheme, more than a historical fact—it is the fact itself. It is as universal as all get-out, and as concrete as a metaphor.

Even so, I missed something in these essays. What I missed, I soon realized, was an essay or two from Ransom's economist period, dating I would say from 1928 when Ransom published "The South—Old or New?" in the *Sewanee Review,* XXVI (April, 1928), to 1937, when he left Vanderbilt University to found the *Kenyon Review* at Kenyon College. Although primarily a poet from 1917 to 1927, he did publish a few bits of criticism in some literary magazines and in *The Fugitive,* the herald for one of the more profound literary renaissances in American literature. During the later years, 1928 to 1937, in which he was an economic polemicist, Ransom developed his critical sensibility and sharpened a pointed prose style that served him in good stead when he turned to literary criticism. Ransom's very characteristic personal idiom employs sharp and even shocking associations of the colloquial and the pedantic. Moreover, he matured under fire during the ideational battle of the 1930's, taking on such stalwarts as V. F. Calverton, Aubrey Starke, William S. Knickerbocker, H. L. Mencken, as well as a host of wild-eyed zealots. It is this aspect of Ransom's career that I wish to examine briefly here to clarify, I hope, some salient points that appear in his subsequent criticism and poetic theory, taking as my cue and my outline Ransom's statement that "the reasonableness of regionalism refers first to its economic, and second to its aesthetic." I must add that the organization of the paper does not do justice to the clarity and style of Mr. Ransom's essays. I also take responsibility for the interpretation—or misinterpretation.

Ransom's position was that of a conservative (some would say "reactionary")—a Southern agrarian. Pushed for a definition, he wrote in one essay, "There are evidently varieties of agrarians. There are the hard and the soft; there are the thoroughgoing and those up to a certain point; the philosophic and the economic; the Southern and the general; the open and the secret; the baptized and the unbaptized." The agrarian position is well defined in *I'll Take My Stand: The South and the Agrarian Tradition* (1930), to which Ransom contributed the phrasing of its principles and the first article, "Reconstructed but Unregenerate." Confronted with industrial encroachment of the South, the twelve Southerners spoke out bluntly against the accelerating demands on the laborer's enjoyment of his labor. Ransom sounded the keynote in the "principles": "His [the modern employee's] labor is hard, its tempo is fierce, and his employment is insecure. The first principle of a good labor is that it must be effective, but the second principle is that it must be enjoyed. Labor is one of the largest items in the human career; it is a modest demand to ask that it may partake of happiness." This almost hedonistic basis for the agrarian movement, certainly not understood nor heeded by all farmers, is, nevertheless, a cardinal point in Ransom's regional aesthetic. The essays were in defense of a way of life, not of kennel-dog security, but of the fury of enjoyment. After all, enjoyment is private, not universal, or even of the masses. So is security, for that matter.

Ransom deployed his arguments under the aesthetic principle that happiness, both economic and aesthetic, accrues to the subsistence farmer who tills his own soil and enjoys the fruits of this labor, i.e., "All labor should be effective without being arduous; and with the general proviso that the best labor is the one which provides the best field for the exercise of the sensibility—[it] is clearly some form of pastoral or agrarian labor. Agriculture has always held the primacy as a form of labor. At least it has until recently, when it began to be mechanized, hurried, and degraded."

The industrialized, or mechanized, farmer cares little for the land, other than as a money-making concern. Obviously, subsistence is not his primary purpose, or any one of his purposes, in tilling the soil. Farming is to him an enterprise, "a factory," that is always in danger, however, of becoming over-mechanized, over-capitalized, over-productive, and consequently bankrupt, or what is probably worse, subsidized.

The agrarian economy, on the other hand, implies a polity of self-sufficiency with subsistence farming predominating over money-cropping. In a self-sufficient economy, time can be found for the leisure on which "a good life" depends. Leisure is discipline, but it is discipline which is not apparent, discipline which creates time to spend and gives the mind an opportunity to develop its own tastes and desires. Ransom says, "An agrarian economy does not conceive of the land as a capital to earn with, not primarily at least; but as a direct source of subsistence for its population. This is the most ancient of economies, which many times has proved its validity."

The enemy of this economy, in Ransom's view, is science. Science as applied to land denies a leisurely culture which sustains itself, and makes land, along with the farmer, a slave to scientific axioms. Industrialism, or scientific method applied, impoverishes the mind of man by first seducing, and then murdering his sensibility. In a sense, Ransom has applied the Faust myth to modern agricultural economy. I suspect that the application is legitimate. It seems to be successful when applied to baseball players (as in *Damn Yankees,* a musical comedy based on the novel *The Year the Yankees Lost the Pennant*), to voluptuous, seductive movie goddesses and demon-ridden movie magnates (as in *Will Success Spoil Rock Hunter?*).

In the South, where industrialization had not completely gained control, a man's life could still be oriented politically and aesthetically. The Southern way of life inculcated an interest in culture based on traditional arts in which the mind had time to develop an aesthetic sensibility. Ransom's argument is in itself seductive, and more so at present when there is so much unstructured leisure created by a shorter work-week. In a society where the worker's leisure and labor do not coexist, little that is culturally significant can be created. But in Ransom's theory, a leisure that grows out of enjoyed labor has structure and meaning, since it has an aesthetic base. Perhaps we can see in the Old Adam-like fetish of delving in the rose garden by the industrial executives a manifestation of the archaic, protean nostalgia for beauty, a beauty, needless to say, that has absolutely nothing to do with mechanization, or the job in the office or in the physics lab. But to the executive, it is escape into the poetic, pastoral world that he does not recognize or understand, trying to shape where there is no shape. These men may be arrogant, powerful, efficient, and dynamic, dervishly active, but their attempts at play and love are pathetic, almost pitiful. In the agrarian, the individual way of life has form.

Ransom's theory of a regional aesthetic is developed in several essays whose titles give some import of their subject matter: "The South Defends its Heritage," "The State and the Land," "Land! An Answer to the Unemployment Problem," "Trading Culture for War Debts," "The South is a Bulwark," "Happy Farmers," "A Capital for the New Deal," "The Aesthetic of Regionalism," "Hearts and Heads," "What Does the South Want?" and "Modern with a Southern Accent." These articles now seem dated. But I am not sure that they are. First, Ransom stated explicitly that he was not discussing the Old South, scented, frilly, and cavalier. He concerned himself with an agrarian economy rather than with a plantation economy. Second, in order for a regional aesthetic to survive, it must partake in a balanced existence that will allow the individual an optimum development of all his faculties. According to Ransom, this can be done most efficiently in an agrarian society where particulars or objects exist in their multiplicity and infinity. Aesthetically, this way of life consists of a jungle of metaphors existing in a universal order, and certainly basic to Ransom's concrete universal poetic. In other words, there is a fence row there among the wild bushes where the sweet birds sing, where even the copperhead coils, the dogwood blooms, and the predator lurks. Furthermore, the agrarian economy, upheld by small, independent landowners, resides in the "ownership of property," and constitutes "one of the most sobering responsibilities that citizens can have under a free state."

The second point, "a balanced existence," or more specifically
in Ransom's terms, "an order of existence," brings into focus the
strictures on science, "the father of industrialism." To develop this
line of his thought, we need to return to the book *God Without
Thunder: An Unorthodox Defense of Orthodoxy* (1930), Ransom's
first volume of economic and critical prose. It can be described as
a foundation statement for the later and more scrupulously argued
observations about science and its effect on aesthetics. Nonetheless,
as the title implies, Ransom is ostensibly concerned with religion—
or the loss of it. And always the agrarian argument underlies the
defense of religion. First, the religionists are "almost inevitably"
agrarians, since they are closer to the "elemental soil." Second, and
from Ransom's point of view more important, science, which has
taken some of the sting out of orthodox religion, is only half of the
order of existence, the rational half. The rationalist assumes that
all being is explainable in "scientific terms," neglecting to consider
that "there are limits to human understanding," that, regardless of
the universe of discourse, it is impossible to transcend the human
reference point, that as P. W. Bridgman points out in his *Philosophical Implications of Physics,* "We are now approaching a bound
beyond which we are forever stopped from pushing our inquiries,
not by the construction of the world, but by the construction of
ourselves." This one-sidedness will not do. A whole order of existence must necessarily include the contingent, and here we meet
Ransom's "ontological" method, a critical measuring-rod that insists
on accounting for both the rational and the contingent in man or
in a literary work.

A combination of the rational and the contingent exceeds definition,
but still can be summed up in the individual in all his complexity
and richness. Science can abstract only, thereby losing sight of the
unique and complex character of objects as such. In so doing, scientific inquiry can produce merely that which it produces after its own
design—it chases itself. A homely simile describes this much better:
Science resembles the dog that pursues his tail for the sake of pursuit,
and no matter how large the circle, he is still merely pursuing his tail.
He is a tautological dog, pure activism. Ransom says, "As the scientific
mind came to look more and more like God's mind, God began to look
more and more like a simple scientist." To us, soft bulbs that we are,
glowing only intermittently, perhaps this is best. After all the scientist
can only blow us up or toss us to another world, while the old God,

nasty old tyrant that He was, would promptly burn our sins out of us in Hell, probably with some justice.

Scientific investigation, by its nature, cannot admit of the contingent, the inexplicable, the unpredictable, or, if we must, "faith," or, to extend, God, defined as "a universe of a magnitude exceeding its own natural history." Of course there is a margin of error, measurable percentage-wise, bound in numerical limits, wherein lives Mr. Joseph Wood Krutch's "Minimal Man." In contrast, variety exists in the area of contingency. Actually, Ransom comes to terms with science by pointing out that it accounts for a part of the order of existence—the abstract part. Science manhandles objects with abstractions, measurements, predictables. In a regional aesthetic, however, the object, or "concretion"—Ransom's term—is celebrated lovingly and sentimentally, not scientifically. The object takes on mythic properties, "resorts to the supernatural in order to represent the fullness of the natural." Ransom goes on to say, "The myth-maker is a desperate man, for he has a memory. He remembers the remarkable individual in the richness of his private existence. He sees little relation between that individual and the dry generalization into which science would fit him." The myth-maker or artist handles, or should handle, the particular order of experience, and attempts, or should attempt, to account for the whole particularity of existence, the "concrete universal," as is illustrated in Ransom's essay, "The Concrete Universal: Observations on the Understanding of Poetry" (1955).

To demonstrate further how the regional aesthetic, based on agrarianism, affected Ransom's poetic theory would require lengthy quotation from later, purely literary articles. Since this would move us too far from the economist period, it is sufficient to say that the foundation of his argument is solidly built on a regional economy, where, to recapitulate, property becomes something personal, something cherished, and something that has infinite possibilities. The agrarian puts his time and energy into a part of himself and is enriched thereby. His existence is structured, meaningful, substantial, and his way of life is an attitude that pits him against God and against Nature, not against Man and against Society, as the sociologists would have man do. In this state, he does not commit the sin of pride, for he realizes that he is not supreme. He may be awed and humbled, but he has a freedom that allows him to take a second look at himself and at the inexhaustible particularity about him. And above all, he is self-sufficient.

Whether or not the regional economy advanced by Ransom—and others—is pertinent now is a moot question. I suspect that it has been discarded almost entirely, except in the impractical dreams of suburbanites; or in the lives of those tourist attractors, the culture-laggers—called Yankee traders, red necks, or sturdy mountaineers, depending on the prejudices of the name-callers—who live in enclaves such as New England, the Midland South, or the Appalachian Mountains, where, of all things, food is still home-grown and preserved just as though the scientific miracle, or "breakthrough of knowledge," had not occurred, seemingly unaware that a shot-put contest, the like of which the world has never seen, is now being waged. Strange—isn't it?—that Robert Frost, Robert Penn Warren, and William Faulkner originated and matured in such areas. Perhaps it is enough to say that at one time the regional economy had validity, for it was *the* pioneer way of life, based, by the way, on the outmoded, "self-sufficient" individual. That we have "progressed"—"metamorphosed"—out of it is certain, but we are still faced with an unstructured leisure-culture.

Nevertheless, these essays, written during a depression period when economic hysteria was omnipresent, have some of the quality of revelation about them, especially enlightening during an era of great prosperity and technological change when we take note of the plight of mechanized farmers and eternally obligated urbanites and ex-urbanites, who have over-capitalized, produced unsalable surpluses, and mortgaged their lives, or when we remember our own almost dehumanized lives, just so many calculus equations, abstractions that do to fill out a statistic, swell a catastrophe.

Regardless of the present-day value of the essays, the fact that a poetic theory is based ultimately on an agrarian or "regional" economy is important. Furthermore, Ransom says, the poets and critics who originally subscribed to the agrarian economy matured under its influence. Fifteen years after the battle, Ransom wrote, "And now, for example, whatever may be the politics of the agrarians, I believe it may be observed that they are defending the freedom of the arts whose function they understand. Not so much can be said for some intemperate exponents of the economic progress."

LOVE AS SYMBOL IN THE POETRY OF RANSOM

Karl F. Knight

John Crowe Ransom repeatedly uses love as a symbol in developing his major poetic theme of the fragmented personality, the individual who has lost the sense of unity in his life and cannot find satisfactory expression or realization in any of the compartments into which his life has been artificially divided.* Several critics have pointed out this theme in Ransom's poetry. "To an astonishing degree," writes Cleanth Brooks, "the problems which engage Ransom's attention turn out to be aspects of one situation: that of man's divided sensibility." Robert Penn Warren defines the center of Ransom's poetry as "that sensibility whose decay Ransom, along with various other critics, has bewailed. . . . To an astonishing degree, in far more than a majority of cases, the hero or heroine of the poem is a sufferer from that complaint of 'dissociation of sensibility.'" In similar terms, F. O. Matthiessen says that Ransom's "main theme has been that of the divided sensibility, torn between reason and imagination, between science and faith."

But it has not been noticed that love or physical passion is frequently used as a symbol by Ransom in poems which embody the theme of the dissociated sensibility. Love is a basic human experience, and love between the sexes is normally the most intense and

*This essay originally appeared in *Mississippi Quarterly*, XIII (Summer, 1960), 132–40.

satisfying kind of love, the kind of love which finds its basic and natural expression through physical passion. Thus in dealing with love and physical passion Ransom is able to symbolize the condition of modern man: the incapacity for expression in one experience symbolizes an all-pervasive breakdown of the individual's ability to achieve full and unified experience and expression.

The use of love and physical passion to symbolize aspects of modern life is fairly common in recent literature: Hemingway's Jake Barnes's impotence symbolizes a generation; his Frederick Henry tries to construct meaning for himself through sexual experience; Eliot's Prufrock seeks to dodge life through effeteness; Fitzgerald's Jay Gatsby nervously attempts to build an impossible world based on the fantasy of love for Daisy; and the impotent Popeye symbolizes Faulkner's mechanized modern world.

A great many of Ransom's poems tend to fall into loose groupings about his theme of the fragmented personality. Because of development of that basic theme in terms of one who is withdrawn from life and because of clear use of sexual symbolism, "Necrological" is representative of Ransom's thought and method. The celibate friar who comes out of his monastery surveys a battlefield strewn with the dead. Though he is dedicated to a way of life and its rituals (paternosters and scourging), he is baffled by "much riddling." The things he sees on the battlefield represent a different way of life, and the contrast between the two explains his perplexity. Looking at the corpses, he thinks that "it is easy . . . to die"; his problem is how to live. Scourging and abstinence are not enough. Chivalric warfare and love suggest a better and fuller life than the friar's. The dead men were dedicated to a way of life so important that they laid down their lives for it. The dead include all levels of society, and it is a hazardous life. But the friar, who does not encounter dangers, is a reflective and abstinent man, given to surmising.

Just as he is not involved in chivalric warfare, so also he is not involved in love. The dead leman, who embraces the "mighty knees" of her dead knight and "who with her flame had warmed his tent," symbolizes this other involvement denied the friar. Love exacts the final price of death from her, just as warfare has led to the knight's death; but her love was dedicated in spite of its illicitness, and it is more intensively impressive because as a camp follower she has had to endure "all men's pleasantries"—derision and social unacceptability. By his vow of celibacy the friar has denied his passionate nature, and the way of life to which he is committed stifles a part of his sensibility. There is an area of experience which he cannot recognize, which he must avoid. Consequently he cannot achieve an integrated experience. The poem's title signifies that it is a roll of the dead; the friar

> . . . bowed his head
> As under a riddle, and in a deep surmise
> So still that he likened himself unto those dead
> Whom the kites of Heaven solicited with sweet cries.

He is as good as dead—worse off than those he sees, for in life they had fulfillment and he has nothing but empty riddling. These last three lines establish a fine irony. The friar presumably took monastic vows in order to achieve heaven, yet the birds "of Heaven" seek the dead illicit lovers. The suggestion is that those who achieve an integrated life will assuredly achieve what the friar hopes for.

The abstemious man in "Spectral Lovers," like the friar, is incapable of total involvement in life. He and the girl are lovers, "but why unclasped, unkissed?" She is more aggressive than he, for "of evasions even she made a snare./The heart was bold that clanged within her bosom. . . ." She is ready to yield herself to him "if he but ask it. . . ." But he does not ask. His exaggerated and overly delicate movements and his bodily undulations indicate that he is effeminate (that is, incapable of normal sexual expression) : "gesturing largely to the moon of Easter,/Mincing his steps and swishing the jubilant grass." He rationalizes their situation and concludes: " 'This is that marble fortress not to be conquered,/Lest its white peace in the black flame turn to tinder/And an unutterable cinder.' " His perverted reticence and her boldness reverse the usual roles of male and female. The unnaturalness of their situation is further indicated by their similarity to substanceless apparitions: they are "like spectral lovers" and have "haunted a thicket of April mist. . . ." Like the friar, they are in effect lifeless in their withdrawal.

In conjunction with love and passion Ransom sometimes uses bookishness and abstract learning to symbolize the fragmentation of the modern personality. The frustrated admirer of the title character in "Miller's Daughter" is a "poor bookish hind" who realizes that he comes with "too much pudding in my head/Of learned char-

acters and scraps of love. . . ." He has not the power to make his
passion efficaciously known; he can merely stare, a "learned eye of
our most Christian nation." He cannot integrate his learning with
his passion, which intrudes itself distractingly upon his studies: she
"cleaves my closest thought. . . ." His artificial compartmentalization
of life is not successful, for things which should be unified tend
to spill over into one another. He remains frustrated and she must
remain only a "long-dreamt miller's daughter."

Ransom uses love and bookishness in a different way to symbolize the fragmented personality in the twenty sonnets comprising the
story "Two Gentlemen in Bonds." The personality is literally split
into the two brothers who are the two gentlemen: "Everything that
Paul was, Abbott was not." Paul is the body, the sensuous and
sensual aspect, and Abbott is the head, who "could talk in Latin,
music, mime,/Or sonneteer with Petrarch in his prime. . . ." Edith,
who requires a whole man, loves both brothers and finds it impossible to choose between two parts. Speaking of Abbott's refusal
to take part in the entertainment of the king, a refusal on abstract
principle, she confusedly says: " 'But Paul! there's something splendid about this—or is it/Terrible, rather—or eerie—or what synonym?' "
And after she had been given in marriage to Paul by the king, she
maintains her vacillating position by visiting Abbott's tower and listening outside his door to his "bitter doctrine descending on the
world." The most striking differentiation between the brothers is in
"Epithalamion of a Peach," an extended conceit describing the eating
of a peach as a sexual act. Paul's "two-and-thirty cut-throats doing his
will/Tore off her robe and stripped her bare until/Drunken with appetite, he devoured and ate." But the eating, which is symbolic of the
attitudes of the brothers toward Edith, "is unloverly, bringing the
wry/To squeamish Abbott's face. . . ." Paul's appetite is mere lust;
Abbott's revulsion is the fastidiousness of withdrawal; and either approach is partial and invalid.

The frustratedly passionate modern man is in several instances
developed through contrast between past and present. The disillusioned romantic who is the speaker in "Blackberry Winter" feels
that "pictures of silver and apples of gold are dead . . . ," suggesting the golden apple awarded to Aphrodite and perhaps two of the
ages of man. Like Miniver Cheevy, he yearns for heroic ages: "all
of the wars have dwindled since Troy fell." The symbols of modern
inadequacy are again the lack of warfare and of physical passion, for

the speaker is "Anxious for the flash of whether eyes or swords,/And hoping a little, a little, that either may be." But in Ransom passive hoping is ineffectual.

The important protagonist of "Man Without Sense of Direction" "writhes like an antique man of bronze,/That is beaten by furies visible . . ."; the diction implies a comparison with Greek tragedy, wherein there is unified experience. The man belongs to a degenerate, a bronze, age; he is punished by avenging forces, but not in the manner of Greek drama, in which the tragic hero recognizes his flaw and gains wisdom; the modern man "is punished not knowing his sins. . . ." And though he "won . . . in bridal the loveliest," he cannot express deep love for he is capable only of turning to her in inarticulate terror after being thwarted by the complex world; he has a "clamoring tongue and taste of ashes/And a small passion to feign large."

The old and new are contrasted again in "Antique Harvesters," perhaps the clearest poetic statement of Ransom's agrarianism. The poem does not deal with sexual love, but there is a chivalric personification of the South as a "Proud Lady, of the heart of fire,/The look of snow." The harvest is gathered for her and she is worthy of the deeds of love done for her. There is thus an ideal of romantic love, about which Ransom has said:

Romantic love is among the most delightful of our experiences; most of us would probably name it as the most massive and satisfying of all—provided at least that we do not confine the term to the love between the sexes, but extend it to the love of nature, of works of art, and of God. . . . At the base of romantic love there is probably an impulse fundamental in our biological constitution, *to be in rapport with our environment.*

The people in the poem are characteristically in rapport with their environment, and tradition is a major factor in the rapport. The heroes who died for the Lady are talked about and cherished by the old men. The hunters, "keepers of a rite," are "archetypes of chivalry." Even the fox is a "lovely ritualist," and the fields are figured as willingly taking part in the way of life, for they offer "themselves to harry." When the taint of money from industrialism enters, the "servitors that have drooped" are to be forgotten, and the ideal of the Lady who is old but "hath not stooped" is to be upheld.

In some of the poems which deal with isolation, lovers who are spiritually cut off may be physically near; but in other poems the situation of isolation is varied by making the characters both physically and spiritually cut off. The friar who riddles, for example, although he lacks no particular person, is physically isolated. The "lady in beauty waiting" in "Piazza Piece" also has no particular object of desire. She scorns the "gentleman in a dustcoat" (probably death personified as a lover) who would embrace her, and she substitutes romantic yearning for "young men's whispering and sighing." The woman in "Parting, Without a Sequel," who has just written a letter "With characters venomous and hatefully curved," is different in that she has had a lover. In "Nocturne" the isolated young man in seersucker is the result of centuries of evolution, but the process has only "borne his boats of passion to the sea. . ."; he does not have "the heart, and the head, for a furious antique bacchanal." "Winter Remembered" does not indicate why the speaker is separated from his beloved, except that he has a wound, which suggests that the separation is an artificial enforcement. Whatever the cause, the isolation incapacitates him; he cannot enjoy the warmth of his house, but must wander out into the raw storm to get "past the smart of feeling."

Two of Ransom's isolated spinsters are inordinately involved in nature, and that excessive involvement is an insufficient substitute for the conjugal love which they do not have. The spinster in "Of Margaret" mourns the leaves which have blown off the trees in autumn, for they are "the sons of all her mothering." But "her generations were of the head,/The eyes, the tender fingers, not the blood,/And the issue was all flowers and foliage." In "Miriam Tazewell" the spinster who is afraid of the storm is disturbed like a mother when her "fragile babes" are damaged. She has a "heart full of the flowers." Miriam's withdrawal from the normal course of life is suggested further in her going out "with skirts kilted/To see in the strong sun her lawn deflowered,/. . . and the stalks naked." The skirt which is drawn up away from the grass suggests a distaste even for the environment she has chosen to involve herself in. The wittily ambiguous "lawn deflowered" and "stalks naked" figure the storm in terms of sexual violation and suggest Miriam's perverted attitude towards her botanical charges.

The dramatic irony in "Emily Hardcastle, Spinster" gives an insight into the mind of the spinster who speaks about the dead Emily. The speaker had expected Emily to join the ranks of local spinsters, and now she thinks of death as a "Grizzled Baron" who is taking Emily to "his castle in the gloom." * That marriage is her metaphor for death implies her abnormal attitude towards conjugal relationships. Further, that she thinks of Emily's sisters who married as "unbelievers" suggests a religious kind of devotion to her situation.

Ransom presents couples who could have united but remained apart in "Good Ships" and "Eclogue." "Good Ships" employs extended nautical figures in summarizing the lives of two who are at first "Fleet ships" and then are "unto miserly merchant hulks converted"; they "hailed each other, poised on the loud surge/Of one of Mrs. Grundy's Tuesday teas . . ." and merely "exchanged the nautical technicalities." Jane Sneed and John Black in "Eclogue" discuss the things which came between them. After reminiscing about their young and unself-conscious joys, Jane says: "Those days I could not quit you if I would,/Nor yet quit me could you." But now they are "sly travelers"; that is, they have become overly rational. Considerations of ambition, death, and immortality caused love to have a "most fatal eclipse"; and the lovers realized that they "must not fructify." Nonetheless, there are those "Who when Night comes, when it is fathomless,/Consort their little hands . . ." and "one flame to the other flame cries Courage. . . ." The night of life is fathomless for Jane and John. John's final word recalls the friar's death in life:

> We lovers mournfully
> Exchange our bleak despairs. We are one part love
> And nine parts bitter thought. As well might be
> Beneath ground as above.

This death-like isolation for Jane and John is the result of their resisting a proper consummation of their Love.

But the man who "cannot fathom nor perform his nature" may find that marriage does not rid him of his burden of a fragmented personality. The father in "Prelude to an Evening" who is "dragging his infected wound homeward" brings from the complex world an "invaded mind." He realizes that his wife functions under similar difficulties; he imagines her confused and agonizing dreams, supposes that she feels "poising round the sunny room,/Invisible evil . . . ," and knows that as she does her tasks she listens for "The warning sibilance of pines." The poem presents a marriage situa-

*In *Chills and Fever* the text reads: "for his gloomy halidom."

tion which has a quiet and terrible undercurrent of uncertainty to which they can react only with "gallant fear." They are perhaps like the quarreling couple of "Two in August," "two entities grown almost one" who cannot tell whether the songs of the birds are "of heaven or hell." That Ransom uses the symbol of love in married situations as well as in unconsummated relationships indicates that he calls for something beyond free love or hedonism; it is the lack of full and meaningful experience which he deplores, and sex is his symbol rather than his basic subject.

Physical passion is employed again as a symbol of ineffectuality in the case of the individual in conflict with institutions. The rural youth who goes to the aging prostitute in the early poem "November" tries to think of himself jauntily as one of the "laissez-faires," but he is trapped by his background. His mother has picked a wife for him, a respectable Baptist maiden, "thirty-odd pounds . . . overweight." He had seen a different girl earlier, whom he idealized, "But God . . . cannot answer all that pray." And so he goes to his "scarlet woman," but he is influenced by a morality which makes him consider himself one of the "mutineers." A parallel situation is given a different slant in "Roses," in which the speaker compares the easy favors of his mistress with an artifical rose, "A horrid thing of bric-a-brac." He measures her against some standard when he says, "Red real roses keep a thorn,/And save their loveliness a while/And in their perfect date unfold." This speaker too is conscious of mutineering; he has indulged his passion without due reference to a form whose validity he recognizes. But the utilization of an inhumane morality can be a grave error. The indignant moralist of "The Four Roses" who ravished one of the roses (one of four sisters) was outraged when the other three did not turn "pale for grief " and draw "fragrance back for shame." And so he self-righteously "scourged them bleeding to the ground./All, all are sinners unto God."

The symbolism of unconsummated physical passion and the theme of the individual in conflict with institutions are combined in one of Ransom's best poems, "The Equilibrists." Her body "was a white field ready for love, . . ." but above the body was a "gaunt tower" from which came "doves" (thoughts) which said "Honor." Again a dichotomy of head and heart. Though the body urged him to take its lilies, "If he would pluck and wear them, bruise and break," her doves were relentless and commanded "Eternal distance." The enforced abstinence is not effective, however, because

"They were bound each to each, and they did not forget." They go into an equilibrium; that is, they are influenced by two forces which operate to place them in perilous balance between polarities, with no possibility of achieving either—effective separation or physical passion, heaven or hell. In heaven there is no passion, in hell no honor. Though their epitaph describes them as beautiful as well as perilous, nonetheless they are in death still "Close, but untouching." The painful equilibrium continues.

Ransom sometimes uses love in developing themes of mutability, as in "Piazza Piece," in which the girl who yearns is placed in a setting of dying roses and a ghostly moon, and with Death as her suitor. And the Grizzled Baron who took Emily Hardcastle away was death. In "Vaunting Oak" the tree is used to represent first the happily illusioned attitude of the girl towards her love as an eternal thing and then the disillusioned attitude of the lover, who realizes that all things must end. The girl took her lover to the old oak and said, " 'Established, you see him there! forever.' " But the lover knocked on the tree, whose "dolorous cry/Boomed till its loud reverberance outsounded . . ." even "the tears of a girl remembering her dread." The matter-of-fact lover calls himself "an unbeliever of bitter blood," and he deliberately strikes the tree in order that "her pitiful error be undone. . . ." He is of course quite right, but this lover is probably to be classed with the scientific moderns who cannot retain a faith in poetry. His facts destroy the symbol chosen by the girl; her poetry must defer to his science. And the love which is abused and thwarted is perhaps a more pathetic symbol of decay than is the old oak, for the tree grandly follows its natural course.

Ransom's world is not a pleasant or easy one. His people are aware of death and yet do not know what to do or feel about it; the forms of society do not satisfy the needs of individuals; men often in isolation dribble away their talents and energies without liking what they do; faith and certainty have been replaced by bad dreams and shadow-boxing with spectres. Ransom seems to be saying that modern man has lost the capacity for total experience; or, to put it another way, scientific man has lost his appreciation for poetry (and all that poetry stands for—everything significant, individual, and precious). The failure of modern man to function with his whole being, then, is symbolized by Ransom in a number of instances through representing his characters as being unable to give adequate expression to their love.

JOHN CROWE RANSOM: THE POET AND THE CRITIC

Graham Hough

Those who admire John Crowe Ransom's poetry mostly do more than admire it—they love it.* And it is hard and often seems unrewarding to give reasons for our loves. Or to put it more exactly, to give reasons for our loves is something that cannot be done directly without inadmissible autobiography. We can only circumscribe, define and distinguish, by methods that are often far from loving; yet by them the nature of the object and therefore the reasons for our loving can be seen more clearly. It is by peripheral details, sometimes finicky and often disobliging, that we are enabled to approach the center of a poetic achievement. The shapely mountain that we admire from a distance is actually climbed by cracks and gullies. And it is approached by less exacting declivities that are themselves only detritus from the mountain core.

The modern poet more often than his predecessors has had to be a critic too, to define his presuppositions, since there were few that he could easily inherit. He has had to invent a dialect for himself, or pick out an eclectic one from the stores of the past, for there was none that was settled and generally available. One way of approaching Ransom's poetry would be through his criticism. Another would be through details of language and style. If I begin by picking

*This essay originally appeared in *Southern Review*, (January, 1965) , 1–21.

about in these areas apparently at random, rather than speaking about the South, the Fugitives, and the New Criticism—the large public facts that have conditioned Ransom's career—the above must be my excuse.

The surface feature that first catches the attention in Ransom's writing is a prevailing trickiness of expression, by which expectation is mildly defeated, the mind is made to boggle a little before getting at the meaning. An essay in *The World's Body* begins: "A poetry may be distinguished from a poetry by virtue of subject matter, and subject matter may be differentiated with respect to its ontology, or the reality of its being." This means: "One kind of poetry may be distinguished from another, etc.," and to put it in that way is several degrees off the line of normal usage. And in normal usage ontology does not mean the reality of an object's being; it means a branch of metaphysics. The poem "Armageddon" begins:

> Antichrist, playing his lissome flute and merry
> As was his wont, debouched upon the plain.

A flute can only be "lissome" in some metaphorical sense that is by no means evident; rivers debouch, and things that can be seen as rivers, like marching armies; but it is hard to see how an individual can do so. I am not now thinking of the archaisms and expressions drawn from earlier literary vocabularies that are so common in the poetry. These probably have a different cause. I am thinking of a deliberate intent to lay the flagstones unevenly and to leave small obstructions lying about. For of course it is deliberate; these are not merely the accidents of a personal dialect. It is significant that Ransom finds the same tendency in others. He suggests of Milton's "Lycidas" "that it was written smooth and rewritten rough; . . . he read the formal poem he had written and deformed it." I don't think this is in fact true. A study of the manuscript suggests the contrary, as Fredson Bowers has pointed out. Many things that poets say about other poets are really said about themselves. The essay concludes by saying that "Lycidas," "for the most part a work of great art, is sometimes artful and tricky."

I connect this with a frequent tendency in the criticism to get things oddly wrong. I do not mean matters of critical theory, which are arguable, but simple eccentricities of nomenclature and descrip-

tion and history. Somewhere in his criticism he refers to ordinary
iambic meter as "goliardic" meter, and this not merely en passant,
but repeatedly. Heaven knows why, and I suppose it doesn't matter
much, except that some hapless student may pick up the phrase and
go running round the world with it expecting to be understood. In
the admirable essay on Hardy, "Old Age of an Eagle," the same
iambic or iambic-anapaestic meter is labelled a "university" meter
and contrasted with the "folk-rhythm," meaning the Anglo-Saxon
kind of metric with four stresses balanced around a central pause.
Mr. Ransom knows perfectly well that our normal accentual-syllabic
versification has nothing particular to do with universities and that
there is nothing particularly folksy about the old Germanic line;
but this amiable quirk allows him to introduce gratuitously a picturesque contrast between sophisticated and popular elements in
Hardy's poetry. In the "Lycidas" essay again he attributes the irregular rhyme-scheme and the varied line lengths of the poem to a
free adaptation of the formal stanzas of the Italian canzone. Well,
yes, in part; but there were examples of informal rhyming and linea-
tion in Italian already, notably the choruses of Tasso's Aminta, which
Milton certainly must have known. In the essay "On Shakespeare's
Language" the Latin element in Shakespeare's vocabulary is consistently labelled, by some extraordinary coinage, as "Latinical." "Latinity" we know, and "Latinised" and "Latinistic"; but "Latinical"?
In "Poetry: a Note in Ontology" the meaning of "metaphysical" as
Dryden and Johnson used it in talking of the Metaphysical poets
is given as "supernatural" or "miraculous." That was a sense that
the word could bear, it is true; but manifestly in this context the
true sense is another one, far commoner at the time—"over-subtle"
or "fine-spun."

In Ransom's theoretical criticism, apart from the use of the word
"ontological," much play is made with the philosophers. Plato, Kant,
and Hegel make frequent appearances, not to mention others. Yet
their views are never expounded or stated plainly. They are brought
in with a very cavalier and allusive air, sometimes it would seem
almost playfully, to support positions that would have disconcerted
these thinkers considerably. Yet we know that Ransom studied classics and philosophy—at that irreproachable nursery of orthodoxy,
Christ Church in Oxford. And I collect this anthology of oddities
with a purpose the reverse of malevolent. As far as his public persona
and état civil is concerned Ransom is an academic critic and a pro-

fessor of literature. (He even believes that the academies are the proper places for the practice of criticism.) Perhaps this has been a necessity for him. It is a fate more often enforced on poets in America than in Europe; though in England too it is becoming a common doom. But I suspect that something in him has always resisted this academic status, and the resistance betrays itself in an obstinate intellectual waywardness. However professorial the occasion he seems impelled by some inner necessity to put things in a way that would certainly merit censure in an examination paper or a Ph.D. thesis.

In his poetry this wayward impulse reveals itself in the diction, which is neither the language of the tribe, however purified or personally handled, nor the language of any particular literary tradition, but a highly mannered fusion of many and disparate elements. There is probably a deeper reason for this than the half-conscious revolt against academicism that affects Ransom's criticism. The area in which poetry operates has become more restricted since the nineteenth century. When Tennyson's heyday was past, poetry became disestablished. In our day it has never been able to take its audience for granted. Since it has no longer been required reading, it has felt the need to call attention to itself. This has meant a quite unprecedented demand that poetry should be surprising, that each new poet should have a new manner of his own. Yet good poetry has been recognized in our civilization for over two thousand years; and what makes it good has not changed all that much. The insistence on novelty and surprise is only a tactical operation, irrational but contingently needed in the circumstances of the time. The demure insolence of Mr. Eliot's earlier manner, Pound's flamboyant acts of aggression, the neo-expressionist or neo-dada maneuvers of today are to the discerning eye merely tactics, and have little essential connection with the virtues of the poetry to which they are attached. Sometimes these scattered tactics are fused together into a plan that could properly be called strategic. Such a plan was the whole movement that we can conveniently sum up by the name of Imagism. Under its direction poetry was forbidden to ratiocinate or reflect and was enjoined to proceed solely by a series of snapshots. As an account of the way poetry had actually proceeded it was patently false, as a program it was restrictive. But it fascinated the intelligentsia in more than one country. And by contriving to *épater* the solid citizen who wanted to find his poetry as intelligible as any other kind of discourse it did manage to call attention to itself, and called attention to the questionable status of poetry in general. It also provided a capacious bandwagon on which most of the active poets and their impresarios could be accommodated.

Now Ransom has always stood rather aside from this large movement. Though the course of his argument has sometimes led him to emphasize the virtues of the arbitrary detail, behind this has always stood the firm assertion of the poem as a rational structure. This has kept him away from a much-traveled main road of contemporary verse; one would think it put him closer to Yvor Winters, though they seem to have quarreled pretty continually for one reason or another. The Fugitives, the Southern Agrarians, the only public movement to which Ransom has ever belonged, was too regional and particular to lend him much of an impetus in the wider world. So he has always had to make his own way in poetry, find his own tactic for making his voice heard. The oddities of his criticism, the stylish idiosyncrasy of his poetic vocabulary are his own quietly arresting fashion of making his points—since the modern poet or expositor of poetry is obliged to be arresting in some fashion. Not that I suppose the desire to be arresting forms a very profound part of Ransom's own nature.

II

It is easy to take exception to Ransom's critical formulations; what is less often noticed is that the eccentricities are generally employed in the service of common sense—often some dazzling bit of common sense that has been in danger of being forgotten. Many of the statements in literary criticism are not of the kind that can be strictly true or false; some however are capable of verification. The statements of this latter kind in Ransom's "Lycidas" essay are as often as not false. Yet the essay as a whole is not only one of the most genial but one of the most valuable studies of "Lycidas." Its title is "A Poem Nearly Anonymous," and its central theme is the virtual disappearance of the author, with his historic personality, his private and social passions, behind the formal and conventional structure of the elegy. I quoted a sentence from the conclusion: "So *Lycidas,* for the most part a work of great art, is sometimes artful and tricky." The paragraph goes on: "We are disturbingly conscious of the man behind the artist." We might surmise that it is this near-anonymity, this just-less-than-total submission to a convention that particularly engages Ransom's affections. At all events we have an essay full of eccentricities in detail yet in its general tenor a sage and pregnant account of the relation between tradition and personal experience in a great poem.

In his essay on Hardy he confronts the problem of the manifest greatness of a poet whose work is nevertheless riddled with failures of diction, stylistic collapses, and absurdities. I cannot say he solves it; with our current critical apparatus it is extremely difficult, and the solution of difficult critical puzzles is not Ransom's forte. But he says right out what the disinterested reader of poetry must say— what the unsophisticated reader would say out of the depths of his simplicity, even though Ransom himself is an extremely sophisticated reader:

> The fact is that we are severe with our artists, and one rule which holds for most of us is this: That is simply a bad poem whose unfashionable or dated diction the plain reader spots at the first reading. The admirers of Hardy, both English and American, seem always too wary of committing themselves in the face of his objectors. I think I would fight the objectors, if I were spokesman for this poet. There is too much force in his representations . . . to have them set aside for finicky reasons. And there is too much greatness of heart.

Ransom's central position about poetry—he states it frequently with but slight variation of terms—is that it consists of a logical *structure* to which is added an irrelevant but delightful *texture*. I have never been able to persuade myself that this is a satisfactory formula—surely too rough and ready for the plane of critical rigor on which Ransom professes to be operating. And a reading of the trade journals will reveal that most of the professionals are equally unpersuaded. Yet Ransom is undoubtedly saying what the common reader would say if he got round to saying anything on these matters—the common reader who obstinately continues to demand that his poetry shall (a) make sense, and (b) have a gratuitous abundance of local beauties. We should always rejoice to concur with the common reader, and to meet a learned critic who in however oblique a fashion finds himself able to do so.

By considering isolated passages it would seem possible to attack Ransom on two opposite counts—as an amateur of textural beauties regarded as something added, like trimmings to a hat; and as a too-traditional upholder of the logical structure of the poem. But to take his work as a whole it is remarkable how sanely he preserves the mean, with only occasional sallies in one direction or the other according to the nature of the opposition. In "Poetry: a Note in Ontology" he finds the theory of Physical poetry insufficient: its ideational basis is not absent, as it alleges, but merely concealed. (Physical poetry means what I have called Imagist poetry.) Platonic poetry is even less satisfying for its images have no independent life of their own, they are merely illustrations of an idea. And he finds the desired synthesis in Metaphysical poetry where image and idea are truly fused. We may find a strangeness in the terms of this Hegelian triad—physical, metaphysical, and platonic here cover both more and less than their usual significations: but the end to which they are used is not eccentric, it is a central and reconciling one.

We associate Ransom with what is still sometimes called the New Criticism. He is not quite the inventor of the label, but it was his revival of the phrase, formerly used by Spingarn for another critical movement, that brought it into common currency. He is felt to be himself a practitioner of this once novel art; and indeed his distinguished work as teacher and editor has provided a focus and a forum for active critical experiment these many years. We cannot yet say what will be the fate of the immense burst of critical excitement in the twenties, thirties, and forties of this century. Tasso's disputations with the Della-Cruscan academy were no doubt exciting in their day; and some of the New Critical hubbub already looks irrelevant and remote. It was not an unmixed advantage to Ransom to be so much in the middle of this turbulent scholasticism. Controversy is not his strong suit, nor I believe is critical theory. Yet if we attend carefully to his critical work we shall find that his role has been commonly misconceived. His book *The New Criticism* is not a manifesto or a defense, and he appears in it more as a slightly skeptical fellow-traveler than as a fully paid-up party member. Deeply impressed by the strenuousness and insight released by a new literary movement, he says of the critical writing of our time: "In depth and precision at once it is beyond all earlier criticism in our language." Yet his book is compact of dubieties and reservations. He is not for a moment taken in by the unredeemable psychological promises of Richards' earlier critical theory; he doubts whether irony is more than a special and occasional device in poetry; he is less than convinced by Eliot's method of allusive nudges; and of that celebrated unity of sensibility that the seventeenth century was supposed to possess and we are supposed to have lost, he writes: "I incline to think there was nothing of the kind there." The successes of his criticism generally come when poetic theory has been forgotten and we meet Ransom the poet simply talking of his craft.

It is possible then to see Ransom as an uneasy contender on the darkling plain where rival academies clashed for so many years, from which poetry, the object of the conflict, so often quietly removed herself. His best work was done at the times when he managed to elope in her company. It is true that he tried to turn himself into a New Critic, but happily he failed.

III

Most of Ransom's poetry comes fairly early in his career, and he has allowed much of it to disappear. It is not quite true that the *Poems About God* (1919) have never been reprinted, for some of them come in *Grace After Meat*, an English selection of 1924, where they won the commendation of Robert Graves. But effectively his reputation rests on the *Selected Poems* of 1945 (only forty-five of them), reprinted in *Poems and Essays* (1955). It is a slender output for a long life, but unlike many more voluminous *oeuvres* it needs no winnowing. Ransom has done it himself. And in the poems that survive there is something studied and fastidious that sorts well with such a limited production. It is one of Ransom's dogmas that the speaker in a poem is never the author in his own person; it is always an assumed personality, a fictitious character, a mask. And he has praised the near-anonymity of "Lycidas." Clearly this suppression of the historical personality of a writer is aided by a drastically restricted production. Links in the chain are broken, the poems stand isolated as self-sufficient entities. Confessional poetry thrives on copiousness and continuity.

But criticism must often proceed by cheating an author's designs, and it is useful to look at some of the largely suppressed *Poems About God,* for they can help to complete the figure in the carpet that has since perhaps been deliberately obscured. The title appears to promise verses of forthright piety, and that may be why they attracted little attention when they came out. Forthright they are indeed, but not pious. Their blunt sceptical home-truths are not acts of devotion. "Grace" is the harshest of them: it was rescued for reprinting against Ransom's wish by the personal intercession of Robert Graves. It tells of a hired man, undemanding, pious, working too hard in too hot a sun. He dies out in the fields, a sudden, pointless, physically revolting death. The sun that kills him is equated with God's grace—random general beneficence, but blazing cruelty as well. The speaker is the son of the farmer whose land the hired man is working. This is his comment:

> I will not worship wickedness
> Though it be God's—I am ashamed!
> For all his mercies God be thanked
> But for his tyrannies be blamed!
> He shall not have my love alone,
> With loathing too his name is named.

God—not the figment of men's imagination, but the sum of all the powers that actually rule the universe—is like the sun: relentless ferocity as well as fertilizing warmth: and it is hypocrisy not to say so.

In "By the Riverside" another God-defier is melted, wryly defeated by a day of natural grace. But the bowed old men of "Resurrection" will never straighten up again. They are finished, and no miracle can restore them. In "Under the Locusts" the old men sitting in the sun utter their defeated commonplaces about old age and suffering; but only to each other:

> Parson's coming up the hill,
> Meaning mighty well:
> Thinks he's preached the doubters down,
> And why should old men tell?

In "The School" the over-educated scion of the provinces revolts against the rusticity of his environment:

> Equipped with Grecian thoughts, how could I live
> Among my father's folk? My father's house
> Was narrow and his fields were nauseous.

Then he reveals the forces that actually reconcile him with things as they are—not Christian resignation or any transcendental hope, but love and money. It is God's doing all right, but he works through common instruments:

He sent a pair of providential eyes.
They would have sat in any witless head,
Although I deemed them deep as classic seas

. . . .

Then he commanded me to scrutiny
As to a fingered thing of no great matter,
A circumstantial sorry little coin.

. . . .

And what were dead Greek empires to me then?

These poems have disappeared from Ransom's publicly presented work; but they were written, and they are part of its background. And without venturing on any forbidden biographical fallacy I believe they are an important part. Death as violent and horrifying, old age as unavoidable pain, love seen ironically as a biological trap, money as a seductive necessity—these form a counterpoint to the better-known pieces in *Selected Poems*, where the tone-values have been lightened, the presentation stylized, and the life-experience deliberately set at a distance. There are those who find in Ransom's later poems a sort of evasive elegance, a world of courteous and chivalrous domesticity seen through a veil of literary allusion. They are wrong, as could be shown on the strictest critical principles from the poems themselves; but this could be more easily perceived if the earlier work were more obviously extant.

Every poet takes his own kind of risk—even if it is only the risk of being unadventurous. The kind of risk most in the air at the moment is the nakedly confessional, the exposure of breakdown and personal disintegration. I quote some words of Sylvia Plath about her own poignant and terrible last poems:

I've been very excited by what I feel is the new breakthrough that came with, say, Robert Lowell's *Life Studies*. This intense breakthrough into very serious, very personal emotional experience, which I feel has been partly taboo. Robert Lowell's poems about his experiences in a mental hospital, for example, interest me very much. These peculiar private and taboo subjects I feel have been explored in recent American poetry.

This represents one kind of risk. Ransom's poetry has been willing to take another kind—that of presenting experiences which fall considerably short of driving his characters into mental hospitals:

The spring transpired in that year with no flowers
But the regular stars went busily on their courses,
Suppers and cards were calendared, and some bridals,
And the birds demurely sang in the bitten poplars.

To Miriam Tazewell the whole world was villain
To prosper when the fragile babes were fallen,
And not to unstop her own storm and be maudlin,
For weeks she went untidy, she went sullen.

Often he has dared to choose material that has been taboo in
modern poetry for reasons quite other than those suggested by Sylvia
Plath. When Mr. Ransom reads his own work he is apt to say
deprecatingly that it is mostly domestic poetry; he tends to play
it down, both in what he says of it and in his manner of presentation. He does not mention that it opens the door to vistas and
sonorities beyond its apparent surface. But I think there is a quality
that we should praise here—the willingness to embark on the chal-
lengingly familiar and affectionate theme, the theme that in other
hands would almost inevitably become trivial or sentimental. A classic example is "Janet Waking." Charming, slight, and not nearly so
fragile as it looks. To write a poem about a little daughter's pet
hen that died is indeed adventurous for a modern poet. Of course
there is an evident displacement here; the theme is not the death of
a hen, it is the child's inability to comprehend the fact of death—
the theme, in fact, of Wordsworth's "We Are Seven." It is hard to
write with tenderness about the limited perceptions of childhood
without denying one's own adult status, and so falling into platitude
or the kind of falseness we call sentimentality. Ransom has found
his way out of this restriction. First, by the rhythm of his poem;
it is an unassuming, rather prosaic rhythm that does not make emotional demands. Then by his diction. It is colloquial and natural,
but one that is colloquial and natural only in the mouth of a
cultivated man, with much verbal taste and a touch of fantasti-
cal dexterity. So that we are not falsely or affectedly plunged into
Janet's simple view of the situation. In the end, three views are
presented, at the same time and in the same words, Janet's; that
of Janet's father, who is affectionately sympathetic; and that of a
detached and slightly quizzical observer who also inhabits Janet's
father's skin, who cannot help knowing how small a place in the
scheme of things is occupied by the deaths of hens. This is not very

like Wordsworth; this combination of tenderness and irony is much more like Andrew Marvell; and we remember that Marvell wrote of a nymph complaining of the death of her fawn, and of little T. C. in a prospect of flowers.

This suggests a balance between a scholarly poetic procedure and a familiar current actuality. One way in which the balance is achieved is to re-engage, quite consciously and deliberately, one of the archetypal lyric themes with a distinctly modern situation. "Blue Girls" works in this way, with its antithesis between the girls, chattering bluebirds, and the terrible old woman who not long ago was lovelier than any of them. It is an old topic; it is in Horace and Catullus, in the "Coy Mistress," "Gather ye Rosebuds," and "Go Lovely Rose"—the transience of beauty and the necessity to enjoy it while you may. But the blue girls are modern co-eds from some neighboring school or college; and this is perhaps the only time they have been celebrated in such courtly fashion. What makes this small poem more than merely charming (which it obviously is) is that modernity and the lingering hint of the seventeenth-century lyric, the actuality and the removed contemplative quality given by a long perspective have an equal right to be present. They combine to form a stronger whole.

IV

Shortly after *Poems About God* Ransom published, surprising to relate, a work of religious polemic called *God Without Thunder*. He disclaims all authority as a theologian, and indeed the book will not rank as a theological classic. It is a curiously personal statement, though I doubt whether this was intended; and it forms a complement to the preceding poems. In part it is a diatribe against the conception of God promulgated by liberal Christianity—a God reduced to the author of a few vague ethical-social precepts, the purveyor of an inauthentic comfort denied at every turn by the actual course of the world. To Ransom the God who speaks out of the thunder, the God who tested Job, is the only one worthy of an honest man's acknowledgement.

In *Poems About God* such a deity was greeted with hate as well as love, resistance as well as gratitude. Yet in the prose treatise it is some reactivation of traditional Protestantism that is finally recommended. I confess that I cannot understand how the attitude in this astonishing work can be reconciled with Christianity of any kind; a stoical skepticism seems the most that it could reach to.

Yet the *mood* is plainly far nearer to one of reconciliation than that of the earlier poems. Ransom feels strongly that a culture cannot survive without a religion, and that a religion cannot survive without local and habitual roots. His own sense of rootedness in the culture of his own particular part of the United States is powerful, and this culture could not help being Protestant if it tried. Yet with the intellectual waywardness that was noticed in his criticism he is quite willing to give the traditional Protestantism of his region a quite unaccustomed content. No purely intellectual formulation could make this possible: the method must be that of mythology—mythology by which contraries can be retained coexistently in fruitful tension. Religion is most fully expressed in mythology; it is in fact a kind of poetry. Ransom says this, as Arnold said it. But he perceives, as Arnold never clearly did, that religion is a poetic myth to which we pledge an active and continued allegiance, unlike the merely provisional consent we give to the myths of poetry. So we may take it that *God Without Thunder* marks the settling of a philosophy of life, and the possibility of reconciling it in some way with the ethos of his region. What his Methodist ancestors would have said of the accommodation is hard to imagine; that must be left to settle itself. Our concern is with what appears in the poetry.

Beneath the more reticent and allusive poems in the selected edition are the same foundations as those of *Poems About God*. But the tone has changed. Resignation, acceptance are not the appropriate words. The world is what it is, and the powers that rule it. There is no use saying any more about *that,* directly. It is only the reflections of this uncompromising actuality in various facets of various human lives that Ransom's poetry feels called upon to deal with. Usually small facets. His poetry delights in putting massive and ineluctable facts in small or delicate settings. The child learns about death, the most massive and ineluctable fact she will ever have to learn, through the death of her pet hen. It is a group of chattering schoolgirls who are presented with the picture of bleareyed decrepitude. The justly famous "Bells for John Whiteside's Daughter" presents the whole of insatiable youthful vitality in the recollection of the little girl harrying the geese round the pond, and the whole incredible outrage of its extinction in the picture of her still lifelike little body in its coffin. But there is no more troubling deaf heaven with bootless cries. The facts being as they are it is more bearable to look at them in cross-lights than full face—

as in "Dead Boy," where the pathos of the child's death is approached only by contrasting the mother's grief with the far from lovable nature of the boy in life, and both are subordinated to the deep dynastic wound suffered by the old family. Yet these small, pathetic, and understated deaths are the same Death as that of the hired man in "Grace," dropping among his vomit under the killing sun, for which the speaker arraigned his God.

It is now possible to speak of these matters quietly. The only thing that would be unforgivable would be to idealize them or to "platonize" them away. Yet a propensity to see the world as it is not is inherent in human life, so that our consciousness is always divided. A series of vaguely parallel dichotomies that indicate this division is pervasive in Ransom's writing; structure and texture in poetry is paralleled by reason and sensibility in psychology; and both are probably, as John L. Stewart* has suggested, aspects of the ancient soul-body antithesis. This balance of irreconcilable opposites receives one of its most elaborate expressions in "The Equilibrists." Not that there is anything arcane about the structural idea—two lovers who between "honour" and desire can live neither with nor without each other. But on this frame is extended an extremely rich textural embroidery—doves, swords, flowers, jacinth, and myrrh—and among this eclectic décor an echo of the fate reserved for Luxuria in the second circle of Dante's hell. In the poem (and the implied suggestion is, so too in life) it is the rich overgrowth of particulars, beautiful, appealing, arresting, that holds together with precarious tendrils two stark incompatibles—which remain just as starkly incompatible in the end, to be celebrated in an epitaph that is compassionate but concludes nothing. Anyone who imagines for himself a soothing or anodyne quality in Ransom's poetry has not read it with much care.

A more intricate antithesis is found in "Painted Head," the most truly Metaphysical of Ransom's poems. I do not believe that poetry of this quality is served by guide-book "explication," so I will not provide any. The experience of picking one's own way through the obliquities of syntax and imagery is essential to its appreciation. It is enough to remark that the central figure of a portrait head (head alone, not bust or full-length) is used as a figure for the "platonizing" tendency of the human mind that has always been one of Ransom's main targets—the instinct of the head, the intellect, to make

*In *John Crowe Ransom* (University of Minnesota Pamphlets, 1962).

itself absolute and to play truant from the body it should serve.
The poem ends in a flare of splendid obscurity, celebrating the
beauty of body in a collocation of images that seems designed to
illustrate Ransom's theory about the rich "irrelevance" of texture:
a theory I have never been able fully to accept, which nevertheless
seems pragmatically justified in these beautiful, hardly explicable,
but wholly convincing lines:

> Beauty is of body.
> The flesh contouring shallowly on a head
> Is a rock-garden needing body's love
> And best bodiness to colorify
>
> The big blue birds sitting and sea-shell flats
> And caves, and on the iron acropolis
> To spread the hyacinthine hair and rear
> The olive garden for the nightingales.

One aspect of the conflict between the-world-as-it-is and the-world-
as-it-is-not I shall hardly deal with. It is the divided attitude toward
a politically defeated Southern culture of which Ransom has been
so conscious a champion. Did this culture ever really exist? What
were its true values? A stranger can have no useful view; I hesitate
even to suggest that the Captain Carpenter of Ransom's most celebrated poem is a direct symbol of the old South, obstinate, romantic
and doomed. The question is never raised of the causes for which
Captain Carpenter was fighting. But the plot of the poem, what it
says in the elementary sense, displays a natural sympathy with the
Quixote figure, the cussed old devotee of personal honour, inevitably worsted in any encounter with those who are more guileful
or realistic than himself. Yet its rhetoric is pure burlesque; the style
archaic, quaintly obsolete, a parody of a popular ballad, and not
even a ballad of a good period. Nothing said *about* Captain Carpenter could be as effective as this subtly chosen manner of telling
his story. It looks like a comment on a political situation; and the
same situation is treated without irony in another place. The most
highly wrought treatment of the old and failing that still commands
passion and devotion is the exquisite "Antique Harvesters," specific
in its setting, but with a theme and a handling that quite transcend the banks of the Ohio and the Mississippi.

V

To the English reader the sense that Ransom's poetry is rooted in a
society is strong, welcome, and on the whole un-American. Not that I
wish to make anything of a supposed similarity between English culture and that of the Southern states; this does not amount to much.
Ransom wrote a poem, "Philomela," on the subject, and it goes out of
its way to emphasize the differences. It is the sense of springing from a
society rather than from an unoccupied metaphysical area that is remarked. Indeed the feeling of contact with a close-knit world of friends,
neighbors, aunts, children, and families is stronger in Ransom's work
than in any English poetry that I can recall. We are used to the am-
bience of sexual love and masculine friendship, but not to this well-
populated, mainly domestic world. Yet how is this atmosphere brought
about? For many of the poems are strictly myths and fables, without
any obvious local habitation; and the diction is in the highest degree
artful, not really familiar at all. The answer I think is that even in
those poems that are manifestly fictions much of the imagery is drawn
from domestically familiar sources, from fairy-tale and folk-tale, from
ballads and the more accessible kinds of romance:

> But the Queen of Heaven on the other side of the road
> In the likeness, I hear, of a plain motherly woman
> Made a wry face, despite it was so common
> To be worsted by the smooth ladies of Hell,
> And crisped her sweet tongue: "This will never come to good!—
> Just an old woman, my pet, that wishes you well."
> ("The Tall Girl")

> Tell this to the ladies: how a hero man
> Assail a thick and scandalous giant
> Who casts true shadow in the sun,
> And die, but play no truant.
> ("Man Without Sense of Direction")

> Now which shall die, the roundel, rose, and hall,
> Or else the tonsured beadsman's monkery?
> ("Armageddon")

I had almost spoken of *décor;* for this looks like a deliberate stage
setting, for themes which on examination turn out to be far from
gently picturesque. Sometimes the presented surface is almost that

of a sunlit or moonlit, magnolia-dappled Old South, as in "Piazza
Piece" or "Vision by Sweetwater":

> Go and ask Robin to bring the girls over
> To Sweetwater, said my Aunt; and that was why
> It was like a dream of ladies sweeping by
> The willows, clouds, deep meadowgrass and the river.

This is of course a calculated risk. What Ransom has done is to
use this kind of surface material, not naively or unreflectingly, but
as a quite conscious literary device. It serves two purposes: first it
gives his verse a persistent link with the unstrenuous culture of his
own region; and secondly it allows him, by virtue of his own in-
finitely wider literary sophistication, to extend what might have been
a banal range of imagery, to execute his own arabesques upon it;
to write *Kunstlieder* with some of the virtues of the *Volkslied*. It is
said that much in Southern manners, the conscious chivalry and
courtesy and so forth, was a borrowing from the novels of Sir Walter
Scott and other secondary nineteenth-century romantic sources. Ransom of course knows this well enough; and he has accepted these
paraphernalia with their slightly faded charm, enriched them from
his own vastly wider and more original reading, and used them not
to create effects of faded charm, but for his own quite different purposes. "Vision by Sweetwater," of which I quoted the idyllic opening, ends with the child speaker suddenly grown old at hearing a
dreadful scream from the white throat of one of the ladies.

There has been much misunderstanding of these matters. The
most elementary is seen in a conversation with Robert Creely, reported in the English periodical the *Review* for January, 1964.
Creeley, after saying that "the Ransom-Tate nexus" gives no particular sense of how to deal with contemporary reality, goes on: "I
would rather have to do with men who are trying to think in terms
of contemporary realities, instead of being awfully-old-Southern-
gentleman—I enjoy antiques, but I don't want to *make* antiques. I hate
fakes, in other words." I enjoy Robert Creeley's poetry; but I think
this remark shows a total misunderstanding of Ransom's poetry—and
if it is meant as more than the statement of a personal program, a
misunderstanding of poetry in general. The pastoral convention of
"Lycidas," half the medieval lyric, most of the Petrarchan sonnet literature of Europe could come under the same ban. What is at issue is the

nature of poetic convention. Creeley calls a convention a fake, and says by implication that authentic poetry does without one. Ransom has stated repeatedly and unequivocally that all poetry is within one. Creeley is in the now quite common position of preferring to use a contemporary convention without knowing that it is a convention—and no harm in this, if this is the way he can work best. Ransom is in the less common position of feeling strongly the omnipresence of convention in poetry and of having to devise one for himself.

A backward glance at *God Without Thunder* will show why he had to devise one for himself. In a late chapter of that book, having realized that a culture cannot long survive without a religion, he inspects the rival suasions of Judaism, Catholicism, the Greek Orthodox, and the Anglican churches, and decides not without regret that none of them has any roots in his soil, nor, for that reason, any hold on his own nature. Whether he wishes it or not, he must elect the kind of Protestantism that grows around his own home. We then observe, however, that he proceeds to give it a new content. So in poetry. It has always been clear to him that he must speak from his own soil, out of his inherited, native, circumambient situation. Robert Graves speaking of his earlier poems hailed him, not without reason on the evidence then available, as a kind of Robert Frost who happened to come from Tennessee instead of north of Boston. Since Tennessee is where he comes from he cannot speak simply with the voice of English poetry, or even with the voice of New England. Frost does not come from nothing; he has Emerson, Thoreau, and Whitman behind him. But Ransom's part of America has no literary tradition, only a rather worn assemblage of romantic and rhetorical properties. And this, in any simple sense, Ransom has outgrown:

> Equipped with Grecian thoughts, how could I live
> Among my father's folk?

But as *God Without Thunder* makes clear, he is not going to adopt Eliot's course, abandon his father's folk and apply for artificial respiration to European culture and the Anglican church. He does what he must do—accepts his attractive but not very promising heritage of scenes and images and characters, and by the aid of an unconventional, idiosyncratic, but wide and eclectic literary culture of his own, makes that heritage into a workable poetic convention.

He is not of course "making antiques." Not one of his poems
is an imitation or reproduction of an existing poetic mode. His
method is commonly to take stereotyped fragments from older literary modes, then by sharpening or deforming the diction, setting
them in a new context, employing an element almost of parody, to
make the whole into a new thing. This procedure is nearer to
cubist or surrealist *collage* than, say, to Rossetti's laborious recreation of old ballads. But "Captain Carpenter" is a pastiche broadside
ballad? Yes, in a way:

> God's mercy rest on Captain Carpenter now
> I thought him Sirs an honest gentleman
> Citizen husband soldier and scholar enow
> Let jangling kites eat of him if they can.

Could this verse ever have come from an actual broadside ballad?
Not quite; there is a narrow but obvious rift between the poem and
its literary archetype. And it is in such rifts that Ransom's originality does its work. The valuables are hidden and the paths are
never straight. The reader who strides guilelessly down what appears to be a well-trodden avenue is tripped up; he who looks merely for novelty is called back to admire a well-known view. And these
obstructions to a plain progress are an essential part of the journey.

Such effects are of course highly "literary." Since Verlaine's *Art
Poétique* this has been used as a term of reproach. Ransom would
not take it so. What else should literature be? And besides the fact
that he is an outspoken defender of the finesse of art I suppose that
he has another reason for his allusive technique. Deep in his poetry
is the need to keep in touch with the homely, the popular, the
familiar. Equally pressing is the knowledge that he is also the deni-
zen of a wider world, in which he has conversed with many philosophies and many literary traditions. His particular way of working
allows him to do justice to both these strains: to stay in a familiar
room, and on every side of it to open windows over long and unexpected vistas.

VI

The greatest and most arresting poetry of our century has been
that of capacious, unusually equipped and adventurous minds. And
their explorations have led them pretty far from the paths of com-

mon daily experience, as great poetry must often do. Byzantium, the Waste Land, Sigismondo Malatesta—Ransom's poetry is on a smaller scale and belongs to another tradition. Its extreme situations are those common to all—death, old age, love imperfectly fulfilled; and the middle ground is occupied by the affections, perplexities, enchantments, and disenchantments to be met with any Monday or Tuesday. Yet "the extravagant device of art/Unhousing by abstraction" these ordinary vicissitudes has endowed them with strangeness, beauty, and meaning. It is a service that art can render us, and has not often done of late. Perhaps that is the reason that Ransom's poetry is so much loved.

F. H. BRADLEY'S *APPEARANCE AND REALITY* AND THE
CRITICAL THEORY OF JOHN CROWE RANSOM

F. P. Jarvis

The influence of the famous neo-Kantian philosopher F. H. Bradley on the thought of T. S. Eliot has long been held a commonplace, and with the recent publication of Eliot's doctoral dissertation, *Knowledge and Experience in the Philosophy of F. H. Bradley,* Eliot admirers can now determine more precisely the extent to which the poet borrowed from the philosopher.* No such written evidence exists to show Bradley's influence on the critical theory of John Crowe Ransom, and to augment the confusion, his statement, "I am obliged to think of Kant as my own mentor," would seem to preclude any further investigation of the possible sources of his thought. The fact remains, however, that Ransom's debt to F. H. Bradley, under whose tutelage he sat as a Rhodes scholar from 1911 to 1913, is far greater and more immediate than his debt to the eighteenth-century German philosopher, and without an awareness of this Bradleyian element, one's understanding of Ransom's critical theory is severely limited.

Bradley's metaphysic may be outlined as follows: Man as a sentient being lives in a phenomenal world. His experiences of the phenomenal world are appearances—appearances, one might say, of absolutes or of an Absolute; and it is only by means of these appear-

*This essay originally appeared in *Papers on English Language and Literature,* I (Spring, 1965) , 187–91.

ances that the nature of this Absolute is suggested to man. The Absolute is the sum total of its appearances. Man makes judgments on his environment, but as a finite center (like one of Leibnitz's monads) the conclusions he arrives at often differ from those of other men. That is to say, what he experiences of the Absolute, the appearances he receives, seems to be paradoxical and contradictory to the experiences of other men. But these contradictories are only verbal, and in the end they are not mutually exclusive; they merely refer to different parts and perspectives of the Absolute. The true nature of the Absolute lies in the coordination of its countless appearances. But no man is capable of knowing the Absolute entirely; only God has this knowledge.

At the risk of stooping to the ridiculous, I would suggest that Bradley's attitude is much like that of the five blind men who were asked to describe the elephant. Each one did so in terms of that part of the elephant's anatomy he could feel. The experience of any one blind man was so limited that his description nowhere approximated the total elephant, but we have the feeling that if there were enough blind men touching all the different parts of the elephant, we might conceivably know the Absolute-elephant.

Ransom's appropriation of Bradley's metaphysical system is most evident in a work where he tries his own hand at theologizing entitled *God Without Thunder* (1930). It is important for one interested in Ransom's critical thought to recognize this Bradleyian strain because it informs two fundamental aspects of his theory: his skepticism of the claim of science to offer full and adequate knowledge of the phenomenal world, and, secondly, his insistence that poetry offers such knowledge—a theory which he develops fully by means of a structure-texture motif that runs throughout his criticism until 1954. Ransom's appropriation of Bradley's metaphysic might be summarized as follows: Man confronts an object in nature (the equivalent of Bradley's Absolute). Too often he feels that in his limited experience of the object he has exhausted it, much like the blind man who presumes to know the entire elephant by merely touching its trunk. In this condition he is a scientist who feels that he has trapped the object in his formula or definition and can use it at a later date for some practical purpose. Ransom concedes that "A scientific definition of the Object is not false in the sense that it is not the truth, but only in the sense that it is not the whole truth." He goes on to equate the scientist's attempted definition with a kind of quantifying of the object, that is, a fitting of it into a scheme or draft amenable to reason and subsequently to practical use. He further suggests that in such a quantification the scientist all too often overlooks qualities of the object that he fails to detect in his limited experience of it. The scientist is the blind man, then, who, touching the trunk, is unaware that the elephant also has two tusks, four legs, and a tail. The poet or artist, on the other hand, is aware of the whole elephant. For him, the elephant was done an injustice by the blind man who presumed to dispose of it on the basis of his limited experience of the trunk. This gift of the artist or poet for taking the second look, for refusing to make routine dispositions, Ransom calls the aesthetic gift.

Ransom illustrates his practical application of Bradleyian metaphysics in a review of George Santayana's *The Realm of Matter,* written in 1930, the same year that *God Without Thunder* was first published in the United States. He lifts a passage from it as his point of departure: " ' When looking on a palm tree,' " Santayana writes, " 'I say to myself, "How straight!" I have exactly the same clear feeling: and this pure essence, not its irrelevant context, is what fills my soul, and is the essence apprehended.' " * Commenting on this passage, Ransom confirms his readers' suspicions that Santayana's mind at this juncture was not so flooded with the essence of straightness that the manifold of other qualities possessed by the palm tree fell away. After all, he writes: ". . . Mr. Santayana never claims to take an aesthetic joy from straightness in its pure essence, only from straight palm trees. Somehow the palm trees are indispensible." Straightness may be the most blatant of the palm tree's characteristics, but it is only one property existing among an illimitable variety.

Bradley's influence again may be detected in the structure-texture metaphor that Ransom formulated to embody the central ideas of his theory of poetic form, a doctrine that finds its clearest and most concise expression in a passage from *The New Criticism* where Ransom designates the poem as a loose logical structure with an irrelevant local texture. He identifies the poem's structure with its prose content or meaning. It represents what the poet has experienced of life or of the physical universe, and in this respect becomes the equivalent of what Bradley calls an appearance or of what Ran-

*Ransom, "Santayana's Palm Tree," *New Republic,* LXIV (October 22, 1930), 263.

som himself signifies in *God Without Thunder* as the scientist's attempt to quantify an object or reduce it to a handy formula. In *The New Criticism* he writes: "The structure proper is the prose of the poem, being a logical discourse of almost any kind, and dealing with almost any content suited to a logical discourse."

Again, in *The New Criticism*, Ransom explains what he means by the poem's texture: "The texture of a poem is the heterogeneous character of its detail, which either fills in the logical outline very densely or else overflows it a little. And it may be said to be imperatively a character to be looked for in anything living, such as a 'living force,' even if it is not a human force; life is such a prodigal kind of being, so much in excess of its own biological functioning."

If one may equate the poem's structure with the scientist's attempt to quantify his experience of an object or put it into a formula, then, by analogy, one may equate texture with the limitless qualities possessed by the object and located beyond the reach of the scientist's measure or experience. "A poem," Ransom writes in 1943, ". . . is everywhere particularizing itself, repudiating its nice abstract precision, and densifying itself with content which is not relevant to the argument."* This "irrelevant content" is what Ransom calls the "world's body," and is the peculiar value of poetry.

In the end, *The Critique of Judgment* remains the source book for much of Ransom's aesthetic, especially for what he has to say regarding the nature of aesthetic contemplation and the purpose of art. But one is reminded, too, that Ransom served two masters in Kant and Bradley, and that the latter may well have been the source of his metaphysical system as well as the medium through whom he met Kant.

*Ransom, "Positive and Near Positive Aesthetics," *Kenyon Review*, V (1943), 445.

RANSOM AS EDITOR

George Lanning

My house is about a thousand yards from John Crowe Ransom's. He lives to the north and east of me, on the other side of Kenyon's Middle Path (a mile-long walk that divides the village of Gambier into two roughly equal parts). His is a new house, built on a lot just behind the college house in which he lived for many years. "I've told John," Mrs. Ransom said when he retired, "that I'll go back to Nashville or I'll stay here. I don't care which; we know people to play bridge with both places. But I won't go anywhere else." She didn't, mysteriously, mention the Cleveland Indians, to whom they're devoted and who aren't, one supposes, often to be seen in Tennessee.

At any rate, because of the Indians, or the quality of the local bridge players, they stayed in Gambier; or perhaps the truth is that they absentmindedly bought land from the college and started a house before they'd really settled anything. About the design of that house Mrs. Ransom says firmly, "This is John Ransom's doing. I think it's crazy." (When she is speaking disapprovingly, she says "John Ransom"; other times she often says "Pappy"—as do many other people, though rarely in Mr. Ransom's presence.)

The house is one story, white clapboard, with blue-green shutters and window boxes along the front. At the rear is Mr. Ransom's garden—everything separated according to its nature, and lined up firmly and confined squarely. "It's not what *I'd* call a *garden*," a neighbor says every summer. "I wish John would mix things up a little, and stop putting all his plants in *rows*." One is reminded of the famous garden at Nassenheide—for Mr. Ransom, too, is a famous gardener—and how visitors came away invariably to criticize.

Between Mr. Ransom's house and mine are a great many trees and a few buildings, including a dreadfully ugly dormitory, the weekend cottage of a trustee, and the beautiful William Sparrow house, which dates from 1834 and is one of the older dwellings in Gambier. If I got out the trapdoor on my roof and stood up—God forbid—I could probably see Mr. Ransom's place; but I would not feel myself in closer communication with him than I do here, three stories down in my study. Nor would I, either here or there, feel any farther away. I have talked about the distance between our houses in order to suggest another kind of distance: that at which most of his colleagues and students stand from him, though they are a part of his "community."

He is a man of dignity and reserve, and not many of us, as deeply as we like and admire him, feel that we know him well. He is also a man of severe judgment and absolute propriety: in a way, the ordering of his garden seems to reflect the habits of his mind and conduct. A few years ago an eminent critic died who had had a long association with the *Kenyon Review*. He was not an old man, and many of us thought that much of his best work lay ahead. But Mr. Ransom said, gently, firmly, "He'd said all he had to say." Once, a very much younger critic, then at the peak of his fashion, wanted to review for us a new book by Arthur O. Lovejoy. His intentions were not amiable, and perhaps he thought of Lovejoy as the antithesis of what the New Critics stood for—a beautiful sitting duck. Mr. Ransom replied, in no uncertain terms, that the young man didn't "know enough" to review a book by a man as learned as Lovejoy. And I suppose everyone remembers Mr. Ransom's famous interpretation of Joyce Kilmer's "Trees" as a parody of sentimental nature poems. Incensed poetry lovers almost rode him out of one town on a rail after he'd made his comments. (Since he has a streak of mischievousness that comes out most obviously in his public appearances, he must have anticipated the reaction he got.)

I think of two instances when Mr. Ransom's propriety somewhat affected the magazine's relations with contributors. A lady of elegant, though small, literary reputation came through town en route by car to the West Coast. She was traveling with several unbuttoned and unshaven men. It would have been possible to put all of them up at the college guest house, but Mr. Ransom wouldn't entertain the notion. The lady slept under one roof, the men under another. What went on out on the road was their business; what went on in Gambier was the *Review's*, and would reflect on the magazine either creditably or uncreditably.

During the time when we were offering annual fellowships in fiction, poetry, and criticism, a recipient wrote asking whether he could be considered eligible for the larger stipend given to married fellows. To be sure, he was separated from his wife, but he was living with another woman, and his wife with another man. Both households, he went on, were conducted with the utmost propriety, and only the high cost of divorce prevented everyone from establishing the more conventional relationship.

I met that man recently, and he still remembered the letter in which Mr. Ransom turned him down. He was under the impression that the rules imposed on us by the grant-making foundation were so inflexible that we couldn't risk the slightest trespass. I shall have something to say later about Mr. Ransom as author of classically ambiguous letters, but let me note here that this man must have got one of the best of them. Mr. Ransom was obliged to condone an adultery belatedly brought to his attention, but I cannot imagine circumstances in which he would have encouraged it with further monetary assistance.

He is a man of endearing balkiness, and on the *Review* we were never sure what he might resist, or why. When I first went to work on the magazine, in my sophomore year at Kenyon, I was amazed to find we had no cumulative index. We were forever getting back orders and then having to riffle through the annual indexes until we ran down the issue in which the requested material appeared. This was time-consuming and boring; it was also dirty work, since back issues sat around on open shelves, collecting dust, spiders' eggs, and water stains from dripping overhead pipes. A cumulative index would have been useful in the office and in pamphlet form might have been sold to libraries. But the project, though several times proposed, was not to Mr. Ransom's liking. I was sure that its advantages had not been presented to him forcibly enough, and I asked Mary Rahming, the secretary of the magazine, if I might bring the matter up again.

Mr. Ransom heard me out; he was all amiability; he was even enthusiastic; he talked about the problems of editing a literary quarterly; he asked about my courses and commented on his own. "What did he say?" Mary Rahming asked when I returned to the business office.

"I don't know," I told her. "He said quite a lot, but . . ."

The index was launched, though furtively. I must add that it wasn't finished until more than a decade later. After completion of the twenty-fifth volume, the present business manager of the magazine, Elizabeth Browne, took on the awful job. For months she worked at night on her dining room table, and toward the end she said that if fire struck she'd save the index first and the children afterward. So perhaps Mr. Ransom was correct to oppose our tackling such a big, extra job on office time. But he never inquired about what progress we were making, and it may be that, in the course of our expansive and friendly exchange, I somehow failed to make clear what I'd come to ask him about.

We all had a curious problem of communication with him. His conversations were engrossing; they were sometimes spirited; one groped for any topic that would prolong them, and the pleasure of his presence. But later one thought: what decisions were reached? what judgments were pronounced? Mr. Ransom has been hard of hearing for some years, and his *Review* colleagues have speculated occasionally that our perpetual state of confusion in dealings with him is due to his imperfect reception of what we're saying. How else, on the one hand, explain the Alice-in-Wonderland conversations and, on the other, the clarity and order of his best critical writing? But that, if part of the truth, is not the whole of it. The rest is that Mr. Ransom is one of those rare men of intelligence and learning who are too kind to swat down less gifted associates. For their sake as well as his own, he has retreated behind a particularly beguiling kind of double-talk that leaves everyone happy and flattered and everything unsettled—or, rather, perfectly settled as Mr. Ransom meant it to be from the first.

The *Review* offices of those days—I am talking about the late forties and the fifties—deserve comment, for visitors were astonished by the squalor from which the magazine emerged. We were located in Ascension Hall, an old building in the college park which contained the president's, dean's, and other administrative offices, and classrooms for the liberal arts courses. The *Review* occupied two rooms in the basement. The business office was on the east side of a hallway that transected the floor from north to south, and looked out on a parking lot (people were always tugging open our casement windows and asking, "Is John here? or isn't it worth coming in?"). The editorial office was across the hall and down two doors. Because the basement was below ground level on that side of the building, Mr. Ransom's windows faced into a mossy stone well. The room was dark and cheerless, and on gloomy winter days oppressive, but for Mr. Ransom it must have had its congenialities: the study in his new house is also in the basement. Along one wall of this office was a blackboard on which the contents for the next issue were written out, together with reminders, notes on assignments and possible projects, and so on. (The magazine almost folded on the night when a conscientious cleaning woman washed the board.)

Across the hall from Mr. Ransom was the office of the philosophy department, and here his managing editor, Philip Blair Rice, had a desk. I suppose, then, you might say the *Review* had two and a half rooms for itself.

They were terrible rooms. In winter, heat passed without pause through the overhead pipes, and in summer damp and mustiness prevailed. The whitewashed pipes clanked and shook in the cold, and in warm weather were beaded with moisture. To stay in either office for long was to collect so many flecks of whitewash that you appeared to have unmelted snow in your hair. In both offices were double desks whose drawers had to be wrenched open in wet or humid weather—that is, from April to November—and often stayed shut despite the most profane and enraged tuggings. (I regret to say that one of those desks has sullenly followed us on our later travels to other buildings and a better life.)

There was a bookcase in the business office into which all review copies were put. These were fair game for everybody connected with the magazine. Mr. Ransom's humane viewpoint was that we got paid so badly that the books helped take up the salary slack. It was understood, of course, that if he said, "Have you seen———?" it was to be brought back and unobtrusively placed where he would find it. No one was expected to admit to having appropriated the book in the first place. The briskest business, inevitably, was in murder mysteries, and these were guarded jealously and, when carried away, kept track of and asked for after a reasonable period. There was a waiting list, though not of reviewers.

A few years ago, Robie Macauley and I went through some old files of the *Review* and threw away a lot of long-dead correspondence. We had to be drastic, because we were desperate for space, but both of us will always regret having to dispose of the carbons to Mr. Ransom's letters of rejection (unlike his successors, he kept a carbon of everything). Most of the letters he typed himself, and sometimes, we decided, the subconscious was strongly at work. For instance: "I don't appreciate your sending these poems to us, and am happy to return them to you with our thanks. . . ." Often, the double-talk was employed: "There are handsome things here, and fine strong ideas, and we like your wanting us to have these, but not quite enough." When his back was to the wall, and he was dealing with someone he'd either encouraged or published and didn't want to lose, he was inclined to write that the *Review*'s material was selected sub specie aeternitatis, and that excellent as the enclosed matter was it did not quite . . . , etc.

The *Review* was never in everyone's good graces at the college, and one of its critics was Kenyon's then president (who, paradoxically, had been responsible for its founding). He had conceived of a magazine of a more general nature, along the lines of the *Yale Review,* a publication he particularly admired and for which, I think, he sometimes wrote. Though he had the generosity to let the editors take their own course, he was known to consider the magazine "sophomoric." More pertinent comments came from some members of the English department; they disliked the New Criticism and, one rather suspected, the New Critics (who seemed, as one heard more about them, to lead lively and complicated sex lives that might reasonably make lesser men envious and hostile). The New Critics, it was said, were ill-educated; they made staggering points based on misquotations; their ignorance of history and biography led them into elementary errors of interpretation; they were arrogant; and often they seemed willfully obscure.

No doubt plenty of evidence could be found to support each of these charges, but some of the best among those writers had a playfulness that acted as a leaven for their authoritarianism, and made their arrogance rather touching and artless. They were like good teachers proposing exciting if sometimes wacky new ideas to imaginative, restless students. William Empson claimed that he read murder mysteries in order to see whether, from internal evidence, he could guess the copyright date. That casual remark has always, for

me, cast a small but informing light over the joyous venture that
criticism was in those days.

Where obscurity was concerned, Mr. Ransom was seldom daunted
either by his writers or his readers. He came into the business
office once with a manuscript he'd accepted from an eminent regular of those days. He held it up by one corner, as if its sheets needed
fresh air and sunshine, and said, "There's some mighty fancy language here, but it doesn't mean much." Another time, one of the
magazine's less enthusiastic supporters on the faculty brought in his
copy of the latest issue and said, "John, read that first paragraph."
(The piece in question was an essay by R. P. Blackmur on *Anna
Karenina*.)

Mr. Ransom dutifully read the first paragraph.

"Now, tell me," said his colleague, "what the hell that *means*."

"I don't know!" Mr. Ransom replied cheerfully. "I don't know."

As an editor, Mr. Ransom displayed a similar insouciance when
it came to mechanical matters. There was no discernible "house
style" except in the spelling of centuries—20th Century, never twentieth century or Twentieth Century—and "labour" might turn up
in one essay and "labor" in the next. The orthodox, and really only
satisfactory, way of proofreading (one reader holding manuscript,
the other galleys, and each reading aloud in turn) was seldom followed. As a result, some insidious typos now bask complacently sub
specie aeternitatis. Mr. Ransom always insisted on making up an issue in one day—no one knew why, since this is the easiest of jobs
to break off from and return to without getting confused—but he
was oblivious to "widows," those typographical harpies that preside
at paging-up sessions. And he was content, as a rule, with the com-
positor's theory of syllabification, though it often led the *Review*
down strangely original paths. The body type, presumably, had been
selected with some care; and Moholy-Nagy had designed the cover
that most readers probably still associate with the magazine. I didn't
understand then, and don't now, why concern for the appearance
of the *Review* went this far but never farther.

Mr. Ransom was not fond of subscription campaigns, perhaps because the first number of the *Review* was sent free to the entire
alumni body of Kenyon and produced not a single response. Nevertheless, each year before Christmas we did a mailing—usually to our
own subscribers and recent lapses—in the hope that readers would
not only send in renewals but order gift subscriptions at (of course)

a remarkable saving. Mr. Ransom either wrote the copy himself or extensively revised that done by other people; and I am sure there is at least one Ph.D. dissertation to be got from the Stately Subscription Letters of John Crowe Ransom. He began several of them "Dear Literate," which must have occasioned surprise as well as gratification in some of the recipients. The Dear Literates never responded in droves—except in the sense that the volume of manuscript submissions picked up for a month or two, each Dear Literate being persuaded that we would prefer his story, poem, or essay to his check.

Everybody dreaded and hated these campaigns; *we* believed passionately in the *Kenyon Review,* but it was hard to think up reasons why anyone not similarly committed should unload it on relatives or friends instead of a Christmas bottle of bourbon or a box of dish towels or even a subscription to the *Saturday Evening Post.* The annual labor was gone through glumly, and when, weeks later, the last of those reply-paid envelopes came drifting in a euphoria seized the staff. We knew you had to do this kind of thing, and we had done it, but now we could forget the whole business for another year. Who knew? Subscriptions might pick up of their own accord. There was one terrible time when Mary Rahming and I had stuffed and sealed subscription brochures all day long. We had so few facilities that only ingenuity could cope with a big mailing, and we had sorted and tied envelopes and then stored them in borrowed wastebaskets until maintenance men came to cart them away to the post office. That night a new janitor emptied the wastebaskets into trash containers, and we spent the next day getting our envelopes back—they were covered with cigar and cigarette ashes, the decayed peelings from various kinds of fruit, and unspeakable blotches that looked like spit.

I don't recall that this was one of our more successful campaigns.

Mr. Ransom was vague about the circulation of the magazine, and when pressed usually said "around 5000." Mary Rahming must have known better—she had to fill out post office forms, after all—but perhaps she thought Mr. Ransom was speaking in some large sense that embraced our total readership. In fact, the circulation of the *Review,* despite its enormous influence and fame, was about 2000. I didn't find this out until much later, however, and like everyone else I imagined that almost every Dear Literate in the country was already in our fold. When returns came in from a campaign,

I would say, "Well, that takes us up to 5027 or thereabouts, doesn't it?" Blithely, we wrote letters to potential advertisers telling them that our circulation was rapidly approaching the 6000 mark.

Once in a while, Mr. Ransom and Phil Rice would brood on possible features that might make the magazine more popular with the general reader. The only one I can recall Mr. Ransom suggesting—and he came up with it every time—was a crossword puzzle which would occupy the magazine's back page. It would be, of course, of the highest literary order, difficult and yet irresistible. Both of the Ransoms are addicted—the word is too mild—to crossword puzzles, and not above accosting friends and neighbors in the street or at the grocery store with bewildering questions resulting from their weekly struggle with *The Nation*'s puzzles. So I suppose Mr. Ransom envisioned similar addicts scattered about in our colleges and universities, all of whom would have to subscribe to the *Review* in order to work on the puzzle, rather than meanly reading a library or departmental copy.

The New Criticism had done its job by . . . when? One is obliged to be arbitrary, and so let us say 1953. By that time, at least, the enthusiasm for the cause, the pleasure in victory, had palled. Many of the original troupe had become so successful—so rich, too, in a few instances—that they'd gone on to other endeavors. Mr. Ransom's own thinking had changed since publication of *The New Criticism* in 1941, and he had come to dislike the phrase and, one supposes, much that it implied (or, in one of his own favorite terms of that period, "imported"). Since he was always many long strides ahead of his fellow critics, the question can be raised whether the magazine in the mid-fifties represented anything like his own thinking, or even many of his interests. I would suppose that, to some extent at least, it went along on momentum. And by then he had been editing it for a long time; for an extraordinary period, considering the life of most magazines of this sort.

There were internal changes, too. In 1956 his friend and fellow editor, Philip Blair Rice, died from injuries received in a car accident. That was in the winter. In the summer, Charles Coffin, chairman of Kenyon's English department and for many years an informal and always wise adviser to the *Review*, died of a heart attack in California. Phil Rice was succeeded by Ted Bogardus, who had recently had his first book selected for the Yale Series of Younger Poets. Not long afterward, Ted died one night, from carbon monoxide poisoning, in his family home in nearby Mount Vernon. The joy of the enterprise must by then have been gone, and on campus there were the usual rumors—they spring up every two or three years—that the *Review* was going to close down. Certainly, when one stopped in the office, there was no sense of gaiety and adventure, as there had been in the old days (at the time I'm writing of I'd been away from the magazine for five or six years). When I started on the *Review,* the atmosphere was that of a country store, with everybody dropping in and looking at the new books and poking the piles of manuscripts derogatorily and reporting the latest village gossip. Kermit Lansner, now managing editor of *Newsweek,* was one of our manuscript readers, and Kermit appeared every day looking cheery but filled with terrible local stories. (As I write this, I realize that his progress from a literary quarterly to a weekly news magazine makes more sense than it ever has before.) Even Robert Hillyer, no friend to the *Review,* came in occasionally when the coast was clear. He would look over our books and then pick up the latest copy of the magazine and say, "May I take this along and just glance over it?"

I see no way of rounding off these comments gracefully. Those were heady times, and then—as a child might write, finishing off his first story for lack of a better ending—everybody died. In fact, it seemed that way, for the president of the college, the man responsible for the *Review*'s founding, also died, and mortality began to afflict contributors. Though Mr. Ransom continued in good health, he was approaching retirement, and I suppose he was finding the endless flow of manuscripts, the endless correspondence and proofreading and meeting of deadlines, more and more wearisome. At any rate, he was anxious to turn the editorship over to a younger man who would find a fresh direction for the *Review.* There were plenty of candidates, but it must have pleased Mr. Ransom that the man chosen was Robie Macauley, his former student and a frequent writer for the magazine.

In the early years of Robie's tenure, Mr. Ransom almost never came to the office. He explained later that he hadn't wanted Robie to feel that he still wished a hand in editorial matters. More recently, we've seen him as often as business has brought him our way. He seems entirely a visitor; no proprietorial eye is cast around, and an outsider would never guess that, except for him, none of us would be here. I have wondered whether—as he has discarded so much of his poetry, so many of his books and other critical writings—he has discarded his time on the *Review* as irrelevant to his present undertakings. He is still moving ahead, and the old days and the old issues are long gone. For the sense of continuity, if he ever requires it, there is always his garden.

BIBLIOGRAPHY

Mildred Brooks Peters

John Crowe Ransom's published works may be described generally under three headings: poetry, social criticism, and literary criticism. His productive years as a poet began with the preparation of his first volume of verse, *Poems About God* (1919), and extended through the years 1922–25 when Nashville, Tennessee, with its little magazine *The Fugitive*, was one of the principal centers of literary activity in the South. Largely from poems originally published in *The Fugitive* came Ransom's second volume of verse, *Chills and Fever* (1924). His third volume, *Two Gentlemen in Bonds*, appeared in 1927. Since that time, he has written only a handful of new poems, but he has revised many of those written much earlier. Three editions of selected poems have been issued, the first in 1945, the second (a paperback collection of selected poems and essays) in 1955, and the third, the revised edition of *Selected Poems*, in 1963.

With the contribution of an essay to the Agrarian symposium *I'll Take My Stand* (1930), Ransom entered the field of social criticism. He was also represented in a second symposium, *Who Owns America? A Declaration of Independence* (1936), edited by Herbert Agar and Allen Tate. Between the years 1930 and 1936 he published—in such periodicals as the *American Review*, the *New Republic*, and *Scribner's Magazine*—several articles elaborating his agrarian theories.

With *God Without Thunder* (1930), his first book-length prose work, Ransom entered the field of literary criticism and philosophic inquiry. *God Without Thunder* was followed by two volumes of critical essays, *The World's Body* (1938) and *The New Criticism* (1941). These works, together with articles published in periodicals—including the *Kenyon Review* which he edited for many years—have earned Ransom a position as one of the leading twentieth-century critics of English and American literature.

Many of Ransom's essays and a few of his poems have not been collected and are scattered through the pages of various periodicals. Some of these magazines, such as *Contemporary Verse* and the *American Review*, ceased publication in the 1920's or 1930's and are no longer readily available. Although there is no complete bibliography of Ransom's works, Robert Wooster Stallman's checklist (*Sewanee Review*, LVI, Summer, 1948) and the bibliography at the end of Karl F. Knight's *The Poetry of John Crowe Ransom* (The Hague: Mouton and Company, 1964) have been most helpful in this compilation, which, in extending the preliminary work of these two scholars, attempts to record, in a form convenient for use by scholars and students, all of Ransom's writings. In addition, the final section of this bibliography is a listing, with brief annotation, of the critical and interpretative comment on Ransom's writings and literary career.

The first section of the bibliography lists, in chronological order according to publication date, Ransom's twelve books and their contents, beginning with *Poems About God* (1919) and continuing with his additional works of poetry, his volumes of critical essays, and his textbooks. The section concludes with the revised and enlarged edition of *Selected Poems* (1963). Reviews in newspapers and periodicals were located for all of Ransom's books except three—*Topics for Freshman Writing* (1935), *A College Primer of Writing* (1943), and the Vintage paperback edition of *Poems and Essays* (1955). Reviews of the remaining nine books are listed immediately following the outline of each of their contents. Only those newspaper reviews cited by Stallman or Knight or quoted from in *Book Review Digest* are included, but the list of reviews appearing in magazines and professional journals is intended to be complete.

The second section of the bibliography is an alphabetical listing of the 152 poems which have been located. Immediately following the name of each poem is an entry noting the place of initial publication; then the poem is traced through reprintings in Ransom's own collections. It was also necessary to indicate in Section II the poems by Ransom which were included in two anthologies published in the 1920's, *Miscellany of American Poetry*, edited by Louis Untermeyer (New York: Harcourt, Brace and Company, 1925) and *Fugitives: An Anthology of Verse* (New York: Harcourt, Brace and Company, 1928). The entire sonnet sequence "Two Gentlemen in Bonds," with the exception of one sonnet, "Rain," was printed for the first time in Untermeyer's *Miscellany*, and one poem, "What Ducks Require," initially published in the *New Republic*, had its first book publication in the Fugitive anthology.

Some of Ransom's poems appearing both in *Poems About God* and in *Chills and Fever* were first printed, according to Ransom's notes in those two volumes, in the *Philadelphia Evening Public Ledger*, copies of which for the years 1919–24 were not immediately available. Therefore, entries for an undetermined number of Ransom's poems printed in that newspaper have been omitted from this bibliography. In addition, Ransom states in the preface to *Poems About God* that one or more poems in his first collected volume appeared in the *Liberator*. On the assumption that the magazine referred to is the one edited by Max Eastman from March, 1919, to October, 1924, copies of all seven volumes of the *Liberator* were examined at the library of the University of Illinois; no poem by John Crowe Ransom was located.

A preliminary investigation was made of the possibility of indicating the appearance of individual poems in publications other than Ransom's collected volumes. Ransom's publisher, Alfred A. Knopf, furnished a list of publishing companies to whom permission had been granted for the publication of some of Ransom's poems; however, it was not possible for either Ransom's publisher or any of the various publishers requesting publication rights to provide a list of anthologies and other works designed as high school and college textbooks in which Ransom's poems appear.

In order to indicate something of the popularity of Ransom's poems as well as to show which poems are more readily available, three works have been consulted to provide a count of anthologized poems. To those poems in anthologies which are included in *Granger's Index to Poetry*, edited by William F. Bernhardt (New York: Columbia University Press, 1962), have been added the poems contained in two new anthologies: *The Literature of the South* (second edition), edited by Thomas Daniel Young and Floyd C. Watkins (Chicago: Scott, Foresman and Company, 1968), and *The Literature of America*, edited by J. L. Maline and James Berkley (New York: L. W. Singer Company and Random House, 1967). The number of appearances of each poem in the anthologies indexed in *Granger's* and in the two new collections is indicated immediately following the chronology of publication of the poem in Section II. For instance, the legend "A-26" appears as the concluding item of information given for the poem "Bells for John Whiteside's Daughter," indicating that the poem is included in twenty-six of the selected anthologies.

It should also be noted that almost every poem appearing in more than one of Ransom's published works has been revised from one publication to the next. Not only have revisions been made in poems appearing initially in magazines and journals before their publication in a book-length work, but changes have also been made in most of the poems taken from early volumes and republished in Selected Poems. A study of the revisions would undoubtedly produce an informative and meaningful work; unfortunately, because of the extent of the alterations which have been made in many poems, it was not possible to include in the present study a summary statement concerning revisions.

Ransom's writing up to 1927 was not, of course, limited to the composition of poems. The earliest of the 124 essays listed in Section III, "Essays and Articles," carried the title "The Question of Justice" and appeared in the *Yale Review* for July, 1915. Several other essays and articles were printed in *The Fugitive* and elsewhere in the 1920's. The most recent article included in Section III, "Gerontion," appeared in the Spring, 1966, issue of the *Sewanee Review.*

Many of Ransom's essays, particularly those published in the 1930's and 1940's were later reprinted, either in a collection of his own essays or in volumes of representative literary criticism or of collected critical essays pertaining to such prominent literary figures as Wordsworth and Yeats. All available information concerning the reprinting of a given essay is placed immediately after the bibliographical entry recording its original appearance. Furthermore, a few articles initially written as book reviews are included in Section III because they were later reprinted, in whole or in part, as essays in collections. These are also included in Section IV, "Book Reviews in Periodicals," where seventy-two of Ransom's book reviews are listed in alphabetical order by author of the book reviewed.

Book reviews listed in Section V include seventy-seven signed reviews contributed to the book page of the *Nashville Tennessean* during the years 1924 to 1930, when Donald Davidson was editor of the book page. Information for this section was taken from microfilm copies of the *Nashville Tennessean* available at the Tennessee State Library. A few reviews may have been omitted since the book page was not available for each week of the seven-year period. Omissions were particularly noticeable for the spring of 1930, as a complete copy of all editions of the newspaper for that period was not available at the time the microfilm was produced.

Entries in Section VII, "Biographical and Critical Material," are limited to those books, articles, and dissertations directly concerned with Ransom's career. It should be pointed out that no effort has been made to cite all of the biographical sketches of Ransom included as introductory material to his poems in textbooks or general anthologies. Furthermore, this section does not purport to be a bibliography of either the Fugitive or the Agrarian movement, of modern poetic criticism, or of the New Criticism. Critical commentary in all of these areas is included when Ransom is mentioned specifically or when his poetry or his critical or social theories are discussed. Indeed, since Ransom's critical pronouncements form an integral part of modern literary criticism, almost every work published since 1935 dealing in any way with literary criticism contains reference to Ransom. Undoubtedly several books and articles making brief references to Ransom and the New Criticism have been overlooked. It is believed, however, that the essential critical estimates of Ransom's poetry, agrarian ideas, and critical theories are cited in Section VII.

I. BOOKS

Poems About God. (Poems.) New York: Henry Holt and Company, 1919.

Contents: "The Swimmer," "Noonday Grace," "The Ingrate," "Sunset," "One Who Rejected Christ," "Grace," "Moonlight," "Street Light," "Darkness," "Geometry," "The Lover," "Dumb-bells," "Overtures," "Under the Locusts," "Worship," "The Cloak Model," "By the Riverside," "The Bachelor," "Roses," "November," "A Christmas Colloquy," "The Power of God," "The Resurrection," "Men," "The Christian," "Morning," "April," "Wrestling," "Prayer," "Friendship," "The Four Roses," "The School," "Sickness."

Signed Reviews

Egan, Maurice F. *Bookman,* L (October, 1919), 222–23.
Stork, Charles W. *Yale Review,* IX (April, 1920), 660–67.
Untermeyer, Louis. *Dial,* LXVI (May 31, 1919), 562–63.

Unsigned Reviews

Current Opinion, LXVI (May, 1919), 324.
Nation, CIX (July 26, 1919), 115–16.
New York Call, April 6, 1919, p. 11.
New York Times Book Review, November 2, 1919, p. 616.
Poetry (A. H.), XVI (April, 1920), 51–52.
Springfield Republican, June 29, 1919.

Chills and Fever. (Poems.) New York: Alfred A. Knopf, 1924.

Contents: "Agitato ma non troppo," "Spectral Lovers," "Bells for John Whiteside's Daughter," "Winter Remembered," "Triumph," "Two Sonnets," "Spring Posy," "To a Lady Celebrating Her Birthday," "Vaunting Oak," "In Process of a Noble Alliance," "Parting at Dawn," "Miriam Tazewell," "Here Lies a Lady," "The Tall Girl," "Fall of Leaf," "Rapunzel Has Submitted Herself to Fashion," "The Vagrant," "Boris of Britain," "April Treason," "First Travels of Max," "Grandgousier," "Miss Euphemia," "Winter's Tale," "Emily Hardcastle, Spinster," "Number Five," "Good Ships," "Youngest Daughter," "Necrological," "Armageddon," "Epitaph," "Judith of Bethulia," "Conrad Sits in Twilight," "Nocturne," "Blackberry Winter," "Lichas to Polydor," "Spiel of the Three Mountebanks," "Night Voices," "Adventure This Side of Pluralism," "On the Road to Wockensutter," "Prometheus in Straits," "Plea in Mitigation," "Tom, Tom, the Piper's Son," "Old Man Playing with Children," "Captain Carpenter," "These Winters," "Old Mansion," "Inland City," "Philomela."

Signed Reviews

Deutsch, Babette. *New Republic*, XLIII (May 27, 1925), 23–24.
Gorman, H. S. *New York Times Book Review*, September 14, 1924, p. 14.
Graves, Robert. *Saturday Review of Literature*, I (December 27, 1924), 412.
Humphries, Rolfe. *The Measure*, No. 49 (March, 1925), 15–17.
Kenyon, Bernice L. *Bookman*, LX (November, 1924), 345–46.
Morley, Christopher. *Vanderbilt Alumnus*, X (October, 1924), 5.
Niles, E. A. *Independent*, CXIII (November 1, 1924), 347.
Percy, William Alexander. *Double Dealer*, VII (January-February, 1925), 114–16.
Tate, Allen. *Guardian*, I (November, 1924), 25.
Untermeyer, Louis. *Yale Review*, XIV (July, 1925), 791–97.

Unsigned Reviews

Boston Evening Transcript, September 20, 1924, p. 5.
Literary Review (W. Y.), V (September 27, 1924), 15.

Grace After Meat. (Poems.) London: Hogarth Press, 1924. (Introduction by Robert Graves.)

Contents: "An American Addresses Philomela," "The School," "Grace," "By the Riverside," "Resurrection," "Winter Remembered," "Under the Locusts," "The Cloak Model," "Wrestling," "The Lover," "Necrological," "Adventure This Side of Pluralism," "Night Voices," "In Process of the Nuptials of the Duke," "At Dawn," "Armageddon," "Two Sonnets," "Judith of Bethulia," "Moonlight," "Ilex Priscus."

Reviews

Deutsch, Babette. *New Republic*, XLIII (May 27, 1925), 23–24.
Muir, Edwin. *Saturday Review of Literature*, I (June 6, 1925), 807.

Two Gentlemen in Bonds. (Poems.) New York: Alfred A. Knopf, 1927.

Contents

The Innocent Doves: "Vision by Sweetwater," "Eclogue," "Piazza Piece," "Moments of Minnie," "Husband Betrayed," "Miller's Daughter," "Blue Girls," "Her Eyes," "Parting, Without a Sequel," "Hilda," "In Mr. Minnit's House," "Janet Waking," "Little Boy Blue," "Lady Lost."
The Manliness of Men: "Our Two Worthies," "Dead Boy," "Puncture," "Semi-Centennial," "Two in August," "Somewhere Is Such a Kingdom," "Persistent Explorer," "Morning," "Dog," "Jack's Letter," "Antique Harvesters," "Man Without Sense of Direction," "Survey of Literature,"

"Amphibious Crocodile," "Fresco: From the Last Judgment," "The Equilibrists."

Two Gentlemen in Bonds: "Pink and Pale," "Thinking, Drinking," "In Air," "Thought, Distraught," "Meeting in a Garden," "Epithalamion of a Peach," "Swine, Wine," "L'état C'est Moi," "Misanthropy," "Vain Protestations," "Tones and Caparisons," "Disappointment of a Thrall," "In Bed, Not Dead," "Primer of Science," "Fait Accompli," "Implacable Tower," "Features of Creatures," "Rain," "Wrong," "Weep or Sleep."

Signed Reviews

Aiken, Conrad. *Independent,* CXVIII (February 26, 1927), 246.

Davidson, Donald. *Nashville Tennessean,* January 23, 1927. Reprinted in *The Spyglass.* Edited by John Tyree Fain. Nashville: Vanderbilt University Press, 1963, p. 105.

Deutsch, Babette. *Bookman,* LXV (April, 1927), 220–21.

Fletcher, John Gould. *Criterion,* VI (July, 1927), 168–72.

Gorman, H. S. *New York Times Book Review,* March 27, 1927, p. 2.

Knickerbocker, William S. *Sewanee Review,* XXXVI (April, 1928), 211–24.

Luhrs, Marie. *Poetry,* XXX (June, 1927), 163–65.

Taggard, Genevieve. *New York Herald Tribune Books,* June 26, 1927, p. 12.

Tate, Allen. *Nation,* CXXIV (March 30, 1927), 346.

Wilson, Edmund. *New Republic,* XLIX (February 2, 1927), 310.

Unsigned Reviews

Booklist, XXIII (May, 1927), 337.

Cleveland Open Shelf, April, 1927, p. 48.

Literary Review, VII (February 5, 1927), 6.

New Statesman, XXIX (May 21, 1927), 188.

Springfield Republican, February 21, 1927, p. 6.

God Without Thunder: An Unorthodox Defense of Orthodoxy. (An Essay.) New York: Harcourt, Brace and Company, 1930. Reprinted by Archon Books, Hamden, Conn., 1965.

Contents

The Dynasty of Heaven Changes: "The New God," "The Old God," "Nature and the Supernatural," "Principles or Gods?" "Religion and Magic," "Satan as Science," "Christ as Science."

The New God's Limits: "What Can He Do?" "We His Poor Followers," "What Does He Know?" "A Table and a Geographical Machine."

Ghosts: Including the Holy: "Finite Ghosts," "Infinite Ghosts," "The Holy Ghost."

Epilogue: "By Way of a Program."

Signed Reviews

Bates, Ernest Sutherland. *Saturday Review of Literature,* VII (February 28, 1931), 627.
Buchanan, Scott. *Virginia Quarterly Review,* VII (July, 1931), 451–57.
Douglas, Lloyd C. *Christian Century,* XLVII (December 3, 1930), 1490–91.
Fletcher, John Gould. *Criterion,* XI (October, 1931), 127–31.
Fergusson, Francis. *Bookman,* LXXIII (March, 1931), 100.
Grattan, C. H. *New York World,* December 7, 1930, p. 3e.
Knickerbocker, William S. *Sewanee Review,* XXXIX (Winter, 1931), 103–11.
Middleton, J. S. *Commonweal,* XIII (February 4, 1931), 385–86.
Morrow, Felix. *Nation,* CXXXI (December 24, 1930), 711.
Sullivan, W. L. *New York Herald Tribune Books,* January 11, 1931, p. 10.

Unsigned Reviews

Boston Evening Transcript, November 29, 1930, p. 8.
Cleveland Open Shelf, September, 1931, p. 115.
Living Church, LXXXV (September 12, 1931), 657.
Times Literary Supplement, December 24, 1931, p. 1036.
World Tomorrow (R. N.), XIV (February, 1931), 59.

Topics for Freshman Writing: Twenty Topics for Writing with Appropriate Materials for Study. (A college textbook.) New York: Henry Holt and Company, 1935.

The World's Body. (Essays.) New York: Charles Scribner's Sons, 1938.

Contents: "A Poem Nearly Anonymous," "Forms and Citizens," "Poets Without Laurels," "The Poet as Woman," "Poetry: A Note in Ontology," "A Psychologist Looks at Poetry," "A Cathedralist Looks at Murder," "The Cathartic Principle," "The Mimetic Principle," "Sentimental Exercise," "The Tense of Poetry," "Contemporaneous Not Contemporary," "Shakespeare at Sonnets," "Art and Mr. Santayana," "Criticism, Inc."

Signed Reviews

Blackmur, R. P. *Virginia Quarterly Review,* XIV (Summer, 1938), 445–50.
Burke, Kenneth. *Poetry,* LV (October, 1939), 50–54.
Canby, Henry S. *Saturday Review of Literature,* XVIII (May 21, 1938), 8–9.
Every, George. *Purpose,* X (1938), 229–32.
Hutchison, Percy. *New York Times Book Review,* December 18, 1938, p. 12.
Jenckes, E. N. *Springfield Republican,* April 23, 1938, p. 6.
Kronenberger, Louis. *Nation,* CXLVII (August 13, 1938), 160–62.
Merton, Thomas. *New York Herald Tribune Books,* XIV (May 8, 1938), 10.
Mizener, Arthur. *Southern Review,* V (Autumn, 1939), 376–400.

Moss, H. J. *Boston Evening Transcript,* May 28, 1938, p. 3.
Pottle, F. A. *Yale Review,* XXVIII (Autumn, 1938), 183–85.
Roberts, Michael. *Criterion,* XVIII (October, 1938–January, 1939), 152–54.
Spencer, Theodore. *New Republic,* XCVI (August 10, 1938), 27–28.

Unsigned Reviews

Booklist, XXXIV (June 15, 1938), 360.
New Yorker, XIV (April 30, 1938), 63.
Time, XXXI (May 9, 1938), 67.
Times Literary Supplement, August 13, 1938, p. 532.

The New Criticism. (Four essays.) Norfolk, Conn.: New Directions, 1941.

Contents: "I. A. Richards: the Psychological Critic. And William Empson,
His Pupil," T. S. Eliot: the Historical Critic" (reprinted in *T. S. Eliot:
A Selected Critique.* Edited by L. Unger. New York: Rinehart and
Company, 1948, pp. 51–74), "Yvor Winters: the Logical Critic,"
"Wanted: an Ontological Critic" (reprinted in *Little Treasury of Ameri-
can Prose: The Major Writers from Colonial Times to the Present Day.*
Edited by George Mayberry. New York: Charles Scribner's Sons, 1949, pp.
645–62).

Signed Reviews

Bogan, Louise. *Nation,* CLIII (July 12, 1941), 37.
Burke, Kenneth. *Kenyon Review,* IV (Winter, 1942), 126–32.
Cowie, Alexander. *Saturday Review of Literature,* XXIV (July 5, 1941), 13.
Deutsch, Babette. *New York Herald Tribune Books,* XVII (June 15, 1941),
11.
Eberhart, Richard. *Accent,* II (Autumn, 1941), 51–55.
Healy, J. V. *Poetry,* LXI (January, 1943), 575–79.
Knickerbocker, William S. *Sewanee Review,* XLIX (October, 1941), 520–36.
Millet, Fred B. *American Literature,* XV (March, 1943), 82–84.
Muller, Herbert J. *Yale Review,* XXXI (March, 1942), 608–11.

A College Primer of Writing. (A college textbook.) New York: Henry Holt
and Company, 1943.

Selected Poems. New York: Alfred A. Knopf, 1945.

Contents: "Winter Remembered," "Miriam Tazewell," "Dead Boy," "Spectral
Lovers," "Necrological," "Bells for John Whiteside's Daughter," "The
Tall Girl," "Good Ships," "Emily Hardcastle, Spinster," "Parting at
Dawn," "Vaunting Oak," "Spiel of the Three Mountebanks," "Here Lies
a Lady," "Tom, Tom, the Piper's Son," "Conrad in Twilight," "Armaged-

don," "Judith of Bethulia," "Blue Girls," "Philomela," "Old Man Playing
with Children," "Captain Carpenter," "Old Mansion," "Piazza Piece,"
"Eclogue," "Her Eyes," "Parting, Without a Sequel," "Janet Waking,"
"Lady Lost," "Two in August," "Somewhere Is Such a Kingdom," "An-
tique Harvesters," "Our Two Worthies," "Puncture," "Dog," "Man With-
out Sense of Direction," "Survey of Literature," "The Equilibrists,"
"What Ducks Require," "Prelude to an Evening," "Of Margaret,"
"Painted Head," "Address to the Scholars of New England."

Signed Reviews

Dupee, F. W. *Nation*, CLXI (August 11, 1945), 138–39.
Eberhart, Richard. *Poetry*, LXVII (January, 1946), 212–15.
Mizener, Arthur. *Quarterly Review of Literature*, II (1945), 366–70.
Moss, Howard. *New York Times Book Review*, July 8, 1945, p. 6.
Norton, Dan S. *Virginia Quarterly Review*, XXII (Summer, 1946), 438–47.
Richman, Robert. *Accent*, VI (Spring, 1946), 206–207.
Spencer, Theodore. *Saturday Review of Literature*, XXVIII (July 14, 1945),
30–31.
Wahl, Jean. *New Republic*, CXIII (August 13, 1945), 196–98.

Unsigned Reviews

Furioso (H. H.), II (Fall, 1946), 65–66.
New Yorker, XXI (July 7, 1945), 67.

Poems and Essays. New York: Vintage Books, 1955. (Paperback.)

Poems: "Winter Remembered," "Miriam Tazewell," "Dead Boy," "Spectral
Lovers," "Necrological," "Bells for John Whiteside's Daughter," "The
Tall Girl," "Good Ships," "Emily Hardcastle, Spinster," "Parting at
Dawn," "Vaunting Oak," "Spiel of the Three Mountebanks," "Here Lies
a Lady," "Tom, Tom, the Piper's Son," "Conrad in Twilight," "Armaged-
don," "Judith of Bethulia," "Blue Girls," "Philomela," "Old Man Play-
ing with Children," "Captain Carpenter," "Old Mansion," "Piazza Piece,"
"Eclogue," "Vision by Sweetwater," "Her Eyes," "Parting, Without a
Sequel," "Janet Waking," "Lady Lost," "Two in August," "Persistent
Explorer," "Somewhere Is Such a Kingdom," "Antique Harvesters," "Our
Two Worthies," "Puncture," "Dog," "Man Without Sense of Direction,"
"Survey of Literature," "The Equilibrists," "Prelude to an Evening,"
"What Ducks Require," "Of Margaret," "Painted Head," "Address to the
Scholars of New England."

Essays: "Old Age of an Eagle," "Humanism at Chicago," "More than Gesture," "The Communities of Letters," "On Shakespeare's Language,"

"Empirics in Politics," "Why Critics Don't Go Mad," "The Concrete Universal: Observations on the Understanding of Poetry."

Selected Poems. Revised and Enlarged Edition. New York: Alfred A. Knopf, 1963.

Contents: "Winter Remembered," "Miriam Tazewell," "Dead Boy," "Spectral Lovers," "Agitato ma non troppo," "Necrological," "Bells for John White-side's Daughter," "The Tall Girl," "First Travels of Max," "Good Ships," "Emily Hardcastle, Spinster," "Parting at Dawn," "Vaunting Oak," "In Process of a Noble Alliance," "Spiel of the Three Mountebanks," "Here Lies a Lady," "The Vanity of Bright Young Men," "Conrad in Twilight," "Armageddon," "Prometheus in Straits," "Judith of Bethulia," "Blue Girls," "Philomela," "Old Man Playing with Children," "Captain Carpenter," "Old Mansion," "Piazza Piece," "Eclogue," "Vision by Sweetwater," "Her Eyes," "Parting, Without a Sequel," "Hilda," "Janet Waking," "Lady Lost," "Two in August," "Persistent Explorer," "Morning," "Somewhere Is Such a Kingdom," "Old Man Pondered," "Antique Harvesters," "Our Two Worthies," "Puncture," "Dog," "Man Without Sense of Direction," "Survey of Literature," "The Equilibrists," "Prelude to an Evening," "What Ducks Require," "Of Margaret," "Painted Head," "Address to the Scholars of New England," "Master's in the Garden Again," "Prelude to an Evening: A Poem Revised and Explicated."

Signed Reviews

Booth, Philip. *Christian Science Monitor,* August 1, 1963, p. 11.
Fraser, G. S. *New York Review of Books,* October 31, 1963, p. 8.
Hecht, Roger. *Sewanee Review,* LXXI (Autumn, 1963), 642–44.
Hyman, Stanley E. *The New Leader,* August 5, 1963, p. 17.
Smith, Ray. *Library Journal,* LXXXVIII (July, 1963), 2709.
Spector, Robert D. *Saturday Review of Literature,* XLVII (February 1, 1964), 37.
Stepanchey, Stephen. *New York Herald Tribune Books,* August 11, 1963, p. 6.

Unsigned Review

Time, LXXXIII (April 3, 1964), 102.

II. POEMS

"Ada Ruel," *The Fugitive,* III (April, 1924), 39. Later published as "The Tall Girl" in *Chills and Fever; Selected Poems,* 1945; *Poems and Essays; Selected Poems,* 1963.

"Address to the Scholars of New England," *Kenyon Review,* I (Autumn, 1939), 406–408; *Selected Poems,* 1945; *Poems and Essays; Selected Poems,* 1963. (A-3)

"Adventure This Side of Pluralism," *The Fugitive,* III (June, 1924), 83–86; *Chills and Fever; Grace After Meat.*

"Agitato ma non troppo," *The Fugitive,* II (April-May, 1923), 56; *Chills and Fever; Selected Poems,* 1963. (A-1)

"Amphibious Crocodile, "*The Fugitive,* IV (December, 1925), 121–23; *Two Gentlemen in Bonds.* (A-2)

"An American Addresses Philomela," *Grace After Meat.* Published as "Philomela" in all United States publications, including *The Fugitive,* II (February-March, 1923), 8–9; *Chills and Fever; Selected Poems,* 1945; *Poems and Essays; Selected Poems,* 1963.

"Antique Harvesters," *Southwest Review,* X (April, 1925), 13–14; *Two Gentlemen in Bonds; Selected Poems,* 1945; *Poems and Essays; Selected Poems,* 1963. (A-14)

"Applied Eleatics," *Palms,* II (1924–25).

"April," *Poems About God.*

"April Absence," *New York Evening Post,* April 24, 1920, p. 10.

"April Treason," *The Fugitive,* II (April-May, 1923), 36–37; *Chills and Fever.*

"Armageddon," The Poetry Society of South Carolina (Charleston), 1923; *Chills and Fever; Grace After Meat; Selected Poems,* 1945; *Poems and Essays; Selected Poems,* 1963. (A-1)

"At Dawn," *Grace After Meat.* Appears as "Parting at Dawn" in *The Fugitive,* III (August, 1924), 99; *Chills and Fever; Selected Poems,* 1945; *Poems and Essays; Selected Poems,* 1963.

"Autumn Grief of Margaret," *Saturday Review of Literature,* XI (September 29, 1934), 137. Published as "Of Margaret" in *Selected Poems,* 1945; *Poems and Essays; Selected Poems,* 1963.

"Autumn Love," *New Republic,* LVIII (February 20, 1929), 10. (A-1)

"Bachelor," *Poems About God.*

"Bells for John Whiteside's Daughter," *The Fugitive,* III (February, 1924), 17; *Chills and Fever; Fugitives: An Anthology of Verse,* 69; *Selected Poems,* 1945; *Poems and Essays; Selected Poems,* 1963. (A-26)

"Blackberry Winter," *The Fugitive,* II (August-September, 1923), 107; *Chills and Fever.* (A-3)

"Blue Girls," *The Fugitive,* III (June, 1924), 82; *Two Gentlemen in Bonds; Selected Poems,* 1945; *Poems and Essays; Selected Poems,* 1963. (A-19)

"Boris of Britain," *The Fugitive,* I (October, 1922), 74–75; *Chills and Fever.*

"By the Riverside," *Poems About God; Grace After Meat.*

"Captain Carpenter," *The Fugitive,* III (February, 1924), 18–20; *Chills and Fever; Fugitives: An Anthology of Verse,* 73–75; *Selected Poems,* 1945; *Poems and Essays; Selected Poems,* 1963. (A-20)

"The Christian," *Poems About God.*

"A Christmas Colloquy," *Poems About God.*

"The Cloak Model," *Poems About God; Grace After Meat.*

"Conrad in Twilight," *The Fugitive,* II (February-March, 1922), 27, as Conrad at Twilight"; *Chills and Fever,* as "Conrad Sits in Twilight"; *Selected Poems,* 1945; *Poems and Essays; Selected Poems,* 1963. A revision of the poem also appears in *Selected Poems,* 1963, under the title, "Master's in the Garden Again." (A-1)

"Darkness," *Independent,* XCVIII (June 28, 1919), 498; *Poems About God.*

"Dead Boy," *New York Evening Post,* February 24, 1920, p. 8; March 1, 1920, p. 8; and March 6, 1920, p. 10, as a three-sonnet sequence entitled "Sonnets of a Selfish Lover"; *Sewanee Review,* XXXII (April, 1924), 129, as "The Dead Boy"; *Two Gentlemen in Bonds; Selected Poems,* 1945; *Poems and Essays; Selected Poems,* 1963. (A-5)

"Destitution Raiseth Her Voice," *The Fugitive,* I (June, 1922), 48.

"Disappointment of a Thrall" (from the sonnet sequence "Two Gentlemen in Bonds"), *Miscellany of American Poetry,* 156; *Two Gentlemen in Bonds.*

"Dog," *Guardian,* I (October, 1925), 440-41; *Two Gentlemen in Bonds; Selected Poems,* 1945; *Poems and Essays; Selected Poems,* 1963. (A-1)

"Dumb-bells," *Poems About God.*

"Eclogue," *The Fugitive,* IV (March, 1925), 22-24; excerpt in *Literary Digest,* LXXXV (April 11, 1925), 34; *Two Gentlemen in Bonds; Selected Poems,* 1945; *Poems and Essays; Selected Poems,* 1963.

"Ego," *The Fugitive,* I (April, 1922), 3-4. Published in *Chills and Fever* as "Plea in Mitigation."

"Emily Hardcastle, Spinster," *Literary Review,* IV (November 3, 1923), 201; *Chills and Fever; Selected Poems,* 1945; *Poems and Essays; Selected Poems,* 1963. (A-3)

"Epitaph," *The Fugitive,* I (June, 1922), 35; *Chills and Fever.* (A-1)

"Epithalamion of a Peach" (from the sonnet sequence "Two Gentlemen in Bonds"), *Miscellany of American Poetry,* 150; *Two Gentlemen in Bonds.*

"The Equilibrists," *The Fugitive,* IV (September, 1925), 87-88, as "History of Two Simple Lovers"; *Two Gentlemen in Bonds; Fugitives: An Anthology of Verse,* 79-81; *Selected Poems,* 1945; *Poems and Essays; Selected Poems,* 1963. (A-14)

"Fait Accompli" (from the sonnet sequence "Two Gentlemen in Bonds"), *Miscellany of American Poetry,* 159; *Two Gentlemen in Bonds.*

"Fall of Leaf," *The Fugitive,* I (October, 1922), 94-95; *Chills and Fever.*

"The Feasting of Maionides and Stephen Dedalus," *New Republic,* LIX (August 14, 1929), 342.

"Features of Creatures" (from the sonnet sequence "Two Gentlemen in Bonds"), *Miscellany of American Poetry,* 161; *Two Gentlemen in Bonds.*

"First Travels of Max," *The Fugitive,* II (June-July, 1923), 86–87; *Chills and Fever; Selected Poems,* 1963. (A-2)

"The Four Roses," *Poems About God.*

"Fresco: From the Last Judgment," *Two Gentlemen in Bonds.* Appears in *The Fugitive,* III (December, 1924), 148–50, as "The Last Judgment (A Fresco)."

"Friendship," *Poems About God.*

"Garden Sonnets" ("I. Sweet Will His Sonnet Set Out," and "II. He Burns for Her"), *New York Evening Post,* February 13, 1920, p. 10, and February 16, 1920, p. 8.

"Geometry," *Poems About God.*

"Ghosts," *Harper's Magazine,* CLIV (December, 1926), 50. Published in *Two Gentlemen in Bonds* and *Selected Poems,* 1963, as the second part of "Hilda."

"Good Ships," *The Fugitive,* II (October, 1923), 131; *Chills and Fever; Selected Poems,* 1945; *Poems and Essays; Selected Poems,* 1963.

"Grace," *Poems About God; Grace After Meat.*

"Grandgousier," *The Fugitive,* II (February-March, 1923), 12–13; *Chills and Fever.*

"The Handmaidens," *The Fugitive,* I (April, 1922), 26–32. Published in *Poems About God* as "The Power of God."

"Here Lies a Lady," *Literary Review,* III (March 24, 1923), 545; *Chills and Fever; Literary Digest,* LXXXIV (February 7, 1925), 34; *Selected Poems,* 1945; *Poems and Essays; Selected Poems,* 1963. (A-22)

"Her Eyes," *Two Gentlemen in Bonds; Selected Poems,* 1945; *Poems and Essays; Selected Poems,* 1963. (A-2)

"Hilda," *Two Gentlemen in Bonds; Selected Poems,* 1963. Part two of the poem as it appears in *Two Gentlemen in Bonds* and in *Selected Poems,* 1963, was first published as "Ghosts" in *Harper's Magazine,* CLIV (December, 1926), 50.

"History of Two Simple Lovers," *The Fugitive,* IV (September, 1925), 87–88. Published as "The Equilibrists" in *Two Gentlemen in Bonds; Fugitives: An Anthology of Verse,* 79–81; *Selected Poems,* 1945; *Poems and Essays; Selected Poems,* 1963.

"Husband Betrayed," *The Fugitive,* IV (September, 1925), 85; *Two Gentlemen in Bonds.* (A-1)

"Ilex Priscus," *Grace After Meat.* Appears as "Vaunting Oak" in *The Fugitive,* II (December, 1923), 174–75; *Chills and Fever; Selected Poems,* 1945; *Poems and Essays; Selected Poems,* 1963.

"Implacable Tower" (from the sonnet sequence "Two Gentlemen in Bonds"), *Miscellany of American Poetry,* 160; *Two Gentlemen in Bonds.*

"In Air" (from the sonnet sequence "Two Gentlemen in Bonds"), *Miscellany of American Poetry,* 147; *Two Gentlemen in Bonds.*

"In Bed, Not Dead" (from the sonnet sequence "Two Gentlemen in Bonds"), *Miscellany of American Poetry*, 157; *Two Gentlemen in Bonds.*

"The Ingrate," *Poems About God.*

"The Inland City," *The Fugitive*, II (April-May, 1923), 53; *Chills and Fever.* (A-1)

"In Mr. Minnit's House," *Two Gentlemen in Bonds.*

"In Process of a Noble Alliance," *The Fugitive*, I (December, 1922), 126; *Bookman*, LVII (March, 1923), 36; *Chills and Fever; Grace After Meat*, as "In Process of the Nuptials of the Duke"; *Selected Poems*, 1963.

"In Process of the Nuptials of the Duke," *Grace After Meat.* Appears in all volumes published in the United States as "In Process of a Noble Alliance."

"Jack's Letter," *The Fugitive*, IV (June, 1925), 57; *Two Gentlemen in Bonds.*

"Janet Waking," *The Fugitive*, IV (September, 1925), 86; *Two Gentlemen in Bonds; Selected Poems*, 1945; *Poems and Essays; Selected Poems*, 1963. (A-10)

"Judith of Bethulia," *The Fugitive*, II (October, 1923), 140–41; *Chills and Fever; Grace After Meat; Fugitives: An Anthology of Verse*, 70–72; *Selected Poems*, 1945; *Poems and Essays; Selected Poems*, 1963. (A-9)

"Lady Lost," *The Fugitive*, IV (December, 1925), 119; *Literary Digest*, LXXXVIII (February 13, 1926), 34; *Two Gentlemen in Bonds; Selected Poems*, 1945; *Poems and Essays; Selected Poems*, 1963. (A-8)

"The Last Judgment (A Fresco)," *The Fugitive*, III (December, 1924), 148–50. Printed in *Two Gentlemen in Bonds*, as "Fresco: From the Last Judgment."

"L'état C'est Moi" (from the sonnet sequence "Two Gentlemen in Bonds"), *Miscellany of American Poetry*, 152; *Two Gentlemen in Bonds.*

"Lichas to Polydor," *The Fugitive*, II (August-September, 1923), 118; *Chills and Fever.*

"Little Boy Blue," *New Republic*, XLVIII (September 22, 1926), 122; *Two Gentlemen in Bonds.* (A-2)

"The Lover," *Poems About God; Grace After Meat; Fugitives: An Anthology of Verse*, 63–64. (A-1)

"Man Without Sense of Direction," *Two Gentlemen in Bonds; Selected Poems*, 1945; *Poems and Essays; Selected Poems*, 1963. (A-2)

"Master's in the Garden Again," *Kenyon Review*, XXIV (Summer, 1962), 439–40; *Selected Poems*, 1963. (Revision of "Conrad in Twilight.")

"Meeting in a Garden" (from the sonnet sequence "Two Gentlemen in Bonds"), *Miscellany of American Poetry*, 149; *Two Gentlemen in Bonds.*

"Men," *Poems About God.*

"The Miller's Daughter," *The Fugitive*, IV (June, 1925), 55–56; *Two Gentlemen in Bonds.* (A-1)

"Miriam Tazewell," *Literary Review*, IV (August 2, 1924), 929; *Chills and Fever; Selected Poems*, 1945; *Poems and Essays; Selected Poems*, 1963.

"Miss Euphemia," *Chills and Fever*. (A-1)

"Misanthropy" (from the sonnet sequence "Two Gentlemen in Bonds"), *Miscellany of American Poetry*, 153; *Two Gentlemen in Bonds*.

"Moments of Minnie," *The Fugitive*, IV (December, 1925), 120; *Two Gentlemen in Bonds*.

"Moonlight," *Poems About God*.

"Morning," *Poems About God*.

"Morning," *Harper's Magazine*, CLIV (December, 1926), 50; *Two Gentlemen in Bonds; Selected Poems*, 1963. (A-1)

"Necrological," *The Fugitive*, I (June, 1922), 62–63; *Chills and Fever; Grace After Meat; Fugitives: An Anthology of Verse*, 67–68; *Selected Poems*, 1945; *Poems and Essays; Selected Poems*, 1963. (A-2)

"Night Voices," *The Fugitive*, I (April, 1922), 10–11; *Chills and Fever; Grace After Meat*.

"Nocturne," *The Fugitive*, II (June-July, 1923), 82; *Chills and Fever*.

"Noonday Grace," *Independent*, XCVIII (April 12, 1919), 66; *Poems About God*. (A-1)

"Nostri in Memoriam Doctissimi," *In Memoriam: Herbert Cushing Tolman*. Nashville: Alpha of Tennessee, Phi Beta Kappa, 1926, pp. 70–71.

"November," *Poems About God*.

"Number Five," *The Fugitive*, II (December, 1923), 166; *Chills and Fever*. (A-1)

"Of Margaret," *Saturday Review of Literature*, XI (September 29, 1934), 137, as "Autumn Grief of Margaret"; *Selected Poems*, 1945; *Poems and Essays; Selected Poems*, 1963.

"Old Man Playing with Children," *The Fugitive*, II (December, 1923), 183; *Chills and Fever; Selected Poems*, 1945; *Poems and Essays; Selected Poems*, 1963. (A-1)

"Old Man Pondered," *Saturday Review of Literature*, V (June 15, 1929), 1107; *Selected Poems*, 1963. (A-2)

"Old Mansion," *The Fugitive*, III (April, 1924), 40–41; *Chills and Fever; Selected Poems*, 1945; *Poems and Essays; Selected Poems*, 1963. (A-2)

"On a Superior Woman," *New York Evening Post*, April 5, 1920, p 8. Appears in *Chills and Fever* as "Triumph."

"On the Road to Wockensutter," *Double Dealer*, IV (November, 1922), 233; *Chills and Fever*.

"One Who Rejected Christ," *Independent*, XCV (July 27, 1918), 116; *Poems About God*.

"Our Two Worthies," *The Fugitive*, IV (September, 1925), 83–84, as "The Two Worthies"; *Two Gentlemen in Bonds; Fugitives: An Anthology of Verse*, 76–78; *Selected Poems*, 1945; *Poems and Essays; Selected Poems*, 1963. (A-2)

"Overtures," *Poems About God.*

"Painted Head," *New Republic,* LXXXI (December 26, 1934), 185; *Selected Poems,* 1945; *Poems and Essays; Selected Poems,* 1963. (A-12)

"Parting at Dawn," *The Fugitive,* III (August, 1924), 99; *Chills and Fever; Grace After Meat* as "At Dawn"; *Selected Poems,* 1945; *Poems and Essays; Selected Poems,* 1963. (A-2)

"Parting, Without a Sequel," *Atlantic Monthly,* CXXXVIII (October, 1926), 517; *Two Gentlemen in Bonds; Selected Poems,* 1945; *Poems and Essays; Selected Poems,* 1963. (A-8)

"Persistent Explorer," *Two Gentlemen in Bonds; Poems and Essays; Selected Poems,* 1963. (A-1)

"Philomela," *The Fugitive,* II (February-March, 1923), 8–9; *Chills and Fever; Grace After Meat* as "An American Addresses Philomela"; *Selected Poems,* 1945; *Poems and Essays; Selected Poems,* 1963. (A-6)

"Piazza Piece," *The Fugitive,* IV (March, 1925), 21; *Two Gentlemen in Bonds; Selected Poems,* 1945; *Poems and Essays; Selected Poems,* 1963. (A-16)

"Pink and Pale" (from the sonnet sequence "Two Gentlemen in Bonds"), *Miscellany of American Poetry,* 145; *Two Gentlemen in Bonds.*

"Plea in Mitigation," *The Fugitive,* I (April, 1922), 3–4, as "Ego"; *Chills and Fever.*

"Poets Have Chanted Mortality," *The Fugitive,* I (October, 1922), 86.

"The Power of God," *Poems About God; The Fugitive,* I (April, 1922), 26–32, as "The Handmaidens."

"Prayer," *Poems About God.*

"Prelude to an Evening," *American Review,* III (May, 1934), 262–63; *New Verse,* No. 10 (August, 1934), 9–10; *Selected Poems,* 1945; *Poems and Essays; Selected Poems,* 1963. (A-9)

"Prelude to an Evening: A Poem Revised and Explicated," *Kenyon Review,* XXV (Winter, 1963), 70–71; *Selected Poems,* 1963. (Revision of the preceding poem.)

"Primer of Science" (from the sonnet sequence "Two Gentlemen in Bonds"), *Miscellany of American Poetry,* 158; *Two Gentlemen in Bonds.*

"Prometheus in Straits," *The Fugitive,* III (February, 1924), 21; *Chills and Fever; Selected Poems,* 1963.

"Proud Heart Rained Upon," *The Measure,* No. 52 (June, 1925), 11. Appears as "Rain," part of the sonnet sequence "Two Gentlemen in Bonds," in *Miscellany of American Poetry,* 162, and in *Two Gentlemen in Bonds.*

"Puncture," *Two Gentlemen in Bonds; Selected Poems,* 1945; *Poems and Essays; Selected Poems,* 1963.

"Rain" (from the sonnet sequence "Two Gentlemen in Bonds"), *The Measure,* No. 52 (June, 1925), 11, as "Proud Heart Rained Upon"; *Miscellany of American Poetry,* 162; *Two Gentlemen in Bonds.*

"Rapunzel Has Submitted Herself to Fashion," *The Fugitive*, II (October, 1923), 151; *Chills and Fever*.

"The Resurrection," *Poems About God; Grace After Meat*.

"Roses," *Contemporary Verse*, VI (December, 1918), 86; *Poems About God*.

"The School," *Poems About God; Grace After Meat*.

"Semi-Centennial," *The Fugitive*, IV (June, 1925), 58–59; *Two Gentlemen in Bonds*.

"Somewhere Is Such a Kingdom," *Two Gentlemen in Bonds; Selected Poems*, 1945; *Poems and Essays; Selected Poems*, 1963.

"Sickness," *Poems About God*.

"Sonnet of a Sure Heart," *New York Evening Post*, February 18, 1920, p. 8.

"Sonnets of a Pastoral Pair" ("I. They Take to the Fields," "II. They Praise the Sun," and "III. They Hail the Sunrise"), *New York Evening Post*, March 12, 1920, p. 10; March 18, 1920, p. 8; and March 25, 1920, p. 8.

"Sonnets of a Selfish Lover," *New York Evening Post*, February 24, 1920, p. 8; March 1, 1920, p. 8; and March 6, 1920, p. 10. Appears in a revised form as "Dead Boy" in *Sewanee Review*, XXXII (April, 1924), 129; *Two Gentlemen in Bonds; Selected Poems*, 1945; *Poems and Essays;* and *Selected Poems*, 1963.

"Spectral Lovers," *The Fugitive*, II (June-July, 1923), 68; *Chills and Fever; Selected Poems*, 1945; *Poems and Essays; Selected Poems*, 1963. (A-4)

"Spiel of the Three Mountebanks," *The Fugitive*, II (October, 1923), 146–48; *Chills and Fever; Selected Poems*, 1945; *Poems and Essays; Selected Poems*, 1963. (A-3)

"Spring Posy," *The Fugitive*, I (June, 1922), 54, as "The Sure Heart"; *Chills and Fever*.

"Street Light," *Poems About God*.

"Sunset," *Independent*, XCVII (February 22, 1919), 261; *Poems About God*.

"The Sure Heart," *The Fugitive*, I (June, 1922), 54; *Chills and Fever* as "Spring Posy."

"Survey of Literature," *Two Gentlemen in Bonds; Selected Poems*, 1945; *Poems and Essays; Selected Poems*, 1963. (A-5)

"The Swimmer," *Poems About God*. (A-1)

"Swine, Wine" (from the sonnet sequence "Two Gentlemen in Bonds"), *Miscellany of American Poetry*, 151; *Two Gentlemen in Bonds*.

"The Tall Girl," *The Fugitive*, III (April, 1924), 39, as "Ada Ruel"; *Chills and Fever; Selected Poems*, 1945; *Poems and Essays; Selected Poems*, 1963. (A-1)

"These Winters," *Chills and Fever*.

"Thinking, Drinking" (from the sonnet sequence "Two Gentlemen in Bonds"), *Miscellany of American Poetry*, 146; *Two Gentlemen in Bonds*.

"Thought, Distraught" (from the sonnet sequence "Two Gentlemen in Bonds"), *Miscellany of American Poetry*, 148; *Two Gentlemen in Bonds*.

"To a Lady Celebrating Her Birthday," *The Fugitive*, I (April, 1922), 21–23; *Chills and Fever*.

"Tom, Tom, the Piper's Son," *The Fugitive*, III (August, 1924), 100–101; *Chills and Fever; Selected Poems*, 1945; *Poems and Essays; Selected Poems*, 1963, as "The Vanity of Bright Young Men." (A-1)

"Tone and Caparisons" (from the sonnet sequence "Two Gentlemen in Bonds"), *Miscellany of American Poetry*, 155; *Two Gentlemen in Bonds*.

"Triumph," *New York Evening Post*, April 5, 1920, p. 8, as "On a Superior Woman"; *Chills and Fever*. (A-1)

"Two Gentlemen in Bonds" (sonnet sequence), *Miscellany of American Poetry*, 145–64; *Two Gentlemen in Bonds*. One sonnet in the sequence, "Rain," was first published in *The Measure*, No. 52 (June, 1925), 11, as "Proud Heart Rained Upon."

"Two in August," *Two Gentlemen in Bonds; Selected Poems*, 1945; *Poems and Essays; Selected Poems*, 1963. (A-7)

"Two Sonnets," *Chills and Fever; Grace After Meat*.

"The Two Worthies," *The Fugitive*, IV (September, 1925), 83–84. Appears as "Our Two Worthies" in *Two Gentlemen in Bonds; Fugitives: An Anthology of Verse*, 76–78; *Selected Poems*, 1945; *Poems and Essays*; and *Selected Poems*, 1963.

"Under the Locusts," *Independent*, XCVIII (June 28, 1919), 498; *Poems About God; Grace After Meat; Fugitives: An Anthology of Verse*, 65–66. (A-1)

"The Vagrant," *The Fugitive*, I (October, 1922), 80; *Chills and Fever*. (A-1)

"Vain Protestations" (from the sonnet sequence "Two Gentlemen in Bonds"), *Miscellany of American Poetry*, 154; *Two Gentlemen in Bonds*.

"The Vanity of Bright Young Men," *Selected Poems*, 1963. Published as "Tom, Tom, the Piper's Son" in *The Fugitive*, III (August, 1924), 100–101; *Chills and Fever; Selected Poems*, 1945; *Poems and Essays*.

"Vaunting Oak," *The Fugitive*, II (December, 1923), 174–75; *Chills and Fever; Grace After Meat* as "Ilex Priscus"; *Selected Poems*, 1945; *Poems and Essays; Selected Poems*, 1963. (A-1)

"Virga," *The Fugitive*, III (December, 1924), 151–52.

"Vision by Sweetwater," *Two Gentlemen in Bonds; Poems and Essays; Selected Poems*, 1963. (A-5)

"Weep or Sleep" (from the sonnet sequence "Two Gentlemen in Bonds"), *Miscellany of American Poetry*, 164; *Two Gentlemen in Bonds*.

"What Ducks Require," *New Republic*, L (April 27, 1927), 273; *Fugitives: An Anthology of Verse*, 82–83; *Poems and Essay; Selected Poems*, 1963. (A-1)

"Winter Remembered," *Sewanee Review*, XXX (January, 1922), 1; *Chills*

240 BIBLIOGRAPHY

and Fever; Grace After Meat; Selected Poems, 1945; *Poems and Essays; Selected Poems,* 1963. (A-4)
"Winter's Tale," *Chills and Fever.*
"Worship," *Poems About God.*
"Wrestling," *Poems About God; Grace After Meat.* (A-1)
"Wrong," (from the sonnet sequence "Two Gentlemen in Bonds"), *Miscellany of American Poetry,* 163; *Two Gentlemen in Bonds.*
"Youngest Daughter," *The Fugitive,* I (December, 1922), 104; *Chills and Fever.*

III. ESSAYS AND ARTICLES

"The ABC of Aesthetics," *New Republic,* LIII (December 14, 1927), 104. (Letter.)
"The Aesthetics of *Finnegan's Wake,*" in *Kenyon Review,* I (Autumn, 1939), 424–28.
"The Aesthetics of Music," *Kenyon Review,* III (Autumn, 1941), 494–97.
"The Aesthetics of Regionalism," *American Review,* II (January, 1934), 290–310. Reprinted in *Literary Opinion in America.* Edited by Morton Dauwen Zabel. New York: Harper and Brothers, 1937, pp. 106–21.
"An Address to Kenneth Burke," *Kenyon Review,* IV (Spring, 1942), 218–37.
"An Age of Criticism," *New Republic,* CXXVI (March 31, 1952), 18–19. Reprinted in *The Arts at Mid-Century.* Edited by Robert Richman. New York: Horizon Press, 1954, pp. 24–27.
"Alienation a Century Ago," *Kenyon Review,* XV (Spring, 1953), 335–36.
"All the King's Men: A Symposium," *Folio,* XV (May, 1950), 2–22. Ransom's sketch of Robert Penn Warren's literary career appears on pages 2–3; other contributors are George Gerhard, Richard B. Hudson, Joseph Raben, and Newton P. Stallknecht.
"All Verse Is Not Poetry," *Hika,* IX (December, 1941), 22–25.
"Apologia for Modernism," *Kenyon Review,* II (Spring, 1940), 247–51.
"Art and the Human Economy," *Kenyon Review,* VII (Autumn, 1945), 683–88.
"Art and Mr. Santayana," *Virginia Quarterly Review,* XIII (Summer, 1937), 420–36. Reprinted in *The World's Body.*
"Artists, Soldiers, Positivists," *Kenyon Review,* VI (Spring, 1944), 276–81.
"Art Needs a Little Separating," *Kenyon Review,* VI (Winter, 1944), 114–22.
"The Arts and the Philosophers," *Kenyon Review,* I (Spring, 1939), 194–99.
"Arts Worries the Naturalists," *Kenyon Review,* VII (Spring, 1945), 282–99.

"The Bases of Criticism," *Sewanee Review*, LII (Autumn, 1944), 556-71.

"A Capital for the New Deal," *American Review*, II (December, 1933), 129-42.

"The Cathartic Principle," *American Review*, V (Summer, 1935), 287-300. Reprinted in *The World's Body*.

"A Cathedralist Looks at Murder," *Southern Review*, I (Winter, 1936), 609-23. Excerpt reprinted in *The World's Body*.

"Characters and Character," *American Review*, VI (January, 1936), 271-88.

"Classical and Romantic," *Saturday Review of Literature*, VI (September 14, 1929), 125-27.

"The Communities of Letters," *Confluence*, I (December, 1952), 86-92. Reprinted in *Poems and Essays*.

"The Concrete Universal: Observations on the Understanding of Poetry. I," *Kenyon Review*, XVI (Autumn, 1954), 554-64.

"The Concrete Universal: Observations on the Understanding of Poetry. II," *Kenyon Review*, XVII (Summer, 1955), 383-407. Reprinted in *Poems and Essays*.

"The Contents of the Novel: Notes Toward a Critique of Fiction," *American Review*, VII (Summer, 1936), 301-18.

"Criticism as Pure Speculation," *The Intent of the Critic*. Edited by Donald A. Stauffer. Princeton: Princeton University Press, 1941, pp. 91-124. Reprinted in *Essays in Modern Criticism*. Edited by Ray Benedict West. New York: Rinehart and Company, 1952, pp. 228-45. Reprinted in *Literary Opinion in America*. Edited by Morton Dauwen Zabel. Revised edition. New York: Harper and Brothers, 1951, pp. 639-54.

"Criticism, Inc.," *Virginia Quarterly Review*, XIII (Autumn, 1937), 586-602. Reprinted in *The World's Body*. Reprinted in *American Literary Criticism, 1900-1950*. Edited by Charles I. Glicksberg. New York: Hendricks House, 1951, pp. 453-67.

"A Doctrine of Relativity," *The Fugitive*, IV (September, 1925), 93-94.

"Editorial," *The Fugitive*, I (October, 1922), 66-68.

"Editorial Notes," *Kenyon Review*, II (Winter, 1940), 92-93.

"Eliot and the Metaphysicals," *Accent*, I (Spring, 1941), 148-56. Printed as a part of "T. S. Eliot: the Historical Critic" in *The New Criticism*.

"Empirics in Politics," *Kenyon Review*, XV (Autumn, 1953), 648-50. Reprinted in *Poems and Essays*.

"E. M. Forster," *Kenyon Review*, V (Autumn, 1943), 618-23.

"Emily Dickinson: A Poet Restored," *Perspectives USA*, XV (Spring, 1956), 5-20. Reprinted in *Emily Dickinson: A Collection of Critical Essays*. Edited by Richard B. Sewall. Englewood Cliffs: Prentice-Hall, 1963, pp. 88-100.

"Fiction Harvest," *Southern Review*, II (Autumn, 1936), 339-418. Excerpt reprinted as "Contemporaneous Not Contemporary" in *The World's Body*.

"Flux and Blur in Contemporary Art," *Sewanee Review*, XXXVII (July, 1929), 353–66.

"Foreword," *Daemon in the Rock*, by Edwin Richardson Frost. New York: G. P. Putnam's Sons, 1934, ix–x.

"Foreword," *The Noise That Time Makes, a First Volume of 101 Sonnets, by Merrill Moore, and Some Reviews of This Book*. New York: Harcourt, Brace and Company, 1929, pp. 3–5.

"The Future of Poetry," *The Fugitive*, III (February, 1924), 2–4.

"Gerontion," *Sewanee Review*, LXXIV (Spring, 1966), 389–414.

"Happy Farmers," *American Review*, I (October, 1933), 513–35. Reprinted in *Contemporary Southern Prose*. Edited by Richmond Croom Beatty and W. P. Fidler. Boston: D. C. Heath Company, 1940, pp. 150–66. Reprinted in pamphlet form as *Happy Farmers*. Tyron, N. C.: Woods Press, n.d.

"Hardy—Old Poet," *New Republic*, CXXVI (May 12, 1952), 16, 30–31. Revised and reprinted in *Poems and Essays* as "Old Age of an Eagle."

"Hearts and Heads," *American Review*, II (March, 1934), 554–71.

"Honey and Gall," *Southern Review*, VI (Summer, 1940), 2–19.

"Humanism at Chicago," *Kenyon Review*, XIV (Autumn, 1952), 647–59. Reprinted in *Poems and Essays*.

"The Idea of a Literary Anthropologist and What He Might Say of the *Paradise Lost* of Milton," *Kenyon Review*, XXI (Winter, 1959), 121–40.

"In amicitia," *Sewanee Review*, LXVII (Fall, 1959), 528–39.

"The Inorganic Muses," *Kenyon Review*, V (Spring, 1943), 278–300.

"Introduction," *Selected Poems of Thomas Hardy*. Edited by John Crowe Ransom. New York: The Macmillan Company, 1960, ix–xxxiii. Also printed in *Kenyon Review*, XXII (Spring, 1960), 169–93, as "Thomas Hardy's Poems."

"Introduction," *The Kenyon Critics: Studies in Modern Literature from the Kenyon Review*. Edited by John Crowe Ransom. Cleveland: World Publishing Company, 1951, vii–ix.

"The Irish, the Gaelic, the Byzantine," *Southern Review*, VII (1941–42), 517–46.

"Joyce Kilmer's 'Trees': A Criticism," *Hika*, V (March, 1939), 9–10, 21–24.

"Land! An Answer to the Unemployment Problem," *Harper's Magazine*, CLXV (July, 1932), 216–24.

"The Literary Criticism of Aristotle," *Kenyon Review*, X (Summer, 1948), 382–402. Reprinted in *Lectures in Criticism: The Johns Hopkins University*. The Bollingen Series, XVI. New York: Pantheon Books, 1949, pp. 15–42.

"The Making of a Modern: The Poetry of George Marion O'Donnell," *Southern Review*, I (Spring, 1936), 864–74.

"A Man Without a Country," *Sewanee Review*, XXXIII (July, 1925), 301–307.

"The Mimetic Principle," *American Review*, V (October, 1935), 536–51. Reprinted in *The World's Body*.

"Mr. Empson's Muddles," *Southern Review*, IV (1938–39), 322–39.

"Mr. Ransom Replies," *Literary Review*, August 11, 1923. (Letter.)

"Mr. Russell and Mr. Schorer," *Kenyon Review*, IV (Autumn, 1942), 406–407.

"Mr. Tate and the Professors," *Kenyon Review*, II (Summer, 1940), 348–50.

"Mixed Modes," *The Fugitive*, IV (March, 1925), 28–29.

"Modern with the Southern Accent," *Virginia Quarterly Review*, XI (April, 1935), 184–200.

"Moholy-Nagy's New Arts," *Kenyon Review*, III (Summer, 1941), 372–74.

"More than Gesture," *Partisan Review*, XX (January-February, 1953), 108–11. Reprinted in *Poems and Essays*.

"Muses and Amazons," *Kenyon Review*, III (Spring, 1941), 240–42.

"New Poets and Old Muses," *American Poetry at Mid-Century*, Lectures presented under the auspices of the Gertrude Clarke Whittall Poetry and Literature Fund by John Crowe Ransom, Delmore Schwartz, and John Hall Wheelock. Washington: Reference Department, Library of Congress, 1958, pp. 1–14.

"Old Age of a Poet," *Kenyon Review*, II (Summer, 1940), 345–47.

"On Being Modern with Distinction," *Quarterly Review of Literature*, IV (1948), 136–42.

"On 'Master's in the Garden Again,'" *The Contemporary Poet as Artist and Critic*. Edited by Anthony Ostroff. Boston: Little, Brown and Company, 1964, pp. 134–40.

"On Shakespeare's Language," *Sewanee Review*, LV (Spring, 1947), 181–98. Reprinted in *Poems and Essays*. Reprinted in *The Modern Critical Spectrum*. Edited by G. J. and N. H. Goldberg. New York: Prentice-Hall, 1962, pp. 48–57.

"On the Brooks–MacLeish Thesis," *Partisan Review*, IX (January, 1942), 40–41. Ransom is one of eight critics responding to a question posed by the editor of *Partisan Review*.

"The Planetary Poet," *Kenyon Review*, XXVI (Winter, 1964), 233–64.

"A Poem Nearly Anonymous," *American Review*, I (May, 1933), 179–203. Reprinted in *The World's Body*. Reprinted in *Criticism*. Edited by Mark Schorer *et al.* New York: Harcourt, Brace and Company, 1948, pp. 333–42; revised edition, 1958, pp. 333–41. Reprinted in *Milton Criticism*. Edited by James Thorpe. New York: Rinehart and Company, 1950, pp. 225–38.

"A Poem Nearly Anonymous: The Poet and His Formal Tradition," *American Review*, I (September, 1933), 444–67. Reprinted as "Forms and Citizens" in *The World's Body*.

"The Poet and Critic," *New Republic*, LI (June 22, 1927), 125–26. (Letter.)

"The Poet as Woman," *Southern Review,* II (Spring, 1937), 783–806. Reprinted in *The World's Body.*

"The Poet Laureate," *Literary Review,* IV (March 29, 1924), 625–26.

"Poetry: A Note in Ontology," *American Review,* III (May, 1934), 172–200. Reprinted in *The World's Body.* Reprinted in *Critiques and Essays in Criticism, 1920–1948.* Edited by Robert Wooster Stallman. New York: The Ronald Press Company, 1949, pp. 30–48. Reprinted in *The Great Critics.* Edited by James Harry Smith and Edd Winfield Parks. Third edition. New York: W. W. Norton, 1951, pp. 769–87. Reprinted in *Modern Criticism.* Edited by Walter Sutton and Richard Foster. New York: Odyssey Press, 1963, pp. 221–32.

"Poetry as Primitive Language," *Michigan Alumnus Quarterly Review,* XLVIII (Summer, 1942), 278–84. Reprinted in *The Writer and His Craft,* Hopwood Lectures, 1932–1952. Ann Arbor: University of Michigan Press, 1954, pp. 146–57.

"The Poetry of 1900–1950," *Kenyon Review,* XIII (Summer, 1951), 445–54. Reprinted in *Journal of English Literary History,* XVIII (June, 1951), 155–62.

"Poetry: I. The Formal Analysis," *Kenyon Review,* IX (Summer, 1947), 436–56.

"Poetry: II. The Final Cause," *Kenyon Review,* IX (Autumn, 1947), 640–58.

"Poets Without Laurels," *Yale Review,* XXIV (March, 1935), 503–18. Reprinted in *The World's Body.* Reprinted in *America Through the Essay.* Edited by A. T. Johnson and Allen Tate. New York: Oxford University Press, 1938, pp. 348–61. Reprinted in *A Vanderbilt Miscellany: 1919–1944.* Edited by Richmond Croom Beatty. Nashville: Vanderbilt University Press, 1944, pp. 289–302. Reprinted in *The Literature of the South.* Edited by Richmond Croom Beatty, Floyd C. Watkins, and Thomas Daniel Young. Chicago: Scott, Foresman and Company, 1952, pp. 757–66. Reprinted in *Literary Criticism in America.* Edited by Albert D. Van Nostrand. New York: The Liberal Arts Press, 1957, pp. 273–87.

"Positive and Near-Positive Aesthetics," *Kenyon Review,* V (Summer, 1943), 443–47.

"Postscript," *The Fugitive: Clippings and Comments About the Magazine and Members of the Group That Published It.* Collected by Merrill Moore. Boston: Privately printed, 1939, p. 11.

"The Pragmatics of Art," *Kenyon Review,* II (Winter, 1940), 76–87. This essay appears in a revised form as a part of "Wanted: an Ontological Critic" in *The New Criticism.*

" 'Prelude to an Evening': A Poem Revised and Explicated," *Kenyon Review,* XXV (Winter, 1963), 70–80.

"Prose: A Doctrine of Relativity," *The Fugitive,* IV (September, 1925), 93–94.

"A Psychologist Looks at Poetry," *Virginia Quarterly Review,* XI (October, 1935), 575–92. Reprinted in *The World's Body.*

"The Question of Justice," *Yale Review,* IV (July, 1915), 684–98.

"Reconstructed but Unregenerate," *I'll Take My Stand: The South and the Agrarian Tradition,* by Twelve Southerners. New York: Harper and Brothers, 1930, pp. 1–27. Reprinted by Harper Torchbooks, 1962.

"Regionalism in the South," *New Mexico Quarterly,* IV (May, 1934), 108–13.

"A Reply to Wayne Booth," *Kenyon Review,* XV (Spring, 1953), 301–304.

"Sentimental Exercises," *Yale Review,* XXVI (December, 1936), 353–68. Reprinted in *The World's Body.*

"The Severity of Mr. Savage," *Kenyon Review,* VII (Winter, 1945), 114–17.

"Shakespeare at Sonnets," *Southern Review,* III (Winter, 1938), 531–53. Reprinted in *The World's Body.*

"Shall We Complete the Trade?" *Sewanee Review,* XLI (April, 1933), 182–90. Excerpt reprinted in *Review of Reviews,* LXXXVIII (August, 1933), 53, as "Trading Culture for War Debts."

"The South Defends Its Heritage," *Harper's Magazine,* CLIX (June, 1929), 108–18.

"The South Is a Bulwark," *Scribner's Magazine,* XCIX (May, 1936), 229–303.

"The South—Old or New," *Sewanee Review,* XXXVI (April, 1928), 139–47. Reprinted in pamphlet form.

"The State and the Land," *New Republic,* LXX (February 17, 1932), 8–10.

"Statement of Principles," *I'll Take My Stand: The South and the Agrarian Tradition,* by Twelve Southerners. New York: Harper and Brothers, 1930, ix-xxi. Reprinted by Harper Torchbooks, 1962.

"The Strange Music of English Verse," *Kenyon Review,* XVIII (Summer, 1956), 460–77.

"Strategy for English Studies," *Southern Review,* VI (Autumn, 1940), 226–35.

"Symbolism: American Style," *New Republic,* CXXIX (November 2, 1953), 18–20. Reprinted in *The Arts at Mid-Century.* Edited by Robert Richman. New York: Horizon Press, 1954, pp. 50–58.

"A Symposium: The Agrarians Today: Five Questions," *Shenandoah,* III (Summer, 1952), 14–33. Ransom's response to the questions posed by the editor appears on pages 14–16; other participants in the symposium are Donald Davidson, Frank L. Owsley, Allen Tate, Herman C. Nixon, Andrew Lytle, and John D. Wade.

"The Teaching of Poetry," *Kenyon Review,* I (Winter, 1939), 81–83.

"The Tense of Poetry," *Southern Review,* I (Autumn, 1935), 221–38. Reprinted in *The World's Body.*

"These Little Magazines," *American Scholar,* XV (October, 1946), 550–51.

"The Thing About Poetry," *Hika,* VI (May, 1940), 9–11. Reprinted in *The New Criticism.*

"Thoughts on the Poetic Discontent," *The Fugitive,* IV (June, 1925), 63–64. Reprinted in *Calendar of Modern Letters,* I (August, 1925), 460–63.

"Ubiquitous Moralists," *Kenyon Review,* III (Winter, 1941), 95–100.

"The Understanding of Fiction," *Kenyon Review,* XII (Spring, 1950), 189–218.

"War and Publication," *Kenyon Review,* IV (Spring, 1942), 217–18.

"Was Shakespeare a Philosopher?" *Kenyon Review,* I (Winter, 1939), 75–80.

"Waste Lands," *Literary Review,* III (July 14, 1923), 825–26. Reprinted in *Modern Essays, Second Series.* Edited by Christopher Morley. New York: Harcourt, Brace and Company, 1924, pp. 345–59

"We Resume," *Kenyon Review,* IV (Autumn, 1942), 405–406.

"What Does the South Want?" *Virginia Quarterly Review,* XII (April, 1936), 180–94. Reprinted in *Who Owns America? A Declaration of Independence.* Edited by Herbert Agar and Allen Tate. Boston: Houghton Mifflin Company, 1936, pp. 178–93.

"Why Critics Don't Go Mad," *Kenyon Review,* XIV (Spring, 1952), 331–39. Reprinted in *Poems and Essays.*

"William Faulkner: An Impression," *The Harvard Advocate,* CXXXV (November, 1951), 17.

"William Wordsworth: Notes Toward an Understanding of Poetry," *Kenyon Review,* XII (Summer, 1950), 498–519. Reprinted in *Wordsworth: Centenary Studies.* Edited by G. T. Dunklin. Princeton: Princeton University Press, 1951, pp. 91–113.

"Yeats and His Symbols," *Kenyon Review,* I (Summer, 1939), 309–22. Reprinted in *The Permanence of Yeats: Selected Criticism.* Edited by James Hall and Martin Steinmann. New York: The Macmillan Company, 1950, pp. 95–107.

"The Younger Poets," *Kenyon Review,* III (Autumn, 1941), 491–94.

"Yvor Winters: the Logical Critic," *Southern Review,* VI (Winter, 1941), 558–83. Abridgement of a chapter in *The New Criticism.*

IV. Book Reviews in Periodicals

Anderson, Forrest. *Sea Pieces,* in *Southern Review,* I (Winter, 1936), 609–23.

Atkins, Elizabeth. *Edna St. Vincent Millay and Her Times,* in *Southern Review,* II (Spring, 1937), 783–806.

Bateson, F. W. *English Poetry and the English Language,* in *Saturday Review of Literature,* XII (August 31, 1935), 17.

Benét, William Rose. *Golden Fleece,* in *Saturday Review of Literature,* XII (July 27, 1935), 6.

Bethell, S. C. *Shakespeare and the Popular Dramatic Traditions,* in *Kenyon Review,* VII (Summer, 1945), 515–20.

Blackmur, R. P. "A Burden for Critics" (in *Hudson Review,* Summer, 1948), *Kenyon Review,* X (Autumn, 1948), 682–88. Also discusses "The Imagery of Killing" by Kenneth Burke *(Hudson Review,* Summer, 1948), and *The Armed Vision,* by Stanley Edgar Hyman.

———. *Language as Gesture,* in *Partisan Review,* XX (January-February, 1953), 108–11.

Brooks, Cleanth. *Modren Poetry and the Tradition,* in *Kenyon Review,* II (Spring, 1940), 247–51.

Brown, Alec. *Daughters of Albion,* in *Southern Review,* II (Autumn, 1936), 399–418.

Buckley, Jerome Hamilton. *William Ernest Henley,* in *Kenyon Review,* VIII (Spring, 1946), 338–39.

Burke, Kenneth. *A Grammar of Motives,* in *New Republic,* CXIV (February 18, 1946), 257–58.

———. "The Imagery of Killing" (in *Hudson Review,* Summer, 1948), *Kenyon Review,* X (Autumn, 1948), 682–88. Also discusses "A Burden for Critics" by R. P. Blackmur *(Hudson Review,* Summer, 1948), and *The Armed Vision,* by Stanley Edgar Hyman.

Childers, James Saxon. *In the Deep South,* in *Southern Review,* II (Autumn, 1936), 399–418.

Comfort, Alex. *The Power House,* in *Kenyon Review,* VII (Summer, 1945), 522–23.

Davidson, Donald. *The Long Street,* in *Sewanee Review,* LXX (Spring, 1962), 202–207.

Eastman, Max. *The Enjoyment of Poetry, with Anthology for the Enjoyment of Poetry,* in *Kenyon Review,* XIV (Winter, 1952), 157–62.

Eberhart, Richard. *Song and Idea,* in *Furioso,* I (Summer, 1941), 68–70.

Eliot, T. S. *The Complete Poems and Plays of T. S. Eliot,* in *New Republic,* CXXVII (December 8, 1952), 16–17.

———. *The Family Reunion,* in *Poetry,* LIV (August, 1939), 264–71.

———. *Murder in the Cathedral,* in *Southern Review,* I (Winter, 1936), 609–23.

———. *The Use of Poetry,* in *Saturday Review of Literature,* X (March 24, 1934), 574.

5 Young American Poets [George Marion O'Donnell, Randall Jarrell, John Berryman, Mary Barnard, and W. R. Moses], *Kenyon Review,* III (Summer, 1941), 377–80.

Fleming, Archibald. *The Island Called Pharos,* in *Southern Review,* I (Winter, 1936), 609–23.

Forster, E. M. *Abinger Harvest,* in *Yale Review,* XXVI (September, 1936), 181–83.

Freud, Sigmund. *Beyond the Pleasure Principle,* in *Saturday Review of Literature,* I (October 4, 1924), 161–62.

―――. *Group Psychology,* in *Saturday Review of Literature,* I (October 4, 1924), 161–62.

Gilby, Thomas. *Poetic Experience,* in *Saturday Review of Literature,* XII (August 31, 1935), 17.

Graves, Robert. *On English Poetry,* in *The Fugitive,* I (October, 1922), 68.

Gregory, Horace. *The Shield of Achilles,* in *Kenyon Review,* VI (Summer, 1944), 469–73.

Hickey, D. W. *Call Back the Spring,* in *Southern Review,* I (Winter, 1936), 609–23.

Huxley, Aldous, *Eyeless in Gaza,* in *Southern Review,* II (Autumn, 1936), 399–418.

Hyman, Stanley Edgar. *The Armed Vision,* in *Kenyon Review,* X (Autumn, 1948), 682–88.

James, Henry. *The American Scene,* in *Nation,* CLXIII (December 7, 1946), 650, 652.

Johnson, Charles S. *Shadow of the Plantation,* in *American Review,* IV (December, 1934), 147–54.

Johnson, E. D. H. *The Alien Vision of Victorian Poetry,* in *Kenyon Review,* XV (Spring, 1953), 335–36.

Kirk, Russell. *The Conservative Mind: From Burke to Santayana,* in *Kenyon Review,* XV (Autumn, 1953), 648–54.

Levin, Harry. *James Joyce: A Critical Introduction,* in *Kenyon Review,* IV (Autumn, 1942), 430–32.

Lewis, Wyndham. *Time and Western Man,* in *Sewanee Review,* XXXVII (July, 1929), 353–66.

Lytle, Andrew. *The Long Night,* in *Southern Review,* II (Autumn, 1936), 399–418.

Mackail, Denis. *Barrie,* in *Kenyon Review,* III (Autumn, 1941), 519–20.

Malraux, André. *Days of Wrath,* in *Southern Review,* II (Autumn, 1936), 399–418.

Maritain, Jacques. *The Dream of Descartes,* in *Sewanee Review,* LIV (Winter, 1946), 153–56.

Masters, Edgar Lee. *Invisible Landscapes,* in *Southern Review,* I (Winter, 1936), 609–23.

Millet, Fred B. *The Rebirth of Liberal Education,* in *Kenyon Review,* VIII (Winter, 1946), 176–77.

Mitchell, Margaret. *Gone with the Wind,* in *Southern Review,* II (Autumn, 1936), 399–418.

Moore, Merrill. *M: One Thousand Autobiographical Sonnets,* in *Kenyon Review,* I (Spring, 1939), 229–31.

Morgan, Charles. *Sparkenbroke,* in *Southern Review,* II (Autumn, 1936), 399–418.

Ortega y Gasset, José. *Mission of the University,* in *Kenyon Review,* VII (Summer, 1945), 524–25.

Patchen, Kenneth. *Memoirs of a Shy Pornographer,* in *Kenyon Review,* VIII (Winter, 1946), 171.

Pitter, Ruth. *A Mad Lady's Garland,* in *Southern Review,* I (Winter, 1936), 609–23.

Pottle, F. A. *The Idiom of Poetry,* in *Modern Language Notes,* LVIII (April, 1943), 321.

Pound, Ezra. *ABC of Reading,* in *Saturday Review of Literature,* XI (January 19, 1935), 434–35.

———. *Eleven New Cantos,* in *Saturday Review of Literature,* XI (January 19, 1935), 434–35.

Read, Herbert. *English Prose Style,* in *New Republic,* CXXVII (October 6, 1952), 17–18.

Robertson, William J. *The Changing South,* in *Forum,* LXXIX (May, 1928), xxiv.

Robinson, Edwin Arlington. *King Jasper,* in *Southern Review,* I (Winter, 1936), 609–23.

Ruykeyser, Muriel. *Theory of Flight,* in *Southern Review,* I (Winter, 1936), 609–23.

Santayana, George. *The Realm of Matter,* in *New Republic,* LXIII (October 22, 1930), 262–63.

Smith, Bernard. *Forces in American Criticism,* in *Free America,* IV (January, 1940), 19–20.

Steinbeck, John. *Cannery Row,* in *Kenyon Review,* VII (Summer, 1945), 526–27.

Tolstoi, Alexei. *Darkness and Dawn,* in *Southern Review,* II (Autumn, 1936), 399–418.

Van Doren, Mark. *The Last Look,* in *New York Herald Tribune Books,* XIV (November 21, 1937), 20.

Warren, Robert Penn. *Selected Poems,* in *Saturday Review of Literature,* XXVII (May 20, 1944), 10–11.

Welty, Eudora. *Delta Wedding,* in *Kenyon Review,* VIII (Summer, 1946), 503–507.

West, Rebecca. *The Thinking Reed,* in *Southern Review,* II (Autumn, 1936), 399–418.

Williams, Tennessee. *27 Wagons Full of Cotton and Other One Act Plays,* in *Kenyon Review,* VIII (Spring, 1946), 344–45.

Wimsatt, W. K., Jr. *The Verbal Icon,* in *Kenyon Review,* XVI (Autumn, 1954), 554–64.

Winters, Yvor. *Edwin Arlington Robinson,* in *New York Times Book Review,* January 19, 1947, pp. 7, 28.

Winther, Sophus Keith. *Take All to Nebraska,* in *Southern Review,* II (Autumn, 1936), 399–418.

Winslow, Ann. *Trial Balances,* in *Southern Review,* I (Winter, 1936), 609–23.

V. *NASHVILLE TENNESSEAN* BOOK PAGE REVIEWS

Austin, Mary. *Everyman's Genius,* June 28, 1925.
Bennett, Arnold. *Elsie and the Child, and Other Stories,* November 30, 1924.
———. *Riceyman Steps,* March 2, 1924.
Boswell, Young. *People You Know,* June 8, 1924.
Cabell, James Branch. *Straws and Prayers,* March 29, 1925.
Canfield, Dorothy. *The Home Maker,* July 27, 1924.
Chevalier, Jaques. *Henri Bergson,* March 17, 1929.
Coffin, Robert P. Tristram. *Christchurch,* February 15, 1925.
Cooke, Edmund Vance. *Companionable Poems,* March 30, 1924.
Davidson, Donald. *The Tall Men,* October 2, 1927.
Dawson, Coningsby. *The Coast of Folly,* April 27, 1924.
Dehan, Richard. *The Pipers of the Marketplace,* September 7, 1924.
H. D. *Heliodora,* August 24, 1924.
Ferber, Edna. *So Big,* March 16, 1924.
Freud, Sigmund. *Beyond the Pleasure Principle,* September 14, 1924.
———. *Group Psychology,* September 14, 1924.
Gale, Zona. *Birth,* April 13, 1924.
Galsworthy, John. *The White Monkey,* December 14, 1924.
Glyn, Elinor. *Six Days,* March 23, 1924.
Gorman, H. S. *Gold by Gold,* April 12, 1925.
Graves, Robert. *The Meaning of Dreams,* May 31, 1925.
Guedalla, Philip. *A Gallery,* February 1, 1925.
———. *Supers and Supermen,* September 28, 1924.
Gwynn, Stephen. *Collected Poems,* March 30, 1924.
Hardy, Thomas. *Collected Poems of Thomas Hardy,* June 12, 1927.
Hibbard, Addison (ed.). *The Lyric South,* July 15, 1928.
Hirsch, Nathaniel D. Mttron. *Twins,* July 20, 1930.
Housman, Laurence. *Trimblerigg,* August 16, 1925.
Hutchinson, Vere. *Great Waters,* May 4, 1924.
Irwin, Wallace. *The Golden Bed,* August 17, 1924.
Jeans, Sir James. *The Universe Around Us,* May 4, 1930.
Johnson, Owen. *Blue Blood,* May 18, 1924.
Keyes, Frances Parkinson. *Letters from a Senator's Wife,* August 10, 1924.
Macauley, Rose. *Orphan Island,* March 8, 1925.
MacGruder, Mary Lanier. *Wages,* April 6, 1924.
McKenna, Stephen. *Vindication,* April 6, 1924.
MacLeish, Archibald. *The Happy Marriage,* March 23, 1924.
Marsh, Charles Fielding. *After Harvest,* September 7, 1924.

Mencken, H. L. *Prejudices: Fourth Series,* February 8, 1925.

Millikan, Robert A. *Science and the New Civilization,* May 4, 1930.

Morley, Christopher, and Don Marquis. *Pandora Lifts the Lid,* June 29, 1924.

Morley, Christopher. *Parson's Pleasure,* February 17, 1924.

Morton, David. *Harvest,* June 1, 1924.

The New Economic Order. A Symposium by Twenty-Four Economists, May 4, 1930.

Newman, Frances. *The Short Story's Mutations,* February 22, 1925.

Percy, William Alexander. *Enzio's Kingdom,* May 11, 1924.

Phelps, William Lyon. *Howells, James, Bryant, and Other Essays,* May 25, 1924.

Philpotts, Eden. *A Human Boy's Diary,* May 18, 1924.

————. *Redcliff,* November 9, 1924.

Powys, Llewelyn. *An Hour on Christianity,* September 28, 1930.

Pupin, Michael. *The Romance of the Machine,* May 4, 1930.

Radin, Paul. *The Story of the American Indian,* March 4, 1928.

Ramsey, Janet. *High Road,* June 15, 1924.

Richards, I. A. *Science and Poetry,* March 6, 1927.

Robinson, Edwin Arlington. *Dionysus in Doubt,* May 3, 1925.

Rung, Otto. *Shadows That Pass,* August 3, 1924.

Russell, Bertrand. *Philosophy,* February 5, 1928.

Sachs, Emanie N. *Talk,* September 21, 1924.

Sackville-West, V. *Seducers in Ecuador,* August 9, 1925.

Schnittkind, Henry T. *The Poets of the Future* (Vol. VII), January 4, 1925.

Sedgwick, Anne Douglas. *The Little French Girl,* October 12, 1924.

Sinclair, May. *Arnold Waterlow,* November 16, 1924.

————. *A Cure of Souls,* February 10, 1924.

————. *The Dark Night,* June 22, 1924.

Spengler, Oswald. *The Decline of the West,* July 11, 1926.

Spitzer, Marian. *Who Would Be Free?* October 5, 1924.

Stein, Leo. *The A.B.C. of Aesthetics,* November 20, 1927.

Strong, L. A. G. (ed.). *The Best Poems of 1924,* January 4, 1925.

Suckow, Ruth. *Country People,* June 13, 1924.

Thomson, D. C., and F. W. Bateson (eds.). *Oxford Poetry, 1923,* March 30, 1924.

Torrence, Ridgely. *Hesperides,* June 21, 1925.

Wade, John D. *John Wesley,* October 19, 1930.

Waldo, Frank. *Salvos,* March 9, 1924.

Weirick, Bruce. *From Whitman to Sandburg in American Poetry,* April 24, 1924.

Werner, M. R. *Brigham Young,* August 23, 1925.

Wharton, Edith. *Old New York,* July 6, 1924.

Wodehouse, P. G. *Golf Without Tears,* July 20, 1924.

VI. MISCELLANEA

American Rhodes Scholars, Oxford, 1910–1913. Edited by Christopher Morley
with John Crowe Ransom and Elmer Davis, 1913.

Dedicatory Address, printed in a pamphlet entitled "Exercises on the Occasion
of the Dedication of the New Phi Beta Kappa Hall, College of William
and Mary in Virginia, Williamsburg, Saturday, May the Eighteenth,
1957." Printed in 1958.

VII. BIOGRAPHICAL AND CRITICAL MATERIAL

BOOKS AND ESSAYS IN COLLECTIONS

Adams, Leonie. "On John Crowe Ransom's 'Master's in the Garden Again,' "
The Contemporary Poet as Artist and Critic. Edited by Anthony Ostroff.
Boston: Little, Brown and Company, 1964, pp. 121–27.
  Compares the revision of "Conrad in Twilight" with the earlier version
of the poem.
Anderson, Sherwood. *Sherwood Anderson's Memoirs.* New York: Harcourt,
Brace and Company, 1942, pp. 458–59.
  Ransom's connection with the Agrarians is mentioned.
Arms, George, and Joseph M. Kuntz. *Poetry Explication.* Revised edition.
New York: Swallow Press and Morrow, 1962, pp. 205–11.
  Cites books and articles containing explications of thirty poems by
Ransom.
Beatty, Richmond Croom. "By Way of Background," *A Vanderbilt Miscel-
lany.* Edited by Richmond Croom Beatty. Nashville: Vanderbilt Uni-
versity Press, 1944, pp. 11–27. Reprinted from *Tennessee Historical
Quarterly,* III (March, 1944), 3–23.
  Contains a brief history of the Fugitive and Agrarian movements.
————. "Donald Davidson as Fugitive-Agrarian," *Southern Renascence:
The Literature of the Modern South.* Edited by Louis D. Rubin, Jr.,
and Robert D. Jacobs. Baltimore: The Johns Hopkins Press, 1953, pp.
392–412.
  Ransom is mentioned in connection with an examination of Davidson's
agrarianism and poetic theories.
————, Floyd C. Watkins, and Thomas Daniel Young (eds.). *The Litera-
ture of the South.* Chicago: Scott, Foresman and Company, 1952, p. 751.
  Includes a biographical note introducing selections from Ransom's
work and a brief discussion of the Fugitive-Agrarian movement.
Boyle, Robert S. J. *Metaphor in Hopkins.* Chapel Hill: University of North
Carolina Press, 1961, pp. 177–83.
  Relies upon Ransom's discussion of the use of metaphor (in *The
World's Body*) in explaining Hopkins' use of metaphor.

Boynton, Percy. *Literature and American Life.* Boston: Ginn and Company, 1936, pp. 868–71.

Emphasizes regionalism as the major thesis of the essays included in *I'll Take My Stand.*

Bradbury, John M. *The Fugitives: A Critical Account.* Chapel Hill: University of North Carolina Press, 1958.

A critical analysis of the works, poetical and critical, of the major Fugitives; Ransom's poetry and criticism are discussed in Chapters III and IX.

————. *Renaissance in the South: A Critical History of the Literature, 1920–1960.* Chapel Hill: University of North Carolina Press, 1963, pp. 25–26 *et passim.*

A brief biographical and critical estimate of Ransom's poetry and critical ideas.

Braithwaite, William S. "Introduction," *Anthology of Magazine Verse for 1925.* Edited by William S. Braithwaite. Boston: B. J. Brimmer, 1925, xv.

Comments on Ransom's volume of poetry *Chills and Fever.*

Brooks, Cleanth. *Modern Poetry and the Tradition.* Chapel Hill: University of North Carolina Press, 1939, pp. 88–95.

In an essay entitled "The Modern Poet and the Tradition," Brooks examines the effects of Ransom's use of irony.

————. *The Well Wrought Urn.* New York: Harcourt, Brace and Company, 1947, pp. 225, 243–47.

In Appendix I, "Criticism, History, and Critical Relativism," Brooks examines Ransom's essay "Shakespeare at Sonnets."

Brooks, Van Wyck. *Opinions of Oliver Allston.* New York: E. P. Dutton, 1941, p. 230 *et passim.*

Mentions, in a spirit of contention, some of Ransom's critical statements.

Burke, Kenneth. *The Philosophy of Literary Form: Studies in Symbolic Action.* Baton Rouge: Louisiana State University Press, 1941, pp. 5, 19, 31, 116, 154.

Refers to some of Ransom's critical pronouncements, largely from *The World's Body.*

Cash, W. J. *The Mind of the South.* Garden City: Doubleday and Company, 1956, p. 380.

The Nashville Agrarians are called "spiritual heirs of Thomas Nelson Page."

Ciardi, John. *How Does a Poem Mean.* Boston: Houghton Mifflin Company, 1959, pp. 803–804.

Quotes and comments on Ransom's poem "Blue Girls."

Cohen, J. M. *Robert Graves.* Edinburgh: Oliver and Boyd, 1960. pp. 43–44.

Suggests a similarity between the ironic manner of Graves and Ransom and concludes that Ransom may have derived the manner from Graves.

Couch, W. T. (ed.). *Culture in the South*. Chapel Hill: University of North Carolina Press, 1934, pp. 180, 181, 187, *et passim*.
Ransom is mentioned briefly in connection with both his poetry and his espousal of agrarianism.

Cowan, Louise. *The Fugitive Group: A Literary History*. Baton Rouge: Louisiana State University Press, 1959.
A definitive history of the Fugitive movement from its beginnings to 1928; Ransom's function as intellectual leader is stressed.

————. "The Pietas of Southern Poetry," *South: Modern Southern Literature in Its Cultural Setting*. Edited by Louis D. Rubin, Jr., and Robert Jacobs. Garden City: Doubleday and Company, 1961, pp. 95–114.
Ransom is included in a group of Southern poets whose works are said to reflect the Southern attitude.

Cowley, Malcolm. *The Literary Situation*. New York: The Viking Press, 1958, pp. 12–13 *et passim*.
Ransom is called the founder of ontological criticism.

Crane, R. S. "The Critical Monism of Cleanth Brooks," *Critics and Criticism: Ancient and Modern*. Edited by R. S. Crane. Chicago: University of Chicago Press, 1952, pp. 83–107.
Finds in Ransom's principle of texture a tendency toward "monistic reduction of critical concepts."

Daiches, David. "The Proper Sphere of Poetry," *Critical Approaches to Literature*. Englewood Cliffs: Prentice-Hall, 1956, pp. 143–57.
Prints and comments on an excerpt from "Poetry: A Note in Ontology," in *The World's Body*, 111–22, 126–28.

Daniels, Jonathan. *A Southerner Discovers the South*. New York: The Macmillan Company, 1938.
The author's conversation with Donald Davidson is recorded in a chapter entitled "Night in Nashville"; Ransom is mentioned in connection with agrarianism.

Davidson, Donald. *Southern Writers in the Modern World*. Athens, Ga.: University of Georgia Press, 1958.
The work includes lectures delivered at Mercer University. The first lecture is the story of the Fugitive group told by one of its members. The second lecture gives the social and philosophical backgrounds of *I'll Take My Stand*, together with a biographical note on each contributor. The third lecture is concerned in part with the influence of Vanderbilt University, or any other university, on its faculty-student writers.

Deusen, Marshall Van. *A Metaphor for the History of American Criticism*. Pamphlet XIII of *Essays and Studies on American Language and Litera-*

ture. Edited by S. B. Liljegren. Copenhagen: Ejnar Munksgaard, 1961, pp. 49–51.
Discusses Ransom's idea of structure and texture in poetry.
Deutsch, Babette. *Poetry in Our Time.* New York: Henry Holt, 1952, pp. 204–10 *et passim.*
Reviews some qualities of Ransom's poetry.
———. *This Modern Poetry,* New York: W. W. Norton, 1935, pp. 156–59 *et passim.*
Characterizes Ransom's poetry as metaphysical.
Douglas, Wallace W. "Deliberate Exiles: The Social Sources of Agrarian Poetics," *Aspects of American Poetry.* Edited by Richard M. Ludwig. Columbus: Ohio State University Press, 1962, pp. 273–300.
Finds "a thematic or logical unity of a sort" between the social theories of the Nashville Agrarians and the development of the New Criticism.
Drew, Elizabeth, and John L. Sweeney. *Directions in Modern Poetry.* New York: W. W. Norton, 1940, pp. 75–78.
A brief characterization of Ransom's poetry.
Duncan, Joseph E. *The Revival of Metaphysical Poetry: The History of a Style, 1800 to the Present.* Minneapolis: University of Minnesota Press, 1959, pp. 174–88.
Discusses the approach of the New Critics to metaphysical poetry.
Dwivedi, Rama Wadh, and Vikramgditya Rah. *Literary Criticism.* Delhi, India: Motilal Banarsidass, 1965, pp. 375, 401.
Mentions the influence of Eliot and Richards on the critical theories of the "Southern group," including Ransom, Tate, and Brooks.
Emerson, O. B. "Prophet Next Door," *Reality and Myth: Essays in American Literature in Memory of Richmond Croom Beatty.* Edited by William E. Walker and Robert L. Welker. Nashville: Vanderbilt University Press, 1964, pp. 237–74.
Cites Ransom's contribution to Faulkner criticism.
England, Kenneth. "Sidney Lanier in C Major," *Reality and Myth: Essays in American Literature in Memory of Richmond Croom Beatty.* Edited by William E. Walker and Robert L. Welker. Nashville: Vanderbilt University Press, 1964, pp. 60–79.
Finds the ideal of the Old South in Ransom's poetry.
Ethridge, James M. (ed.). *Contemporary Authors: A Bio-Bibliographical Guide to the Current Authors and Their Works.* Vols. 7–8. Detroit: Gale Research Company, 1963, p. 446.
A brief biographical sketch, list of major works, and one-paragraph critical estimate of Ransom.
Fain, John Tyree. *The Spyglass: Views and Reviews, 1924–1930 by Donald Davidson.* Nashville: Vanderbilt University Press, 1963, vii.
Notes Ransom's contribution of book reviews to Davidson's book page in the *Nashville Tennessean.*

Fletcher, John Gould. *Life Is My Song: The Autobiography of John Gould Fletcher.* New York: Farrar and Rinehart, 1937, pp. 339–43.
Mentions Ransom in a discussion of the Fugitives.
Foster, Richard. *The New Romantics: A Reappraisal of the New Criticism.* Bloomington: Indiana University Press, 1962, pp. 138–44, 199–200, *et passim.*
Discusses Ransom's differentiation between structure and texture in poetry and notes certain alterations in his general critical theory.
Garrett, George P. "The Recent Poetry of Robert Penn Warren," *Robert Penn Warren: A Collection of Critical Essays.* Edited by John Lewis Langley, Jr. New York: New York University Press, 1965, pp. 223–36.
The Fugitives' poetry, especially that of Ransom and Tate, is described as "traditional and traditionally Southern."
Glicksberg, Charles I. *American Literary Criticism, 1900–1950.* New York: Hendricks House, 1951, pp. 450–67 *et passim.*
Summarizes Ransom's critical theory and reprints his essay "Criticism, Inc."
Graves, Robert. "Introduction," *Grace After Meat.* London: Hogarth Press, 1924.
A brief comment on Ransom's literary career; Graves discovers an affinity between Ransom's and Frost's poetry.
Gregory, Horace, and Marya Zaturenska. *A History of American Poetry: 1900–1940.* New York: Harcourt, Brace and Company, 1946, pp. 360–72.
A brief biographical note and summary of Ransom's critical views and characteristics of his poetry.
Gross, Harvey. *Sound and Form in Modern Poetry.* Ann Arbor: University of Michigan Press, 1964, pp. 72–78.
Discusses Ransom's critical views and poetry under the heading of "Modern Poetry in the Metrical Tradition"; certain revisions in his critical principles are remarked.
Handy, William J. *Kant and the Southern New Critics.* Austin: University of Texas Press, 1963.
Discusses the influence of Kant upon the critical theories of Ransom, Tate, and Brooks.
Hardy, John Edward. "The Achievement of Cleanth Brooks," *Southern Renascence: The Literature of the Modern South.* Edited by Louis D. Rubin, Jr., and Robert D. Jacobs. Baltimore: The John Hopkins Press, 1953, pp. 413–26.
Remarks some points of difference in the doctrine of the New Critics.
——. "Poets and Critics," *South: Modern Southern Literature in Its Cultural Setting.* Edited by Louis D. Rubin, Jr., and Robert Jacobs. Garden City: Doubleday and Company, 1961, pp. 260–75.
Discusses Ransom's poetry and criticism in connection with an assess-

ment of the major Fugitives as Southern writers within the entire tradition of Western literature.

Hart, James D. (ed.). *The Oxford Companion to American Literature.* Fourth edition. New York: Oxford University Press, 1965, pp. 694–95.
    A brief biographical sketch.

Heilman, Robert B. "The Southern Temper," *South: Modern Southern Literature in Its Cultural Setting.* Edited by Louis D. Rubin, Jr., and Robert Jacobs. Garden City: Doubleday and Company, 1961, pp. 48–59. Essay also appears in *Southern Renascence: The Literature of the Modern South,* 1953, pp. 3–13.
    Mentions Ransom's poetry and criticism in connection with certain characteristics of Southern writers, including concreteness and a sense of the elemental and ornamental.

Herzberg, Max J. *The Reader's Encyclopedia of American Literature.* New York: Thomas Y. Crowell Company, 1962, pp. 938–39.
    A brief biographical sketch and critical estimate.

Heyl, Bernard C. *New Bearings in Esthetics and Art Criticism.* New Haven: Yale University Press, 1943, pp. 12, 13, 21, *et passim.*
    Scattered references to some of Ransom's critical essays.

Hicks, Granville. *The Great Tradition: An Interpretation of American Literature Since the Civil War.* Revised edition. New York: The Macmillan Company, 1935, pp. 270, 282.
    Remarks Ransom's defense of Christian faith; dismisses as futile the cause of agrarianism.

Hillyer, Robert. *In Pursuit of Poetry.* New York: McGraw-Hill, 1960.
    Mentions Ransom's leadership in turning the Fugitives from poetry to criticism; dismisses the New Criticism as shortsighted and ineffectual.

Hoffman, Frederick, Charles Allen, and Carolyn Ulrich. *The Little Magazine: A History and a Bibliography.* Princeton: Princeton University Press, 1946, pp. 116–25.
    A brief history of *The Fugitive.*

Holman, C. Hugh. "The Defense of Art: Criticism Since 1930," *The Development of American Literary Criticism.* Edited by Floyd Stovall. Chapel Hill: University of North Carolina Press, 1955, pp. 199–245.
    Ransom's critical theories are included in an assessment of recent literary criticism.

Howard, Leon. *Literature and the American Tradition.* New York: Doubleday and Company, 1960, p. 312.
    Finds Ransom to have been "one of the most influential men" of the 1930's.

Hyman, Stanley Edgar. *The Armed Vision: A Study in the Methods of Modern Literary Criticism.* New York: Alfred A. Knopf, 1948, pp. 92–95 *et passim.*

Summarizes the critical theories of the "Southern school" of critics headed by Ransom.

Jones, Howard Mumford, and Richard M. Ludwig. *Guide to American Literature and Its Background Since 1890*. Third edition. Cambridge: Harvard University Press, 1964, pp. 184, 186.

Three of Ransom's works are listed.

Jordan, Elijah. *Essays in Criticism*. Chicago: University of Chicago Press, 1952, p. 95 *et passim*.

Mentions Ransom's expression of need for a critical theory grounded in philosophy.

Kazin, Alfred. "Criticism at the Poles," *On Native Grounds*. New York: Reynal and Hitchcock, 1942, pp. 400–52. Also printed in *New Republic*, CVII (October 19, 1942), 492–99.

An interpretation of modern American prose literature; identifies Ransom with the literary criticism arising in the 1930's which Kazin characterizes as intense and narrow.

Knight, Karl F. *The Poetry of John Crowe Ransom: A Study of Diction, Metaphor, and Symbol*. Volume II of Studies in American Literature. The Hague: Mouton and Company, 1964.

A critical analysis of Ransom's poetic art.

Kreymborg, Alfred. *Our Singing Strength: An Outline of American Poetry, 1620–1930*. New York: Coward-McCann, 1929, pp. 563–71 *et passim*.

A brief history of *The Fugitive* and a critical estimate of some of the major members of the group.

Krieger, Murray. *The New Apologists for Poetry*. Minneapolis: University of Minnesota Press, 1956, pp. 82–87, 143–47, *et passim*.

Examines Ransom's explanation of structure and texture as it defines the creative process and as it contrasts with other critical theories, including those of Brooks, Winters, and Tate.

Leary, Lewis (ed.). *Contemporary Literary Scholarship: A Critical Review*. New York: Appleton-Century-Crofts, 1958, pp. 458–60 *et passim*.

Uses Ransom's essay "The Aesthetics of Regionalism" as a take-off point for the posing of questions for students concerning regionalism and the New Criticism.

Lemon, Lee T. *The Partial Critics*. New York: Oxford University Press, 1965, pp. 98–103 *et passim*.

Discusses Ransom's idea of perception in the criticism of poetry; also mentions in other parts of the work Ransom's theory of poetic language (118–19) and his distinction between pure and Platonic poetry (59–60).

Levin, Harry. *Contexts of Criticism*. Cambridge: Harvard University Press, 1957, p. 257.

Mentions Ransom's call for ontological criticism.

Ludwig, Richard M. (ed.). *Bibliography Supplement, Literary History of the United States*. New York: The Macmillan Company, 1959, pp. 225–27.

Lists Ransom's major published works; includes under bibliography and criticism some of the otustanding studies of Ransom's poetry and critical and agrarian theories.

MacCaffrey, Isabel Gamble. "Ceremonies of Bravery: John Crowe Ransom," *South: Modern Southern Literature in Its Cultural Setting*. Edited by Louis D. Rubin, Jr., and Robert D. Jacobs. Garden City: Doubleday and Company, 1961, pp. 210–20. Also printed in *Southern Renascence: The Literature of the Modern South*. Edited by Louis D. Rubin, Jr., and Robert D. Jacobs. Baltimore: The Johns Hopkins Press, 1953, pp. 341–51, and in *Hopkins Review*, VI (Spring-Summer, 1953), 105–15.

Considers Ransom's obliqueness of style in relation to his major subject, "the war of death with life."

Millet, Fred B. *Contemporary American Authors: A Critical Survey and 219 Bio-Bibliographies*. New York: Harcourt, Brace and Company, 1940, pp. 146–47, 535–36.

A note on the Fugitives names Ransom as the leader; also includes a brief biographical sketch.

Mims, Edwin. *The Advancing South*. Garden City: Doubleday, Page and Company, 1926, pp. 198–201.

A brief history of the Fugitives; notes that Ransom's poetry is not consciously Southern.

————. *History of Vanderbilt University*. Nashville: Vanderbilt University Press, 1946, pp. 414–17 *et passim*.

A brief account of the Fugitive group and the publications of some of the members.

Monroe, Harriet. *A Poet's Life*. New York: The Macmillan Company, 1938.

In a list of contributors to *Poetry* in its second decade (1922–32), names the "southern regionalists"—Ransom, Tate, Davidson, and Warren.

Moore, Merrill. *The Fugitive: Clippings and Comments, Collected by Merrill Moore*. Boston: Privately printed, 1939.

Moore's own observations on the Fugitives are interwoven with reprints of various clippings concerning the magazine and the anthology.

Muller, Herbert J. *Science and Criticism: The Humanistic Tradition in Contemporary Thought*. New Haven: Yale University Press, 1943.

Scattered references to Ransom's critical doctrines; see index.

Nyren, Dorothy (ed.). *A Library of Literary Criticism*. New York: Frederick Ungar Publishing Company, 1960, pp. 386–89.

Quotes twelve statements by various critics concerning Ransom's poetry and criticism.

O'Connor, William Van. *Sense and Sensibility in Modern Poetry*. Chicago: University of Chicago Press, 1948, pp. 138–40, 217–18, 234–36, *et passim*.

Discusses Ransom's ironic temper, his distrust of "progress," and his distinction between pure and obscure poetry.

Owen, Guy. "John Crowe Ransom: The Evolution of His Style," *The Twenties: Poetry and Prose*. Edited by Richard E. Langford and William E. Taylor. Deland, Fla.: Everett Edwards Press, 1966, pp. 46–52.
    Summarizes critical opinions of Ransom's poetry.
Parks, Edd Winfield. *Segments of Southern Thought*. Athens: University of Georgia Press, 1938, pp. 116–18.
    In a brief consideration of the major Fugitives, mentions some characteristics of Ransom's poetic art.
Pottle, F. A. *The Idiom of Poetry*. Revised edition. Bloomington: Indiana University Press, 1963, pp. 90, 150.
    Alludes to Ransom's consideration of poetry and science; cites the interest of contemporary critics, including Ransom, Brooks, and Warren, in metaphysical poetry.
Pratt, William. "In Pursuit of the Fugitives," *The Fugitive Poets: Modern Southern Poetry in Perspective*. New York: E. P. Dutton, 1965, pp. 13–46.
    A history of the Fugitives with a brief commentary on each major figure; also contains a collection of Fugitive verse.
Preminger, Alex (ed.). *Encyclopedia of Poetry and Poetics*. Princeton: Princeton University Press, 1965, pp. 516–17, 568, *et passim*.
    Under the heading "Modern Poetics," discusses Ransom's preference for metaphysical poetry; under "New Criticism," lists Ransom's *The New Criticism* in the selected bibliography.
Pritchard, John Paul. *Criticism in America: An Account of the Development of Critical Techniques from the Early Period of the Republic to the Middle Years of the Twentieth Century*. Norman, Okla.: University of Oklahoma Press, 1956, pp. 238–46 *et passim*.
    Summarizes Ransom's critical theories expressed in *God Without Thunder, The World's Body*, and *The New Criticism*.
———. *Literary Wise Men of Gotham: Criticism in New York, 1815–1860*. Baton Rouge: Louisiana State University Press, 1963, pp. 27, 45.
    Mentions parallels between early literary criticism in New York and that of Ransom in the twentieth century.
Purdy, Rob Roy (ed.). *Fugitives' Reunion: Conversations at Vanderbilt, May 3–5, 1956*. Nashville: Vanderbilt University Press, 1959.
    The Fugitives discuss literature and their own careers.
Quinn, Arthur Hobson. *The Literature of the American People*. New York: Appleton-Century-Crofts, 1951, pp. 922–23.
    Characterizes the Fugitives and Agrarians as "champions of a regional attitude both in literature and in politics"; sees Ransom's major poetic theme as the divided sensibility.
Raiziss, Sona. *The Metaphysical Passion*. Philadelphia: University of Pennsylvania Press, 1952, pp. 184–211.
    Examines, in a chapter entitled "The Fugitives," metaphysical qualities of the poetry of Ransom, Warren, and Tate.

Riding, Laura. *Contemporaries and Snobs*. Garden City: Doubleday, Doran and Company, 1928, p. 33.
> Refers to Ransom as a "romantic satirist."

──────, and Robert Graves. *A Survey of Modernist Poetry*. Garden City: Doubleday, Doran and Company, 1928, pp. 103–109, 229–30, *et passim*.
> Cites Ransom's "Captain Carpenter" as a poem of a "highly trained literary connoisseur"; mentions his "clownishness."

Rock, Virginia. "The Twelve Southerners: Biographical Essays," *I'll Take My Stand: The South and the Agrarian Tradition*, by Twelve Southerners. New York: Harper Torchbooks, 1962, pp. 360–85.
> A brief biographical and critical estimate of Ransom appears on pages 375–77.

Rosenthal, Macha Louis, and A. J. M. Smith. *Exploring Poetry*. New York: The Macmillan Company, 1955, pp. 6–8.
> Explicates Ransom's poem "Janet Waking."

──────. *The Modern Poets: A Critical Introduction*. New York: Oxford University Press, 1960, pp. 159, 254.
> Finds traditionalism in Ransom's art and thought and "poignant sweetness" in his poetry.

Rossiter, Clinton. *Conservatism in America*. New York: Vintage Books, 1962, pp. 229–32.
> Summarizes the principles of agrarianism as stated in *I'll Take My Stand*.

Rubin, Louis D., Jr. "The Poetry of Agrarianism," *The Faraway Country: Writers of the Modern South*. Seattle: University of Washington Press, 1963, pp. 155–84.
> Analyzes Ransom's poetry from the point of view of agrarian themes (165–72).

──────. "The Serpent in the Mulberry Bush," *Southern Renascence: The Literature of the Modern South*. Edited by Louis D. Rubin, Jr., and Robert D. Jacobs. Baltimore: The Johns Hopkins Press, 1953, pp. 352–67.
> Discusses the Fugitives' relation to the South in an essay on Tate's "Ode to the Confederate Dead."

Rukeyser, Muriel. "On John Crowe Ransom's 'Master's in the Garden Again,'" *The Contemporary Poet as Artist and Critic*. Edited by Anthony Ostroff. Boston: Little, Brown and Company, 1964, pp. 128–33.
> Suggests that the revision of "Conrad in Twilight" carries a meaning which "speaks for a further stage of life."

Schramm, Wilbur L. "Imaginative Writing," *Literary Scholarship: Its Aims and Methods*. Chapel Hill: University of North Carolina Press, 1941, p. 205 *et passim*.
> Uses the gathering of the Fugitives at Vanderbilt as an example of the value of "group apprenticeship" in creative writing and in literary criticism.

Scott, Wilbur S. *Five Approaches of Literary Criticism: An Arrangement of Contemporary Critical Essays.* New York: The Macmillan Company, 1962, pp. 179–224.

In a chapter entitled "The Formalistic Approach: Literature as Aesthetic Structure," examines the basis of the New Criticism; mentions (182) Ransom's interest in the poem as a whole rather than a dissection of parts.

Smith, Bernard. *Forces in American Criticism: A Study in the History of American Literary Thought.* New York: Harcourt, Brace and Company, 1939, pp. 385–86.

Considers Ransom a traditionalist and classicist.

Snodgrass, W. D. "On John Crowe Ransom's 'Master's in the Garden Again,' " *The Contemporary Poet as Artist and Critic.* Boston: Little, Brown and Company, 1964, pp. 114–20.

An explication of Ransom's revision of the poem "Conrad in Twilight."

Spiller, Robert, *et al. A Literary History of the United States.* New York: The Macmillan Company, 1949, III, pp. 56, 61, 64, 67, 156, 158.

Mentions Ransom's critical emphasis upon aesthetic values (61), and lists some of his published works (56, 61, 156, 158).

Stageberg, Norman C., and Wallace L. Anderson. *Poetry as Experience.* New York: American Book Company, 1952, pp. 26–27.

Explicates Ransom's poem "Dead Boy."

Stallman, Robert Wooster (ed.). *The Critic's Notebook.* Minneapolis: University of Minnesota Press, 1950, pp. 28–29, 76–77, 83–84, *et passim.*

Quotes selected passages from various critical essays published by Ransom.

———. "The New Criticism and the Southern Critics," *A Southern Vanguard.* Edited by Allen Tate. New York: Prentice-Hall, 1947, pp. 28–51.

In an essay centering upon Tate's critical theories, Stallman also examines some facets of Ransom's criticism, including dislocation of sensibility and the emphasis upon structure-texture in the poem.

Stauffer, Donald A. *The Nature of Poetry.* New York: W. W. Norton, 1946, p. 14.

Refers briefly to Ransom's idea of the distinguishing mark of poetry (as Stauffer understands it) —"the logical irrelevancy of its local details."

Stewart, John L. *John Crowe Ransom,* University of Minnesota Pamphlets on American Writers, No. 18. Minneapolis: University of Minnesota Press, 1962.

A brief critical biography of Ransom.

———. *The Burden of Time.* Princeton: Princeton University Press, 1965.

Traces the Fugitive-Agrarian movement from the gathering of the Fugitives on the Vanderbilt University campus to post-agrarianism; examines in detail the prose and poetry of Ransom, Tate, and Warren.

Chapter five is devoted to a study of Ransom's poetry and Chapter six to his theories of poetry and criticism.

Stewart, Randall. *American Literature and Christian Doctrine.* Baton Rouge: Louisiana State University Press, 1958, p. 123.
Quotes Ransom's remarks on Faulkner.

Sutton, Walter. *Modern American Criticism.* Englewood Cliffs: Prentice-Hall, 1963, pp. 107–16 *et passim.*
In a study of the New Criticism, summarizes the critical theories found in Ransom's larger works; discusses his attack upon science and draws parallels between the critical theory of Ransom and Eliot.

Sypher, Wylie. "Obscurity as Fetish," *Twentieth Century English.* Edited by William S. Knickerbocker. New York: The Philosophical Library, 1946, pp. 338–40.
Ransom is discussed briefly in connection with the New Criticism.

Tate, Allen. "The Profession of Letters in the South," *Reactionary Essays on Poetry and Ideas.* New York: Charles Scribner's Sons, 1936, pp. 162–64. Reprinted in *On the Limits of Poetry.* New York: Swallow Press, 1948.
Considers and rejects Ransom's fear, expressed in "Modern with the Southern Accent" (*Virginia Quarterly Review,* April, 1935) that Southern writers are losing their identity in aligning themselves with modernism.

———. *Reason in Madness: Critical Essays.* New York: G. P. Putnam's Sons, 1941, pp. 76, 97, 100–101, 160.
Incidental references to Ransom as critic.

———. *Recent American Poetry and Poetic Criticism.* Washington: Library of Congress, 1943, pp. 7, 12.
Lists Ransom's *Chills and Fever* and *The World's Body.*

———. *Sixty American Poets, 1896–1944.* Washington: Library of Congress, 1945, pp. 126–27.
Lists Ransom's major works and selected criticism of his works.

———. *Sixty American Poets, 1896–1944.* Washington: Library of Congress, 1954, pp. 103–104.
Revision of 1945 edition listed above.

Thorp, Willard. *American Writing in the Twentieth Century.* Cambridge: Harvard University Press, 1960, pp. 244–46.
A critical estimate of Ransom's poetry and criticism.

Tuve, Rosemond. *Elizabethan and Metaphysical Imagery: Renaissance Poetics and Twentieth-Century Critics.* Chicago: University of Chicago Press, 1947, pp. 112–14 *et passim.*
Among other brief references to Ransom, uses Ransom's critical terms.

Twentieth Century Authors: First Supplement. Edited by Stanley J. Kunitz. New York: H. W. Wilson Company, 1955, p. 814.
A brief biographical sketch.

Unger, Leonard. *The Man in the Name: Essays on the Experience of Poetry.*

Minneapolis: University of Minnesota Press, 1956, pp. 35–40, 111–19, *et passim*.

Examines Ransom's "categorical" conception of metaphysical poetry; reviews his critical position as expressed in several essays.

Van Doren, Carl, and Mark Van Doren. *American and British Literature Since 1890*. Revised and enlarged edition. New York: D. Appleton-Century, 1940, pp. 51–52, 361.

A brief critical and biographical study.

Venturi, Lionello. *Art Criticism Now*. Baltimore: The Johns Hopkins Press, 1941, ix-x.

Quotes from Ransom's article in the *Southern Review* as a sign of the revival of "aesthetic consciousness."

Vivas, Eliseo. *The Artistic Transaction and Essays on Theory of Literature*. Columbus: Ohio State University Press, 1963, pp. 24, 227, 228.

Mentions Ransom's efforts to distinguish poetry from science and names his "inept idea of loose logical structure and irrelevant texture" as an outcome of his preoccupation with science.

————. "The Objective Correlative of T. S. Eliot," *Critiques and Essays in Criticism, 1920–1948*. Selected by Robert Wooster Stallman. New York: Ronald Press, 1949, pp. 389–400. Reprinted from *American Bookman*, I (Winter, 1944), 7 ff.

Elaborates upon and extends some of Ransom's remarks in *The New Criticism* concerning Eliot's principles of criticism.

Waggoner, Hyatt Howe. *The Heel of Elohim: Science and Values in Modern American Poetry*. Norman: University of Oklahoma Press, 1950, pp. 89, 155, 193, 199.

Quotes from Ransom's critical works including *God Without Thunder*, *The World's Body*, and *The New Criticism*.

Warren, Austin. "Literary Criticism," *Literary Scholarship: Its Aims and Methods*. Chapel Hill: University of North Carolina Press, 1941, p. 140.

Mentions Ransom's poem "The Equilibrists" as a modern poem having a "point of view."

Wellek, René. *Concepts of Criticism*. Edited by Stephen G. Nichols, Jr. New Haven: Yale University Press, 1963, pp. 339–40, 358–59, *et passim*.

Labels Ransom a "Bergsonian"; assesses the New Criticism.

————, and Austin Warren. *Theory of Literature*. New York: Harcourt, Brace and Company, 1949, pp. 22, 163.

Alludes to Ransom's definition of poetry as knowledge and to his evaluation of sound patterns in poetry.

Wells, Henry W. *The American Way of Poetry*. New York: Columbia University Press, 1943, pp. 161–73, 213, 235.

In an essay entitled "Dynastic Wound," Wells calls Ransom the last notable poet to express the South's more enduring qualities.

———. *New Poets from Old*. New York: Columbia University Press, 1940, pp. 145, 202–203, *et passim*.

Mentions Ransom's use of Middle English rhythms in "In Mr. Minnit's House"; remarks the logical development of "Captain Carpenter."

Wilder, Amos N. *The Spiritual Aspects of the New Poetry*. New York: Harper and Brothers, 1940, pp. 15–20, 247.

Quotes from Ransom's definition of modern poetry in his essay "Poets Without Laurels."

———. *Theology and Modern Literature*. Cambridge: Harvard University Press, 1958, p. 22.

In a discussion of the cleavage of literature and religion, uses Ransom's idea of the imagination separated from "The World's Body."

Williamson, George. "Donne and the Poetry of Today," *A Garland for John Donne, 1631–1931*. Edited by Theodore Spencer. Cambridge: Harvard University Press, 1931, pp. 153–76.

Examines briefly Donne's influence upon the Fugitives and especially upon the poetry of Ransom.

Wilson, James Southall. "Poetry of the New South," *Anthology of Magazine Verse for 1926*. Edited by William S. Braithwaite. Boston: B. J. Brimmer, 1926, pp. 58–66.

A brief history of literature in the South, closing with a listing of contemporary Southern poets, including some of the Fugitives; notes the death of "false romanticism" in Southern literature.

Wimsatt, W. K., Jr., and Cleanth Brooks. *Literary Criticism: A Short History*. New York: Alfred A. Knopf, 1957, pp. 626–30.

Examines Ransom's definition of structure and texture of poetry; see index for brief references to other critical views.

Winters, Yvor. "John Crowe Ransom; or, Thunder Without God," *In Defense of Reason*. New York: Swallow Press and William Morrow and Company, 1947, pp. 502–55.

An assessment of Ransom's major poetic theories, arising in part from Ransom's objections to Winters' own critical position.

PERIODICALS

Abel, Darrel. "Intellectual Criticism," *American Scholar*, XII (Autumn, 1943), 414–28.

An investigation and rejection of what Abel describes as the tendency of Tate, Ransom, and Brooks to define poetry as intellectual and to deny an emotional appeal. See response by Cleanth Brooks, *American Scholar*, XIII, 285–95, and reply by Abel, *American Scholar*, XIII, 501–503.

Abrams, Meyer Howard. "Unconscious Expectations in the Reading of Poetry," *ELH*, IX (December, 1942), 235–44.

Mentions (244) Ransom's "Shakespeare at Sonnets" as an example of literary criticism on the basis of the metaphysical school of Donne.

Aiken, Conrad. "Back to Poetry," *Atlantic Monthly,* CLXVI (August, 1940), 217–23.
Quotes from Ransom's poetry in speaking of the decline of poetic energies among contemporary poets.

Allen, Charles. "The Fugitive," *South Atlantic Quarterly,* XLIII (October, 1944), 382–89.
A brief survey of *The Fugitive,* its origin and purpose.

Ames, Van Meter. "Art and Science Inseparable," *Philosophical Review,* LV (March, 1946), 183–89.
A comment upon Ransom's (*Kenyon Review,* Winter, 1944) and Zink's (*Journal of Philosophy,* XLI, 1944) opinions on the separation of art and science.

———. "Expression and Aesthetic Expression," *Journal of Aesthetics and Art Criticism,* VI (December, 1947), 172–79.
Discusses Ransom's distinction between poetry and science.

Arvin, Newton. "Our Haughty Poets," *Current History,* XL (June, 1934), 308–14.
In a discussion of the shortcomings of contemporary poets, characterizes Ransom, Tate, and Davidson as strongly regionalistic.

"Awards," *Wilson Library Bulletin,* XXXVII (January, 1963), 398.
Announces the awarding of the 1962 fellowship for distinguished poetic achievement from the Academy of American Poets to Ransom.

Baker, Joseph E. "The Philosopher and the 'New Critic,'" *Sewanee Review,* L (Spring, 1942), 167–71.
Comments upon Ransom's editorial in *Kenyon Review,* Winter, 1941, praising the New Criticism; Baker contends that Santayana, whom Ransom, it is said, cites as denying moral qualities in art, actually recognized its moral implications.

Barrett, William. "Temptations of St. Yvor," *Kenyon Review,* IX (Autumn, 1947), 532–51.
In considering the critical theories of Yvor Winters, mentions Ransom's attitude toward Winters' criticism.

Battestin, Martin C. "John Crowe Ransom and *Lycidas:* A Reappraisal," *College English,* XVII (January, 1956), 223–28.
Challenges the critical value of Ransom's essay "A Poem Nearly Anonymous."

Beatty, Richmond Croom. "Fugitive and Agrarian Writers at Vanderbilt," *Tennessee Historical Quarterly,* III (March, 1944), 3–23. Reprinted in *A Vanderbilt Miscellany,* 1944.
A brief history of the Fugitive and Agrarian movements.

———. "The Heritage of Symbolism in Modern Poetry," *Yale Review,* XXXVI (March, 1947), 467–77.

Mentions Ransom's "Poets Without Laurels" in discussing the obscurity of symbolism in modern poetry.

————. "John Crowe Ransom as Poet," *Sewanee Review*, LII (Summer, 1944), 344–66.

Examines some major themes of Ransom's poetry.

————. "A Personal Memoir of the Agrarians," *Shenandoah*, III (Summer, 1952), 11–13.

Impressions of the Nashville Agrarians and the symposium *I'll Take My Stand* by a graduate student at Vanderbilt University during 1929–30.

————. "Some Modern Poets and the Gentle Reader," *American Review*, IV (January, 1934), 337–60.

Quotes from Ransom's observations on poetic meter in the essay "A Poem Nearly Anonymous."

Bergonzi, Bernard. "A Poem About the History of Love: 'The Equilibrists' by John Crowe Ransom," *Critical Quarterly*, IV (Summer, 1962), 127–37.

Explicates "The Equilibrists" and discusses the classical and biblical allusions in the poem.

Blackmur, R. P. "San Giovanni in Venere: Allen Tate as Man of Letters," *Sewanee Review*, LXVII (Fall, 1959), 614–31.

Discusses Ransom's idea of "structure" and "texture" in connection with an assessment of Tate's poetry.

Bleifuss, William. "Ransom's 'Here Lies a Lady,'" *Explicator*, XI (May, 1953), Item 51.

Blum, Morgan. "The Fugitive Particular: John Crowe Ransom, Critic," *Western Review*, XIV (Winter, 1950), 85–102.

An analysis of Ransom's critical approach, especially in *The World's Body*.

Bly, Robert. "On the Necessary Aestheticism of Modern Poetry," *Sixties*, No. 6 (Spring, 1962), 22–24.

Rejects Ransom's statement in "Poets Without Laurels" that the aesthetic and moral values in poetry have become separated and that modern poetry retains only the aesthetic; concedes that this may be true of poetry in English but contends that it is not true of French, Spanish, and German poetry.

"Bollingen Award," *Publisher's Weekly*, CLIX (February 3, 1951), 799.

News item announcing the award of the 1950 Bollingen Prize in Poetry to Ransom.

Bradbury, John M. "Ransom as Poet," *Accent*, XI (Winter, 1951), 45–57.

Reviews certain characteristics of Ransom's poetry, including his irony, predicated on dualism, and his diction.

————. Untitled Review of Louise Cowan's *The Fugitive Group*, in *Mississippi Quarterly*, XIII (Spring, 1960), 101–104.

A generally favorable review of Mrs. Cowan's literary history of the

Fugitives; finds Mrs. Cowan's close connection with Davidson a limiting
factor.

Brooks, Cleanth. "The Doric Delicacy," *Sewanee Review,* LVI (Summer,
1948) , 402–15.
Finds a parallel between Ransom and Milton in the development of
a personal idiom and in the achievement of aesthetic distance in poetry.

———. "The Modern Southern Poet and Tradition," *Virginia Quarterly
Review,* XI (April, 1935) , 305–20.
Remarks a lack of preoccupation with Southern tradition and local
color in the poetry of the Fugitives and other Southern poets.

———. "The New Criticism: A Brief for the Defense," *American Scholar,*
XIII (Summer, 1944) , 285–95.
A response to Abel's article in *American Scholar,* XII, 414–28.

Brown, Ashley. "A Note on *God Without Thunder,*" in *Shenandoah,* III
(Summer, 1952) , 34–37.
Summarizes the major theories in *God Without Thunder,* a work
which he describes as providing "a certain metaphysical depth" not
always found in the two Agrarian publications *I'll Take My Stand* and
Who Owns America?

Burgum, Edwin Berry. "An Examination of Modern Critics: John Crowe
Ransom," *Rocky Mountain Review,* VIII (Spring, 1944) , 87–93.
Considers Ransom's criticism in relation to Renaissance humanism.

Calverton, V. F. "The Bankruptcy of Southern Culture," *Scribner's Magazine,* XCIX (May, 1936) , 294–98.
I'll Take My Stand is considered as a pronouncement in favor of
restoration of the antebellum South; Calverton's essay emphasizes the
backwardness of the South. *See also* Ransom's article, "The South Is a
Bulwark," 298–303.

Campbell, Harry M. "John Crowe Ransom," *Southwest Review,* XXIV (July,
1939) , 476–89.
An examination of Ransom's ambiguous attitude toward science.

Carne-Ross, D. C. "Ransom's 'Judith of Bethulia,'" *Nine,* II (Spring, 1949) ,
91–95.
Explicates the poem; finds it is not concerned with divided sensibility
and does not employ an oblique approach; concludes that the ambiv-
alence of the "Mother Goddess," Judith, is well portrayed.

Cater, Catherine. "Four Voices Out of the South," *Michigan Alumnus
Quarterly Review,* L (Winter, 1944) , 168–73.
The voices are those of Davidson, Tate, Warren, and Ransom; Ran-
som's criticism is discussed on pages 167–68 and his poetry on page 172.

Connelly, Thomas Lawrence. "The Vanderbilt Agrarians: Time and Place
in Southern Tradition," *Tennessee Historical Quarterly,* XXII (March,
1963) , 22–37.
A survey of the meaning of agrarianism.

"Contribution to Poetry," *Time*, LVII (February 12, 1951), 94.

Announces the awarding of the 1950 Bollingen Prize in Poetry to Ransom.

Cowan, Louise. "The Communal World of Southern Literature," *Georgia Review*, XIV (Fall, 1960), 248–57.

Examines Ransom's use of a Southern setting in early poetry, and a continuation of the themes, but not directly of the setting, in his later poems.

Crane, R. S. "Cleanth Brooks; or, the Bankruptcy of Critical Monism," *Modern Philology*, XLV (1948), 226–45.

Finds a tendency toward "a monistic reduction of critical concepts" in the theories of the major New Critics, including Ransom.

"Culture and Gallantry," *Newsweek*, LXIII (January 27, 1964), 79–80.

A brief summary of Ransom's literary career on the occasion of the naming of a building at Kenyon College in his honor.

Current-Garcia, Eugene. "The Fugitive-Agrarian Movement: A Symposium. Introduction," *Mississippi Quarterly*, XIII (Spring, 1960), 53–54.

Introductory comments affixed to the papers printed in the same issue which were presented at the Southeastern Area Studies Association–South Atlantic Modern Language Association meeting on November 7, 1959.

Daiches, David. "The New Criticism: Some Qualifications," *English Journal*, XXXIX (February, 1950), 64–72.

Names as a limitation of the New Criticism the implicit suggestion that the "end-product of literary activity is the critical analysis of the work and not the work itself."

Daniel, Robert. "The Critics of Nashville," *Tennessee Studies in Literature*, I (1956), 19–26.

Surveys the importance and influence of the Fugitive group as critics.

Davidson, Donald. " 'I'll Take My Stand': A History," *American Review*, V (Summer, 1935), 301–21.

An explanation of the history, purpose, and reception of *I'll Take My Stand* by one of the contributors.

————. "The Thankless Muse and Her Fugitive Poets," *Sewanee Review*, LXVI (Spring, 1958), 201–28.

The story of the Fugitive group and a summary of its early poetic achievements by one of its members.

Davis, Louise. "John Crowe Ransom and How He Escaped," *Nashville Tennessean Magazine*, June 7, 1964, pp. 10–11, 14.

A conversation with Ransom, April, 1964, and a brief biographical sketch.

Davis, R. G. "New Criticism and the Democratic Tradition," *American Scholar*, XIX (January, 1950), 9–19.

Attacks the "socio-historical patterns of acceptance and rejection" established as a movement by the New Criticism and places the movement outside the democratic tradition; mentions briefly Ransom's place in the movement.

Dupee, F. W. "Verse Chronicle," *Nation,* CLXI (August, 1945), 138–39.
In reviewing several volumes of poetry (not Ransom's), alludes to what he calls Ransom's "mandarin" style.

Elton, William. "A Glossary of the New Criticism," *Poetry,* LXXIII (December, 1948; January, 1949), 153–62, 232–45.
Defines terms frequently used by the New Critics, including Ransom, "who has keenly refined and consolidated the leading concepts."

Emerson, Dorothy. "John Crowe Ransom," *Scholastic,* XXX (February 6, 1937), 12.
A brief biographical sketch and comment on Ransom's literary career.

England, Kenneth. "They Came Home Again: Fugitives Return," *Georgia Review,* XIV (Spring, 1960), 80–89.
Remarks the significance of the Fugitive reunion at Vanderbilt University in 1956.

Farrell, James T. "The Ground of Criticism," *Saturday Review of Literature,* III (July 2, 1927), 939, 942.
In discussing contemporary criticism, refers to a letter by Ransom in the *New Republic* concerning the value of contemporaneity in poetry.

Fergusson, Francis. "A Voice of One's Own: A Note on Mr. Ransom's Style," *Shenandoah,* XIV (Spring, 1963), 13–14.
On the immediacy of Ransom's style as opposed to a studied literary style.

Fiedler, Leslie. "A King of Solution: The Situation of Poetry Now," *Kenyon Review,* XXVI (Winter, 1964), 54–79.
In a survey of trends in modern poetry, Ransom is referred to as a "neo-Genteel" poet whose work reveals a "madness and passion" not found in certain later poets of the same school.

Fishwick, Marshall W. "They Took Their Stand," *Western Review,* II (Summer, 1947), 234–40.
Summarizes the principles underlying *I'll Take My Stand* and compares the stand of the Nashville Agrarians with views expressed by later writers.

Fletcher, John Gould. "The Modern Southern Poets," *Westminster Magazine,* XXIII (Winter, 1935), 229–51.
A critical assessment of the poetry of Ransom, Davidson, Tate, Warren, "minor Fugitives," and John Peale Bishop.

Flynn, Robert. "Ransom's 'Miriam Tazewell,'" *Explicator,* XII (May, 1954), Item 45.

Fogle, Richard Harter. "A Recent Attack on Romanticism," *College English,* IX (April, 1948), 356–61.

Examines the attack of the New Critics upon English poetry of the Romantic period.

———. "Romantic Bards and Metaphysical Reviewers," *ELH*, XII (September, 1945), 221–50.

An examination of the attack of the New Critics, including Eliot, Ransom, Tate, Leavis, and Brooks, upon Romantic poetry.

Ford, Newell F. "Empson's and Ransom's Mutilations of Texts," *Philological Quarterly*, XXIX (May, 1950), 81–84.

Ransom is said to have picked up and approved, in *The New Criticism*, what Ford calls Empson's "mischievous sophistry" in criticizing Wordsworth's "Tintern Abbey."

Foster, Ruel E. "Flight from Mass Culture," *Mississippi Quarterly*, XIII (Spring, 1960), 69–75.

Suggests that the Fugitives were fleeing the corrupting influence of mass culture on art and life in general.

Frank, Joseph. "Force and Form: A Study of John Peale Bishop," *Sewanee Review*, LV (Winter, 1947), 71–107. Expanded and reprinted as "Spatial Form in Modern Literature" in *Critiques and Essays in Criticism, 1920–1948*. Edited by Robert Wooster Stallman. New York: The Ronald Press, 1949, pp. 315–28.

Distinguishes the poetry of Bishop from that of Ransom, Tate, and Warren who treat the theme of "dissociation of sensibility."

Glicksberg, Charles I. "The Character of Modern Criticism," *Antioch Review*, VII (Fall, 1947), 435–46.

Mentions briefly Ransom's work *The New Criticism* in an article emphasizing the value and importance of modern literary criticism.

Grattan, C. Hartley. "The Present Situation in American Literary Criticism," *Sewanee Review*, XL (January-March, 1932), 11–23.

Calls Ransom a "neo-Confederate" in his critical principles.

Graves, Robert. "The Future of the Art of Poetry," *Hogarth Essays* (1928), 172.

Alludes briefly to the "Gothic principle" so named by Ransom.

Grigson, Geoffrey. "John Crowe Ransom," *New Verse*, XVI (August-September, 1935), 12–17.

A biographical summary and a general assessment of Ransom's poems.

Handy, William J. "The Ontological Theory of the Ransom Critics," *University of Texas Studies in English*, XXXV (1956), 32–50.

An examination of the background in Kantian philosophy of critical theory, chiefly that of Ransom, Brooks, and Tate.

Harder, Kelsie B. "John Crowe Ransom as Economist," *Modern Age*, II (Fall, 1958), 389–93.

Considers the effect of Ransom's agrarianism on his poetry and poetic theory.

Hardy, John Edward. "Lycidas," *Kenyon Review,* VII (Winter, 1945), 99–113.
    In a reconsideration of Milton's "Lycidas," Ransom's essay, "A Poem Nearly Anonymous," is mentioned.
Hartsock, Ernest. "Roses in the Desert: A View of Contemporary Southern Verse," *Sewanee Review,* XXXVII (July, 1929), 328–55.
    The Fugitives are included in a survey of Southern poetry.
Heilman, Robert B. "Poetic and Prosaic: Program Notes on Opposite Numbers," *Pacific Spectator,* V (Autumn, 1951), 454–63.
    Examines the poetic effect accomplished in a poem with "a rather prosy rhythm," Ransom's "Bells for John Whiteside's Daughter" (458–60).
Herbert, T. Walter. "Near-Rimes and Paraphones," *Sewanee Review,* XLV (October, 1937), 433–52.
    Ransom's poetry is examined as an example of contemporary use of "near-rimes."
Herschberger, Ruth. "The Structure of Metaphor," *Kenyon Review,* V (Summer, 1943), 433–43.
    A comment on Ransom's explanation of the use of metaphor in an editorial, "The Inorganic Muses," *Kenyon Review,* V (Spring, 1943), 278–300. *See* Ransom's reply, *Kenyon Review,* V (Summer, 1943), 443–47.
Hoepfner, Theodore C. "Economics of Agrarianism," *Mississippi Quarterly,* XIII (Spring, 1960), 61–68.
    Defines the agrarian philosophical position and defends its theories of economics.
Holland, Robert B. "The Agrarian Manifesto: A Generation Later," *Mississippi Quarterly,* X (Springs, 1957), 73–78.
    Summarizes the meaning of *I'll Take My Stand.*
Holman, C. Hugh. "Literature and Culture: The Fugitive–Agrarians," *Social Forces,* XXXVII (October, 1958), 15–19.
    Examines the Fugitive-Agrarian movement in the light of the culture which produced it.
Hough, Graham. "John Crowe Ransom: The Poet and the Critic," *Southern Review,* I (January, 1965), 1–21.
    A critical approach to Ransom's poetry through his criticism and his technique.
———. "Marvell of the Deep South," *Listener,* LXIV (August 4, 1960), 183–85.
    Examines for a British audience some qualities of Ransom's poetry, including his diction, courtliness, and interest in tradition.
Howarth, Herbert. "Eliot: The Expatriate as Fugitive," *Georgia Review,* XIII (Spring, 1959), 5–17.
    An account of Eliot's notice of Ransom and the Fugitives.

Irish, Marion D. "Proposed Roads to the New South, 1941: Chapel Hill Planners versus Nashville Agrarians," *Sewanee Review*, XLIX (January-March, 1941) , 1–27.

  The tenets of agrarianism are explored.

Jarrell, Randall. "John Ransom's Poetry," *Sewanee Review*, LVI (Summer, 1948) , 378–90. Reprinted in *Poetry and the Age*. New York: Alfred A. Knopf, 1953, pp. 96–111.

  An informal essay encompassing Ransom's rhetoric, his use of ambiguity, and his irony.

Jarvis, F. P. "F. H. Bradley's *Appearance and Reality* and the Critical Theory of John Crowe Ransom," *Papers on English Language and Literature*, I (Spring, 1965) , 187–91.

  Finds Ransom's debt to Bradley greater than his debt to Kant, whom he called his mentor.

Jones, Howard Mumford. "Is There a Southern Renaissance?" *Virginia Quarterly Review*, VI (April, 1930) , 184–97.

  Ransom's writings are said to display nostalgia for the "civilization of the slavery system."

———. "The Uninfluentials," *Saturday Review of Literature*, XXIV (October 11, 1941) , 3–4, 20.

  A review of *The Intent of the Critic*, to which Ransom contributed the essay "Criticism as Pure Speculation"; Jones contends that critics are ineffectual in the molding of public opinion concerning literature.

Knickerbocker, William S. "The Fugitives of Nashville," *Sewanee Review*, XXXVI (April, 1928) , 211–24.

  Suggests the possible extent of the Fugitives' contribution to American poetry on the occasion of the publication of *Fugitives: An Anthology of Verse*.

———. "Mr. Ransom and the Old South," *Sewanee Review*, XXXIX (Spring, 1931) , 222–39.

  An estimation of *I'll Take My Stand*, including Ransom's contribution to the symposium.

Knight, Karl F. "John Crowe Ransom's 'gewed,' " *American Speech*, XXXVIII (December, 1963) , 308–309.

  Traces the Old English origins of the word "gewed" used by Ransom in the poem "Fresco: From the Last Judgment."

———. "Love as Symbol in the Poetry of Ransom," *Mississippi Quarterly*, XIII (Summer, 1960) , 132–40.

  An examination of Ransom's use of love as a symbol of the theme of the divided sensibility.

Koch, Vivienne. "The Achievement of John Crowe Ransom," *Sewanee Review*, LVIII (Spring, 1950) , 227–61. Reprinted in *Modern American Poetry*. Edited by B. Rajan. New York: Roy Publishers, 1952, pp. 33–65.

A critical estimate of *Poems About God, Chills and Fever,* and the
five poems written after 1927.
"Look Applauds," *Look,* XXI (December 10, 1957) , 15.
    A brief biographical and critical sketch.
Lowell, Robert. "John Ransom's Conversation," *Sewanee Review,* LVI
(Summer, 1948) , 374–77.
    Lowell finds Ransom's facility of "conversation," or precise use of
    words, one of his major accomplishments.
Lynskey, Winifred. "A Critic in Action: Mr. Ransom," *College English,* V
(February, 1944) , 239–49.
    An assessment of flaws in Ransom's critical theory.
Lytle, Andrew. "Note on a Traditional Sensibility," *Sewanee Review,* LVI
(Summer, 1948) , 370–73.
    Suggests that Ransom's early environment gave him "a coherent view
    of life."
Matthiessen, F. O. "American Poetry, 1920–1940," *Sewanee Review,* LV
(Winter, 1947) , 24–55.
    A brief characterization of Ransom's poetry in an essay written as a
    chapter of *Literary History of the United States.*
————. "Primarily Language," *Sewanee Review,* LVI (Summer, 1948) , 391–
401.
    Discusses Ransom's facility for "characterization by language."
McCormick, Virginia Taylor. "Is Poetry a Live Issue in the South?" *Sewanee
Review,* XXXVII (Fall, 1929) , 399–406.
    Mentions the influence of the Fugitives in the revival of Southern
    poetry.
Mencken, H. L. "The South Astir," *Virginia Quarterly Review,* XI (January,
1935) , 47–60.
    Opposes the stand of the Nashville Agrarians.
Mizener, Arthur. "The Structure of Figurative Language in Shakespeare's
Sonnets," *Southern Review,* V (Spring, 1940) , 730–47.
    Disagrees with certain points made by Ransom in the essay entitled
    "Shakespeare at Sonnets."
Mitchell, Charles. "Ransom's 'Little Boy Blue,'" *Explicator,* XXII (Sep-
tember, 1963) , Item 5.
Moorman, Charles. "Ransom's 'Painted Head,'" *Explicator,* X (December,
1951) , Item 15.
Muller, Herbert J. "The Critic Behind Barbed Wire," *Saturday Review of
Literature,* XXVI (September 25, 1943) , 3–4, 18.
    Mentions Ransom briefly in a consideration of the narrow confines
    set for literary criticism by Ransom and others.
————. "The Function of a Critical Review," *Arizona Quarterly,* IV (Spring,
1948) , 5–20.

Explores the inadequacies of Ransom's idea of a limited type of critical review described in the article, "These Little Magazines."

———. "The New Criticism in Poetry," *Southern Review*, VI (Spring, 1941), 811–39.

Points to certain limitations of the literary criticism, including that of Ransom, which concentrates upon aesthetic values in literature to the exclusion of other considerations.

Nemerov, Howard. "Summer's Flare and Winter's Flaw," *Sewanee Review*, LVI (Summer, 1948), 416–25.

Discusses, under the term "elegance" of vocabulary, Ransom's irony and his emphasis on duality; divides his poems into five major subject classifications.

Nixon, Herman C. "A Thirty Years' Personal View," *Mississippi Quarterly*, XIII (Spring, 1960), 76–79.

An Agrarian reaffirms agrarianism.

Norton, Dan S. "Ten Poets," *Virginia Quarterly Review*, XXII (Summer, 1946), 438–47.

A discussion of poetry published immediately after World War II, including the *Selected Poems* of Ransom.

O'Connor, William Van. "The Influence of the Metaphysicals on Modern Poetry," *College English*, IX (January, 1948), 181–87.

Considers the influence of Donne and other metaphysical poets upon Ransom's poetry, especially in the "tension between the romantic and the real."

———. "The World as Body," *Sewanee Review*, LVI (Summer, 1948), 435–41.

Ransom's contribution to criticism is cited, with emphasis upon "dissociation of sensibility" expressed in *The World's Body* and other critical essays.

Olson, Elder. "William Empson, Contemporary Criticism, and Poetic Diction," *Modern Philology*, XLVII (May, 1950), 222–52. Reprinted in *Criticism: Ancient and Modern*. Edited by R. S. Crane. Chicago: University of Chicago Press, 1952, pp. 45–82.

Mentions Ransom's claims for "unity of method" in the New Criticism.

Osborn, Scott C. "Ransom's 'Blue Girls,'" *Explicator*, XXI (November, 1962), Item 22.

Osborne, William R. "Ransom's 'Blue Girls,'" *Explicator*, XIX (May, 1961), Item 53.

Peck, Virginia L. "Ransom's 'Prelude to an Evening,'" *Explicator*, XX (January, 1962), Item 41.

Pressly, T. J. "Agrarianism: An Autopsy; Appraisal of the Nashville Agrarian Movement," *Sewanee Review*, XLIX (April-June, 1941), 145–63.

An examination of the "nature and fate" of agrarianism.

"Professor on a Hill," *Newsweek*, XXXII (August 2, 1948), 73.

News item concerning the special issue of the *Sewanee Review* (Summer, 1948) in honor of Ransom and his acceptance of the journal on the Kenyon College campus.

"Ransom Harvest," *Time*, LXXI (May 12, 1958), 75.

News item containing a brief biographical sketch.

Redman, Ben R. "Critics in Hobbles and Blinders," *Saturday Review of Literature*, XXXII (November 12, 1949), 8–9, 60–62.

An examination of the limitations of contemporary literary criticism; discusses Ransom and others, including Eliot, Tate, Richards, Brooks.

Rice, P. B. "George Santayana: The Philosopher as Poet," *Kenyon Review*, II (Autumn, 1940), 460–75.

An assessment of Santayana's poetry; mentions Ransom's comments on Platonism in *The World's Body*.

Rock, Virginia. "Dualisms in Agrarian Thought," *Mississippi Quarterly*, XIII (Spring, 1960), 80–89.

Examines dualistic vision of the Fugitive-Agrarians with particular attention to the central dualism of science versus art.

Roellinger, Francis X., Jr. "Two Theories of Poetry as Knowledge," *Southern Review*, VII (Spring, 1942), 690–705.

Summarizes Ransom's and Tate's theories of poetry as knowledge rather than emotion and feeling and pronounces in favor of a middle way—poetry as a "delight of the mind."

Rubin, Louis D., Jr., "The Concept of Nature in Modern Southern Poetry," *American Quarterly*, IX (Spring, 1957), 63–71.

Nature is the basic metaphor of *"I'll Take My Stand* and is central to the aesthetics and poetry of the leading Fugitives.

———. "John Ransom's Cruell Battle," *Shenandoah*, IX (Winter, 1958), 23–35.

Traces the theme of death and the air of masked violence in Ransom's poems.

Schwartz, Delmore. "Instructed of Much Mortality: A Note on the Poetry of John Crowe Ransom," *Sewanee Review*, LIV (Summer, 1946), 439–48.

Assesses briefly a similarity between the poetry of Ransom and of Wallace Stevens in language and often in theme; discusses the theme of death in Ransom's poetry.

———. "The Poetry of Allen Tate," *Southern Review*, V (Winter, 1940), 419–38.

Consider Ransom's influence upon Tate's poetry.

Schwartz, Elias. "Ransom's 'Bells for John Whiteside's Daughter,'" *English Language Notes*, I (June, 1964), 284–85.

A response to Warren's analysis of the poem in "Pure and Impure Poetry," *Kenyon Review*, Spring, 1943.

Sister Mary Janet. "Poetry as Knowledge in the New Criticism," *Western Humanities Review*, XVI (Summer, 1962), 199–210.

Examines the doctrine of poetic knowledge in the New Criticism of Richards, Ransom, and Tate.

Stallman, Robert Wooster. "John Crowe Ransom: A Checklist," *Sewanee Review,* LVI (Summer, 1948) , 442–76.

A preliminary checklist in three sections: Books and Essays, Reviews, and Criticism on Ransom.

Starke, Aubrey. "The Agrarians Deny a Leader," *American Review,* II (March, 1934), 534–53.

Reconsiders *I'll Take My Stand* in light of Tate's and Warren's essays (*New Republic,* August 30, 1933, and *American Review,* November, 1933) showing, it is said, lack of harmony with Sidney Lanier who might be considered an early Agrarian. See response by Ransom immediately following Starke's article (554–71) .

Stauffer, Donald A. "Critical Principles and a Sonnet," *American Scholar,* XII (Winter, 1942) , 52–62.

A record of the analysis of a Shakespearean sonnet by five persons, including Ransom.

————. "Portrait of the Critic-Poet as Equilibrist," *Sewanee Review,* LVI (Summer, 1948) , 426–34.

Reviews Ransom's accomplishments in poetry under the guise of considering what his example might teach a student who wishes to write poetry.

Stevens, Wallace. "John Crowe Ransom: Tennessean," *Sewanee Review,* LVI (Summer, 1948) , 367–69.

Suggests that Ransom's peculiar individuality, stemming from his Tennessee background, is reflected in his poetry to a greater extent than either knowledge or later experience.

Stewart, John L. "The Poetry of John Crowe Ransom," *Shenandoah,* XIV (Spring, 1963) , 33–48.

Discusses one of Ransom's dualities—the disparity between the ideal and real worlds of the characters within the poems and of the poems themselves; finds Ransom's failure in the "insufficiency of the ideal world affirmed by the style and by the too limited people."

Stewart, Randall. "The Relation Between the Fugitives and Agrarians," *Mississippi Quarterly,* XIII (Spring, 1960) , 55–60.

Finds a connection between the philosophy behind the Fugitive movement and the Agrarian movement.

Stocking, Fred H., and Ellsworth Mason. "Ransom's 'Here Lies a Lady.' " *Explicator,* VIII (October, 1949) , Item 1.

Stone, Geoffrey. " 'It is the Virile Part to React,' " *American Review,* VII (Summer, 1936) , 341–52.

Points out similarities between Ransom's views in *God Without Thunder* and Tate's ideas in "Religion and the Old South."

Tate, Allen. "American Poetry Since 1920," *Bookman*, LXVIII (January, 1929), 503-508.

Contains a brief note on the Fugitives and their contribution to the poetry of the 1920's.

———. "Confusion and Poetry," *Sewanee Review*, XXXVIII (April, 1930), 133-49.

Refers briefly to Ransom (148) in a discussion of the state of literary criticism.

———. "For John Ransom at Seventy-Five," *Shenandoah*, XIV (Spring, 1963), 5-8.

Personal reminiscences of Tate's and Ransom's associations at Vanderbilt University.

———. "The Fugitive, 1922-25: A Personal Recollection Twenty Years After," *Princeton University Library Chronicle*, III (April, 1942), 75-84.

The story of the Fugitives.

———. "Modern Poets and Convention," *American Review*, VIII (February, 1937), 427-35.

Calls Ransom's "Captain Carpenter" a "perfectly traditional poem."

———. "A Note on 'Autotelism,' " *Kenyon Review*, XI (Winter, 1949), 13-16. Reprinted in *The Forlorn Demon*. Chicago: Regnery, 1953, pp. 161-64.

Notes Ransom's contributions to literary criticism through his editorship of the *Kenyon Review* and through his essays and articles.

———. "Poetry and the Absolute," *Sewanee Review*, XXXV (January, 1927), 41-52.

Contends that great poets are absolutists rather than dualists, a descriptive term proposed by Ransom in "Thoughts on the Poetic Discontent."

———. "R. P. Blackmur and Others," *Southern Review*, III (Summer, 1937), 183-98. Reprinted in *Reason in Madness*, 160-81.

A brief reference to Ransom's criticism.

———. "Taste and Dr. Johnson," *New Republic*, LXVIII (August 19, 1931), 23-24.

Mentions, in connection with a review of Eliot's introduction to a new edition of two of Johnson's poems, Ransom's defense of orthodoxy in *God Without Thunder*.

Thorpe, Clarence D., and Norman E. Nelson. "Criticism in the Twentieth Century: A Bird's-eye View," *English Journal*, XXXVI (April, 1947), 165-73.

Summarizes (170-71) the theories of the New Critics; mentions Ransom's differentiation between poetry and science.

"To John Crowe Ransom," *Kenyon Review*, XXVI (Winter, 1964), 22-23.

Dedicatory comments upon the publication of the one-hundredth issue of *Kenyon Review* in honor of Ransom.

"Trowbridge, Hoyt. "Aristotle and the 'New Criticism,'" *Sewanee Review,* LII (1944), 537–55.

Distinguishes the Chicago school of critics, following Aristotle, from the New Critics who adopt the dialectical method of Plato.

Waggoner, Hyatt H. "Ransom's 'Blue Girls,'" *Explicator,* XVIII (October, 1959), Item 6.

Wallach, Virginia. "Ransom's 'Painted Head,'" *Explicator,* XIV (April, 1956), Item 45.

Warren, Robert Penn. "John Crowe Ransom: A Study in Irony," *Virginia Quarterly Review,* XI (January, 1935), 93–112.

Considers the wit and irony of Ransom's poetry in relation to twentieth-century trends in science and religion.

——. "A Note on Three Southern Poets," *Poetry,* XL (May, 1932), 103–113.

Discusses the poetry of Ransom, Fletcher, and Davidson; lists "disruption of sensibility" as the central issue in Ransom's poetry.

——. "Pure and Impure Poetry," *Kenyon Review,* V (Spring, 1943), 228–54. Reprinted in *Critiques and Essays in Criticism, 1920–1948.* Edited by Robert Wooster Stallman. New York: The Ronald Press Company, 1949, pp. 85–104.

Ransom's poem, "Bells for John Whiteside's Daughter," is explicated.

——. "Some Random Remarks," *Shenandoah,* XIV (Spring, 1963), 19–21.

Personal reminiscences and a short comment on *Poems About God.*

Wasserman, G. R. "The Irony of John Crowe Ransom," *University of Kansas City Review,* XXIII (Winter, 1956), 151–60.

Defines the term "irony" as applied to modern poetry and examines the means by which Ransom achieves irony.

Watkins, Floyd C. Untitled Review of *Fugitives' Reunion: Conversations at Vanderbilt,* in *Mississippi Quarterly,* XIII (Spring, 1960), 99–101.

The volume serves, Watkins asserts, to point up the individual personalities and philosophies of the Fugitives and Agrarians.

Weaver, Richard M. "The Tennessee Agrarians," *Shenandoah,* III (Summer, 1952), 3–10.

Summarizes the stand of the Nashville Agrarians who presented "one of the few effective challenges to a monolithic culture of unredeemed materialism."

Weiss, Theodore Russell. "The Nonsense of Yvor Winters' *Anatomy,*" in *Quarterly Review of Literature,* I (Summer, 1944), 300–18.

An assessment of Yvor Winters' work in literary criticism entitled *The Anatomy of Nonsense,* which includes an essay on Ransom's critical doctrine.

——. "T. S. Eliot and the Courtyard Revolution," *Sewanee Review,* LIV (Spring, 1946), 289–307.

Assesses Ransom's opinion of Eliot's poetry and criticism.

Welker, Robert L. "An Interview with John Crowe Ransom: Upon Return-ing," *Vanderbilt Alumnus,* XLVII (March-April, 1962), 14–15, 45.
A brief biographical sketch and record of Ransom's reminiscences during a visit to the Vanderbilt University campus.

Wellek, René. "Concepts of Form and Structure in Twentieth Century Criticism," *Neophilologus,* XXI (January, 1958), 2–11.
Compares (6–7) Ransom's and Winters' theories of what Ransom terms "texture" and "structure" in poetry.

West, Ray Benedict, Jr. "Truth, Beauty, and American Criticism," *University of Kansas City Review,* XIV (Winter, 1947), 137–48.
Includes a discussion of *The Fugitive* and of Ransom's literary crit-icism in a review of the history of American criticism.

Williams, Oscar. "The Bollingen Award," *Saturday Review of Literature,* XXXIV (February 3, 1951), 18.
Announcement of the 1950 Bollingen Prize in Poetry awarded to Ransom.

Wimsatt, W. K., Jr. "The Structure of the 'Concrete Universal' in Litera-ture," *Publications of the Modern Language Association,* LXII (March, 1947), 262–80.
Mentions Ransom's use of the term 'concrete universal' in modern literary criticism.

Zoellner, Robert H. "Poetic Cosmology in Pope's *Essay on Man,*" in *College English,* XIX (January, 1958), 157–62.
Uses Ransom's definition of structure and texture in a study of the structural ideas of Epistle I of Pope's *Essay on Man. See also* John M. Aden, "Texture and Structure in Pope: A Dissent," *College English,* XIX (May, 1958), 358; and Walter J. DeMordaunt, "Ransom, Pope, and the Intentional Fallacy," *College English,* XX (May, 1959), 415.

UNPUBLISHED DISSERTATIONS

Auerbach, M. Morton. "Conservatism and Its Contemporary American Ad-vocates." Columbia University, 1958.
A history and critique of modern conservative theory; includes a section on the Vanderbilt Agrarians (123–52).

Bradbury, John M. "The Fugitive Critics: A Critical History." State Uni-versity of Iowa, 1948.
Traces the development of the New Criticism of the Fugitives and their followers from 1922 to the late 1940's; Ransom's poetry and criticism are discussed on pages 17–32, 131–47, 186–91, *et passim.* Revised and published as *The Fugitives: A Critical Account* (1958).

Handy, William J. "Poetry as Knowledge: The Kantian Tradition in Modern Literary Theory." Oklahoma University, 1954.

Ransom is prominent among the modern critics whose theories are discussed in connection with Kantian philosophy; Chapter II is devoted to Ransom's attempted reconciliation of "the moral, the psychological, and the aesthetic."

Karanikas, Alexander. "John Crowe Ransom and Allen Tate: A Study of the Southern Agrarian Theory of Literature." Northwestern University, 1953.

A reconstruction of Ransom's and Tate's literary theories as Agrarians and a discussion of parallels between these theories and the New Criticism.

Knight, Karl F. "Diction, Metaphor, and Symbol in the Poetry of John Crowe Ransom." Emory University, 1962.

Examines the major characteristics of Ransom's poetry. Revised and published as *The Poetry of John Crowe Ransom* (1964).

Mills, Gordon H. "Myth and Ontology in the Thought of John Crowe Ransom." State University of Iowa, 1942.

Discusses the ontology and religious mythology associated with Ransom's theory of literature as knowledge.

Rock, Virginia. "The Making and Meaning of *I'll Take My Stand*: A Study in Utopian Conservatism, 1925–1939." University of Minnesota, 1961.

A reconstruction of the development of agrarianism and the publication of *I'll Take My Stand;* terms the Agrarians "utopian-conservatives, believing in and seeking to embody a myth out of a timeless order of man's universal consciousness into a world of history."

Stallman, Robert Wooster. "Dryden in Modern Poetry and Criticism." University of Wisconsin, 1942.

Examines Ransom's critical theories and his conception of poetry (285–300).

Stewart, John L. "The Fugitive-Agrarian Writers: A History and a Criticism." Ohio State University, 1947.

A critical history of the Fugitives and the Nashville Agrarians. Chapter IV, entitled "Ransom Focuses His Fury," is devoted to a study of Ransom's poetic activity and critical theory from the time of the demise of *The Fugitive* to the publication of *I'll Take My Stand*. Revised and published as *The Burden of Time* (1965).

Stocking, Fred H. "Poetry as Knowledge: The Critical Theory of John Crowe Ransom and Allen Tate." University of Michigan, 1946.

Examines the meaning and historical background of one element of the New Criticism, the doctrine held by Ransom and Tate that poetry is a form of knowledge.

Woodward, Barbara. "Theories of Meaning in Poetry, 1915–1940: A Critical History." University of Michigan, 1946.

Examines the theories of poetry set forth by Ransom, Brooks, and Tate.

INDEX